# SECURING INDIA
## Strategic Thought and Practice

# Securing India

## Strategic Thought and Practice

*Essays by*
GEORGE K. TANHAM

*Commentaries by*
KANTI P. BAJPAI
AMITABH MATTOO
RAHUL ROY-CHAUDHURY
VARUN SAHNI
WAHEGURU PAL SINGH SIDHU

*Edited by*
KANTI P. BAJPAI
AMITABH MATTOO

MANOHAR
2026

First published 1996
Reprinted 2026
First eBook edition 2026



ISBN 978-81-7304-147-1 (hardbound)
ISBN 978-93-7451-731-4 (eBook)

*Published by*
Ajay Kumar Jain for
Manohar Publishers & Distributors
4753/23 Ansari Road, Daryaganj
New Delhi 110 002

Printed and bound in India

TO
THE YOUNG OF INDIA
WHO WILL PONDER
AND HELP SHAPE INDIA'S
FUTURE POLICIES AND STRATEGY

# CONTENTS



* This essay was published by the Rajiv Gandhi Foundation under the title 'Indian Strategic Concerns in the 1990s'.

# PREFACE

This volume is part of an attempt to generate a wider debate on Indian strategy. India's strategic conceptions and choices are of crucial importance for its citizens. They are also of concern to the neighbouring states and to those more distant. The size of the country, its military power and its growing economic strength make it a potential great power. As a great power, India could be a force for stability, but, one must reckon, also a force for disruption. Informed and critical analysis of India's security and strategy is essential, both at home and abroad. Unfortunately, this has been singularly lacking. Debate at home has been confined to a small, nationalistic community located in Delhi. Outside India, few have been persuaded that Indian security and strategy merited much consideration. Fortunately, this is changing—with the momentous reconfigurations of the international system since 1990 and the redrawing of India's foreign and economic policies.

A significant proportion of the change wrought, both in India and outside, must be attributed to George Tanham's provocative and cogent monograph, *Indian Strategic Thought: An Interpretive Essay.* Our volume brings together George Tanham's original essay on India's strategic thought, his more recent appraisal of India's strategic options, and five Indian commentaries. It also includes a select bibliography on India's security issues, which updates and enlarges upon Tanham's original.

A brief word is in order on the antecedents and origins of this volume. In 1991, under the auspices of the RAND Corporation, George Tanham published a short monograph on Indian strategy. The monograph, *Indian Strategic Thought: An Interpretive Essay,* argued that India lacked a tradition of strategic thinking but that elements of a strategy were nonetheless visible. Tanham had spent several months conducting research in India, plumbing Indian opinion through interviews and discussions with members of its security community. The monograph came to be widely referred to within this community. Prime Minister Rao alluded to the monograph in his speeches. Reactions varied. Some Indians were affronted, some reassured, and some saw the thesis as confirming the ideas they had long—and sorrowfully—held.

While word of the monograph spread, the work itself was not widely available, and few could claim to have actually turned its pages. *Indian Strategic Thought* was more often quoted than read. Admirers and critics of Tanham's propositions were aplenty, but a serious reading, particularly from Indians, was absent. This fact emerged clearly in the course of several conversations we had with Tanham in the winter of 1994-5. Out of those conversations grew the feeling that his original intervention should be resurrected and given greater play. It was decided to produce a small 'symposium' on Indian strategy built around Tanham's monograph. His new essay, then in progress for the Rajiv Gandhi Institute for Contemporary Studies, promised to nicely round off the symposium.

We are happy to present the product of our conversations and decision. We hope the volume will go some way in stimulating futher debate on India's strategy. George Tanham has made us look down at our strategic navels and lift our sights and look beyond. In the deepest sense, we dedicate this book to students of Indian strategy, past, present and future.

KANTI P BAJPAI
AMITABH MATTOO

# EDITORS' ACKNOWLEDGMENTS

Our primary thanks, of course, are to George Tanham who, in spite of pressing commitments (including finishing his new essay), joined enthusiastically in producing this volume. We must also thank the RAND Corporation for their speedy permission to reprint the original essay and the Rajiv Gandhi Institute for Contemporary Studies which agreed to a quick reissue of his new essay on Indian strategy. We gratefully acknowledge the role of our commentators who received invitations to produce their essays in very short order, who without exception met the deadline, who revised their essays at our prompting, and who have borne the subsequent delay of the volume with good humour. Last but by no means the least, we wish to record the indefatigable yet cheerful labours of Anurag Yadav who in the midst of a torrid Delhi summer produced the bibliography in signal time.

*Jawaharlal Nehru University*
*New Delhi*

KANTI P BAJPAI
AMITABH MATTOO

# ACKNOWLEDGMENTS

I particularly wish to thank Kanti Bajpai and Amitabh Mattoo for thinking of the idea of this book and preparing the entire manuscript for the publisher. Without them, this volume, which we all hope will be useful for students of security matters, would never have appeared. I am most grateful to them. I would also like to thank Rahul Roy-Chaudhury, Varun Sahni, and Waheguru Pal Singh Sidhu who commented so ably on my essays. The excellent commentaries of these five young Indians suggest that the interest of the younger generation in India's foreign affairs and strategy is increasing and should be in good hands.

For my original essay, I would like to thank Stephen P Cohen for encouraging me at the start of this project, for generously sharing his knowledge and understanding of India, and for helping me with the draft of the report. Jonathan Pollack gave strong support to my work and also carefully reviewed the draft, providing helpful and constructive criticism. Stephen T Hosmer was particularly helpful in organising the report.

Scores of Indians assisted and encouraged me in my research. I want to thank them all for their generous help, kind understanding and patience with a newcomer to India. I particularly want to thank Admiral KK Nayyar, who arranged many interviews and generously shared his firsthand knowledge of the Indian defence community, and PK Singh, former Joint Secretary of External Affairs and now in the Indian High Commission in London, for helping me launch the project in India, for arranging meetings, and assisting in many, many ways. Mrs Mitra Vasisht of the Ministry of External Affairs was most helpful in Delhi and Washington and provided a constructive critique of the report.

K Subrahmanyam gave most generously of his time and knowledge, and patiently explained many facets of the strategic culture, especially the role of the Army. General Krishnaswami Sundarji was particularly generous and forthcoming in his help. Admiral MK Roy assisted me directly and arranged several very useful seminars. Jasjit Singh was most helpful in sharing his knowledge and views. AP Venkateswaran patiently tried to explain Hinduism and Indian culture as a backdrop for Indian strategic culture.

Many other Indians helped me: among them, Bhabani Sen Gupta, Raja Mohan, Eric Gonsalves, Giri Deshingkar, M Dubey, Prakash Shah, Lt Gen. Mathew Thomas (Retd), Vice Admiral S Govil, Lt Gen VK Sood (Retd), Lt Gen. ML Chibber (Retd), Maj. Gen. GK Bhimaya (Retd), Lt Gen. JFR Jacob (Retd), Maj. SC Singh (Retd), Maj. Gen. D Bannerjee, RR Subramaniam, Surjit Mansingh, VP Dutt, HK Dua, Capt. Bharat Verma (Retd), the late Giri Lal Jain, Brigadier VK Nair (Retd) and Capt. CU Bhaskar. Many others helped, and I hope they also will accept my thanks.

In the Indian Embassy in Washington, Lalit Mansingh, the DCM, and Brigadier Sen Gupta, the Defense Attache, were most cooperative. The former political counsellor, Raminder Jassal, was extremely helpful and encouraging.

The two technical reviewers of the RAND report, Leo Rose of the University of California and Gordon McCormick of RAND, provided incisive criticism and thoughful suggestions.

For my Rajiv Gandhi Foundation report, I want to thank Abid Hussain for inviting me to be a visiting fellow in early 1995, which allowed me to write it. I also wish to thank many of the same people who helped me with my first report, *Indian Strategic Thought.* My appreciation also goes to Sunil Das Gupta, Bhashyam Kasturi and Rahul Roy-Chaudhury who met me regularly during the period of my fellowship. Dr Rajesh Kadian, Raminder Jassal, Air Marshal Chandu Gole, C Uday Bhaskar and Surjit Mansingh were particularly helpful. Lastly, I wish to thank my wife, Kathleen, who has patiently seen me through the throes of writing, typed the manuscript several times, and was my most demanding and constructive critic. She has my love and appreciation.

To all these people, my grateful thanks and deep appreciation. For the shortcomings and mistakes, I alone am responsible.

GEORGE K TANHAM

# INTRODUCTION

KANTI P BAJPAI AND AMITABH MATTOO

Strategy is coterminous with human experience. To be human is to strategise: I plan, therefore I am. As we jostle and push our way through the world, we are doomed to define where we are going, who will stand in our way, who will help us move ahead, how we propose to get where we want to go, what our capacities are and how to deploy them to best effect. Nations as much as individuals must strategise. As they jostle and push with other nations, they must articulate their basic goals, identify threats and opportunities along the way, plot alternative courses and allocate their resources to the attainment of fundamental objectives.

For some, strategy flows from the nature of the international system, and one can more or less deduce strategic postures from it. In an anarchic system, that is, where there is no overarching central authority to regulate the relations between states, strategy is essentially about the cultivation of power. Since no state can rely on a higher authority to guarantee its security and survival, this is a 'self-help' system. In a self-help environment, the primary goal of states is the cultivation of power relative to rival states. It may do this by its own efforts (internal balancing) or by allying with others (external balancing). Also, it may cultivate various forms of power. In the end, however, military power is crucial.[1]

This 'structural realist' view, clearly, has wide currency. It is a view that flattens out and homogenises strategy. All states at all times in all places work within the same problematic: states define the same goals (survival), identify the same threats (power imbalances), choose between similar courses of action (internal or external balancing) and divide their resources appropriately (primarily towards military strength).

The spare, deductive logic of structural realism is appealing and instructive, but for many this is inadequate for the task of understanding international relations and strategy.[2] Traditional realists and liberals differ with the structuralists on a number of matters. The limits on the use of force, the role of diplomacy, a broader conception of power, the efficacy of international institutions, the constraints exerted by domestic politics, society, and economics, the influence of social ideas, all these move more traditional realist and liberal analyses.[3] Strategy, in these views, is not flat but inflected by a host of international, regional, national, even subnational, specificities.

The question of course is: beyond international structure, what inflects strategy and how? Digging below international structural influences on strategic postures does not mean a retreat into studying strategy *sui generis*. Rather, a series of *sui generis* studies would be a valuable resource for the comparative study of strategy: they would be mined for the formulation of broader generalisations about strategic goals, threats and opportunities, responses, and allocations of resources. And all this, surely, would be progress towards answering the charge that strategy, as an area of intellectual inquiry, is ethnocentric.

George K Tanham's *Indian Strategic Thought* and his sequel essay 'Indian Strategy in Flux?' fit in this latter kind of programme.[4] While Tanham's is a *sui generis* analysis, it is fodder as it were for the comparative study of strategy. Tanham's excavation of Indian strategic thought and practice describes grand strategy and military strategy and traces back their sources. As Amitabh Mattoo points out, it is this kind of endeavour that will contribute to a less ethnocentric view of strategy. Most of what we know and read about strategy focuses on Europe, the United States and the Soviet Union. While this may have been tolerable—but only tolerable—during the cold war, when these were the central actors in the principal axis of global conflict, it no longer is. A range of powers will matter greatly in the three decades to come: China, Japan, South Korea, Taiwan, Indonesia, Vietnam, Australia, Iran, Egypt, Israel, Nigeria, post-apartheid South Africa, united Germany, Poland, Brazil, Argentina, Mexico, Pakistan and India. These have been relatively neglected in the study of strategy and must find their native and non-native 'informants' and chroniclers.

It hardly needs to be added that this is not just a matter of salvaging the academic study of strategy. The strategies of these mostly 'middle powers' will be deeply consequential for the future of international politics. The comparative study of strategy should help illumine the nature of those strategies, and therefore the future of the international system.

## INDIAN STRATEGIC THOUGHT

Tanham argues that four principal factors account for Indian strategy: Indian geography; the reconstruction of Indian history over the past 150 years; Indian culture, society, and belief systems; and British rule. Geography has caused Indians to see the subcontinent as 'a single strategic entity' and to be fundamentally inward-looking. Culture, society and belief systems have undergirded this unity by stressing diversity, accommodation of contradictions and adaptivity. The reconstruction of Indian history has stressed integration under great empires, alternating with periods of massive strife and disintegration. The British Raj has contributed to Indian strategic views by passing on its geopolitical concepts—the need for buffers in the north, sea denial in and around India, and the existence of a core and periphery in the subcontinent, the core being post-independence India and the periphery being the smaller states ringed around it.

Through the lens of these four factors, Tanham argues, India has assessed its principal threats and opportunities and its strategic responses. Threats and opportunities can be arranged, he suggests, by means of a *mandala* scheme of concentric circles which has domestic politics in the first circle, the smaller neighbours in the second circle, Pakistan, China and the Soviet Union in the third, the Indian Ocean region next, and the rest of the world—comprising the other great powers and distant regions—in the outermost circle.

Indian strategic responses, in Tanham's formula, consist of the following elements: deny the small regional states access to great power support; contain Pakistani influence in the region, and deter and defeat Pakistan; contain and deter China as well and seek symbolic equality with Beijing; use the erstwhile Soviet Union as a balance against both Pakistan and China; increase naval capabilities sufficient to control the Indian Ocean; and develop naval, nuclear and missile capabilities for protection against near and distant great powers.

Below this formulaic surface, Tanham sees a deeper strategic structure. Thus, India is concerned with internal security over external security. It prefers defence to offence. It is primarily a land rather than a sea power. It seeks outright independence and great power status over any form of dependence and middle power status. It will rely principally on 'hard' (military) not 'soft' (economic, cultural) power. And its strategic thought and choices are inchoate and *ad hoc* more than they are precise and systematic.

Three factors, Tanham suggests, could cause the Indian formula to change and the deeper structure to alter: the acquisition of military high technology; domestic politics; and financial constraints. Tanham's identification of these factors turns out to be prophetic. As his more recent essay shows, the latter two were among the factors that since 1991 have led to some major shifts in Indian strategic thinking and practice.

## INDIAN STRATEGY IN FLUX?

Tanham's new essay, 'Indian Strategy in Flux?', is an attempt to chart Indian policies in a new era. The essay maps Indian strategic concerns and responses since 1991 which it sees as a 'watershed'. A variety of domestic and external developments, Tanham suggests, combined to shock the system in that year: internal political disruption; financial and economic crisis; the collapse of the Soviet Union; the Gulf wars; and the rise of Chinese economic and military power.

At least two major strategic changes resulted. First, India instituted a dramatic programme of economic reforms. The reforms stressed deregulation of the economy and greater reliance on market mechanisms, trade and foreign investment. A fundamental goal is high rates of economic growth on the pattern of South-East Asia. Second, India sought a wide-ranging partnership with the United States and, subsidiarily, with the market economies of East and South-East Asia (the Look East policy).

On the other hand, Tanham argues, New Delhi has not yet fashioned a clear response to a number of other challenges. These include: the growth of Chinese economic and military power; Islamic militancy, both internal and external; Pakistani involvement in Afghanistan; Chinese involvement in Myanmar; the opening up of Central Asia; and changes in the Indian Ocean littoral. Above all, New Delhi has not yet produced a 'coherent strategy for domestic law and order'. Nor has it found 'an effective counter to Pakistan's policy of assisting these (i.e. separatist and insurgency) and other movements', especially in Kashmir. Underlying this is a fundamental problem: Indians continue to be relatively neglectful of security issues and to have no institutionalised method of appraising threats and fashioning strategic responses.

Tanham concludes, nonetheless, that 'on the whole India has adjusted its strategies and policies well despite some shortcomings in the strategy-making process'. External shocks seem to be necessary to stir the decision-making system into major reappraisals of basic postures, but, on a day-to-day basis, India continues not to do too badly by an *ad hoc*, informal method of arriving at strategic choices. Also on the positive side, Indians are more strategically aware than before, and the younger generation sees the future in more practical and less ideological ways.

The great service of Tanham's essays is, first, to have cogently organised what is a widespread and therefore influential view of Indian strategy. While there is nothing that altogether surprises—or at least does not surprise Indians—in terms of the overall portrait of India's strategic thinking and practice, Tanham is the first to have drawn the lines so clearly and with a few, slashing brush-strokes. Second, his thesis that India lacks a tradition of and institutional structure for strategic thinking, and that this may not be such a bad thing, is provocative and disturbing. It is this second contribution that has drawn the greatest attention thus far; but it is revealing that the comments in this volume focus on the first.

How has the 'symposium' organized around Tanham's two essays answered or dealt with the various key issues raised in his writings? We discuss these in the following sections: influences on Indian strategic thought; threats and opportunities in Indian security assessments; the absence of Indian strategic thought; and naval and nuclear strategy. In each, a number of tensions and differences are discernible—between Tanham and the commentators, as well as between the commentators themselves—and this has guided our choice of focus.

## INFLUENCES ON INDIAN STRATEGIC THINKING

First of all, Tanham suggests that to understand Indian strategy one must take account of its unique geography, history, culture, political and economic system, and the British legacy. On various matters and in different ways there is disagreement here with Tanham.

Waheguru Pal Singh Sidhu does not doubt that these factors count, but he argues that Tanham is 'more than generous to the contribution made by the British raj' in respect of Indian unity. In fact, the British presence in India over 150 years ruptured India's evolving nationhood. The rupture, moreover, was violent: British policies—divide and rule—created the fissures that continue to rend post-colonial India and complicate its strategic environment. Finally, the much-vaunted strategic legacies of the Raj have their roots in pre-colonial, Mughal conceptions and practices.

Amitabh Mattoo locates Tanham's essays within the genre of writings on strategic culture and argues that the essays are a pioneering attempt at correcting a particularly American ethnocentric bias that has characterised most of strategic studies. Moreover, in a discipline increasingly dominated by structural realism, it is a challenge to discover if strategic choices are influenced by 'values or assumptions with roots deep in a state's ideational history'. But, that said, Mattoo finds Tanham guilty of geographic, historical, and cultural 'determinism'. Thus, 'for every cultural trait or historical factor that . . . has inhibited the development of strategic thought', Mattoo argues, 'one can easily identify an opposing trait or factor which should have promoted such thinking.' Of much greater cause for concern, Mattoo concludes, are the inhibitory role of contemporary Indian institutions and processes.

Varun Sahni takes issue with Tanham's contention that the Indian view of the world is in many ways *sui generis*. Is it, for instance, uniquely Indian to regard neighbours as potential adversaries? Tanham seems to suggest that it is while alluding to Kautilya's *mandala* concept. Sahni disagrees vehemently. He argues that 'far from being distinctly Indian, this strategic notion forms the bedrock of how most large countries view their place in the world' and when 'India seeks to control the actions of its neighbours . . . [i]t is merely acting like a big power, or mimicking the way other big powers behave.'

Similarly, is it peculiarly Indian to have a hierarchical view of the world? Tanham claims that the caste system has played a significant role in reinforcing such a worldview. Sahni's comments draw attention to the all-pervasive hierarchies that are an integral part of the international system, and he suggests that there is nothing typically Indian about such a view of the world. In this context,

Sahni also focusses on a glaring contradiction between India's policy and posture on international affairs. On the one hand, India seeks to reform the international system and erode institutionalised hierarachies. On the other hand, Indian diplomats are feverishly engaged in securing a place for the country in the first league. In short, power and interest rather than cultural idiosyncracies largely dictate India's behaviour on the international stage.

### THREATS AND OPPORTUNITIES

A major element of strategy is to chart the threats and opportunities before nations. Here we wish to highlight two key areas of debate, the first relating to China and the second regarding Pakistan. As Tanham notes in 'Indian Strategy in Flux', 'Of all its external threats, India still sees its traditional adversaries, China and Pakistan, as the most critical'.

In both essays Tanham portrays China as being the primary enemy in the Indian threat cosmology. The first essay refers to 'China: The Major Rival' and the second claims that 'The greatest and longest term strategic challenge to India . . . is China.' One of the sharpest 'exchanges' in the volume occurs on this subject. Joining Tanham is Mattoo. In the opposite corner is Kanti Bajpai.

Mattoo sees China as a very real threat to Indian security. He is alarmed at the 'complacency' over China in the Indian policy community and at the 'revisionist' trend in Indian thinking about the causes of the 1962 war (for which he concedes that India's forward policy was responsible). These are tantamount to sedition. For at least six reasons, China must be watched with great care: China has armed Pakistan with nuclear capability; Chinese disintegration after Deng may help India; its economic and military growth is making it expansionist and will bring it into conflict with India; it is a nuclear threat; Tibetan refugees in India will lead to confrontation; and the Indian public has not forgiven the humiliation of 1962.

Bajpai almost completely disagrees. He argues that China ceased being a threat more or less the day it got what it wanted, which was Aksai Chin. China is the satisfied power with respect to the border, and it is not interested in hostilities, conventional or nuclear. Those who argue that Chinese domestic upheavals may cause it to conjure up external tensions, Bajpai contends, assume that India can play the role of papering over internal quarrels in China. This is doubtful: India simply does not have that kind of place in Chinese threat cosmologies. Finally, the idea that India and China are rivals in South-East Asia is wrong. China has assets that India does not and is not likely to possess for a long time. There is no prospect therefore of an India-China 'race' for influence.

If the Mattoo-Bajpai exchange reveals that China is controversial in India's threat cosmology, Pakistan would seem to be beyond controversy as *the* 'regional destabilizer', to use Tanham's appellation. Yet Sahni makes the case that even this merits deconstruction. A comparison with Bangladesh is instructive, he argues. Bangladesh is 'economically poorer, geographically smaller and militarily weaker', yet its larger population, its quarrels with India, its cultural appeal (to Indian Bengalis), and its location astride India's northeast should make it a formidable concern. What captivates India's strategic imagination though, Sahni suggests, is the view that Pakistan's 'Islamic professions' broke up and then challenged India. As the 'third generation' (to use Stephen Cohen's phrase) comes to power in India, Sahni predicts that the acceptance of Pakistan as 'another country' will reduce its strategic salience.

One might note, in conclusion, that Bajpai and Mattoo also see the diminishment of the Pakistan factor in Indian strategic calculations. Bajpai argues that Indian economic growth over 20–30 years would, at a good clip, make Pakistan an offer its growing business interests could not refuse, leading to an economic entanglement that promises to end the political divide. Mattoo notes in passing that the Pakistani threat has always been exaggerated. He implies that if India reckons the threat of China correctly, Pakistan's salience will decrease.

## THE ABSENCE OF STRATEGIC THOUGHT

One of the most provocative propositions Tanham advances is that India lacks a tradition of strategic thinking. For a country which prides itself on the longevity of its tradition(s), this is a galling judgment. Yet many in India have found Tanham's claim supportive of their complaints. K Subrahmanyam and others have often suggested that the absence of strategic planning and vision must be attributed to India's uneasiness with power, its lack of 'will to power'. Does India lack a tradition of strategic thinking and if so why?

Only Sidhu rejects the argument that India lacks a tradition of strategic thinking. His reply is that Tanham has overlooked the importance of oral history and communication in the Indian tradition. He suggests that the lack of formal writings on strategic studies could be erroneously viewed as the absence of thinking on strategic issues. There is, Sidhu argues, a continuous tradition of 'realism' as a philosophy and as a practical political doctrine from the days of Chandragupta Maurya to Mohandas Gandhi.

Mattoo, by contrast, concedes that Tanham is correct—with an important exception. He tests Tanham's key thesis both against the narrower view of strategy—the art of distributing military means to fulfill the ends of policy, and the grander view of the term—the mating of domestic and international resources to achieve national security. As far as military strategy is concerned, Mattoo is in agreement with Tanham. There has been and remains a singular lack of coordinated military planning in independent India. There is no evidence to suggest that careful thought has gone into devising a plan of action on the basis of which specific policies, related to the armed forces, are being executed.

If it is, however, also Tanham's contention that India has not developed a grand strategy, then Mattoo disagrees. He argues that India's first prime minister, Jawaharlal Nehru, may have seemed like a woolly-headed idealist, but he was arguably one of the most sophisticated grand strategists of this century. Mattoo suggests that Nehru had a clear vision for India and its place in the world, and had devised prudent domestic and international strategies that could enable the country to realise these goals.

To the extent that India lacks a tradition of strategic thinking, why so? Bajpai argues it has little to do with geography or culture. It does have to do with history but not in the particularistic sense Tanham is partial to. A tradition of strategic thought originated and grew in Europe because of two world historical developments: after the Peace of Westphalia, the rise of the nation-state system in Europe which was a perpetual war system; and after Napoleon, the advent of total war which integrated European states and societies as never before. Under the shadow of constant and unlimited war, Europeans were forced to invent and invest in a tradition of systematic thought related to military and grand strategy. India's entry into this nation-state system and the growing integration of its state and society will tend towards a similar development. If this has not happened faster, it is because India's wars promise to be relatively limited and its state-society relationship remains less intimate. With Mattoo, Bajpai is more optimistic about the prospects of grand strategic thinking. In the realm of military strategy, on the other hand, India is not likely to make any signal contributions. The one exception is in the area of counter-insurgency where India has had great experience and continuing 'success'.

## NAVAL AND NUCLEAR STRATEGY

Tanham's original essay paid especial attention to two areas which remain contentious in India, namely, Indian naval strategy and capabilities as also nuclear weapons strategy and capabilities.

It is Tanham's analysis of India's naval policy and maritime interests which form the basis of Rahul Roy-Chaudhury's comments. Roy-Chaudhury is in agreement with Tanham's central thesis about the lack of strategic planning especially with reference to the Indian navy. As he points out, '. . . naval plans have not been prepared on the basis of a comprehensive policy directive provided by the political leadership of the country, which would have set out the major priorities to be kept in mind.' But he does dispute Tanham's contention that Indian naval strategy, however *ad hoc*, aims at both a 'sea denial' strategy and a 'sea control' one.

For Roy-Chaudhury these aims represent normative ideals. In reality, the 'nature of the navy's force of aircraft carriers, destroyers, and frigates . . . should be seen in terms of an attempt to primarily acquire a regional "sea-control", rather than a super or great power "sea-denial" capacity'. Roy-Chaudhury also disagrees with Tanham's suggestion that the development of a blue water Indian navy is rooted in the country's aspiration to acquire great power status. Instead, he argues that the expansion of the Indian navy is directly related to the need to maintain the defence and security needs of its growing maritime interests.

Roy-Chaudhury's view may be counterposed to Sahni's. In his writings elsewhere, Sahni reveals a worry not so much about the lack of sustained planning and budgetary cuts as the Navy's worldview.[5] He notes that while naval proponents outline an ambitious series of tasks, their budgets suggest a more modest function. Yet the Navy, he argues, perceives budgetary constraints as merely a postponement. Naval planners continue to harbour, as it were, 'an inflated vision of naval threats and capabilities'. The

Navy's overambitiousness, he suggests, takes three forms: temporal, structural, and geostrategic. Thus, temporally, protecting the sea lanes of communications (SLOCs) seems premature given the size of India's trade. Also, India's two fleets are already strong enough to contend with any regional navy; anything more is futile. Structurally, Sahni doubts the use of aircraft carriers and nuclear-propelled submarines. At any rate, he would 'cap' the number of carriers at two. Geostrategically, the Indian Navy's vision of the importance of seapower is misplaced, for India is basically a landpower.[7]

Much bigger than the Navy in geopolitical terms is the question of India's nuclear choices and policies. Mattoo, Sidhu, and Bajpai present different perspectives on India's nuclear choices.

Mattoo finds Tanham's thesis on nuclear issues substantially correct but hints that India's policy may be nudging towards a more overt capability. Indian policy, Mattoo complains, has been marked by ambiguity, hobbled by a lack of debate, and constrained by secrecy and by bureaucratic inertia and delay. Moreover, the virtues of this *ad hoc* posturing are overstated and in any case are increasingly open to doubt: the neither-confirm-nor-deny position is losing its diplomatic utility and military credibility. Indeed, regional tensions and international pressures are forcing India to review and reconsider its choices. New Indian thinking may be moving this policy in the direction of a more overt posture.

Sidhu's insightful comments on nuclear strategy tend towards the opposite conclusion. Contrary to the general view, Sidhu holds that clearsightedness not muddling through has marked the Indian policy from the beginning. He suggests that there is ample evidence to demonstrate that as far as India's nuclear weapon and long range missile capabilities are concerned 'the organisations concerned did plan well in advance and, in fact, anticipated the possible hurdles along the way'. Thus, in the nuclear field, there exists a basic Indian posture, which was outlined by Homi Bhabha in the 1940s and 1950s, and this posture has always had an eye to the military uses of the technology. This is true for the missile programme too. While there are debates within the security community, there is a *policy* consensus, which is to keep options open. Thus, Sidhu rejects the idea that Indian policy on these two issues will clarify only in the wake of crisis. Judging by the increasing public debate, which he notes, one is led to the following conclusion: that, contrary to the general perception of the matter, the nuclear and missile debates will continue to be shaped in a thorough and systematic and not sporadic way.

While Mattoo sees a 'maturing' of India's nuclear policy towards a more overt posture and while Sidhu's analysis suggests maintenance of the status quo, Bajpai urges a more fundamental shift. Bajpai argues that an overt posture is unnecessary and that the status quo—'ambiguity'—is dangerous. Abstinence is not utopian and should be India's option. Nuclearisation is unnecessary, Bajpai suggests, because China is not a threat and because Pakistan can be handled without nuclear weapons. If India gave up the bomb, international and even domestic opinion would force Pakistan to do so. If not, and provided the Pakistani nuclear programme was limited, a strategy of massive conventional retaliation could deter Pakistan. Ambiguity, on the other hand, is far more dangerous than its proponents, both Indian and foreign, concede. First, an ambiguous posture will eventually lead the other nuclear powers to train their nuclear weapons on India and to punish it politically and economically. Secondly and ironically, ambiguity has deterred India from retaliating against Pakistani aid to Kashmiri and Sikh insurgents. Finally, while ambiguity may be deterrence-stable it may not be crisis-stable.

## CONCLUSION

George Tanham's two cogent and insightful essays have stimulated us to think anew about Indian strategy. As the range of views here demonstrates, there is both agreement and disagreement between him and the various commentators, and between the commentators themselves. This is all to the good. Whether India has a tradition of strategic thought and debate or not, surely more thought and debate is welcome. If India moves ahead economically in the decades to come, it will be a major global force. As a global player, it must reckon its way as clearly as possible—for itself and for the international system as a whole which will feel the effects of India's growing power and involvement. We offer these writings and comments in the hope that they will play some part in invigorating how Indians come to think about their country and its engagement with the world.

## NOTES

1 The most influential statement of this view of the international system and international relations is of course Kenneth W Waltz, *Theory of International Politics* (New York: Addison-Wesley, 1979).

2 For an appraisal of 'structural' or 'neo-' realism, see the essays in Robert O Keohane, ed., *Neorealism and its Critics* (New York: Columbia University Press, 1986).

3 For a richer realist strategic programme, see George F Kennan (Mr X), 'The Sources of Soviet Conduct', *Foreign Affairs* XXV (July 1947), pp. 566-82. On a broader view of strategy, see Richard Rosecrance and Arthur A Stein, 'Beyond Realism: The Study of Grand Strategy', in *The Domestic Bases of Grand Strategy,* eds., Richard Rosecrance and Arthur A Stein (Ithaca: Cornell University Press, 1993), pp. 3-6.

4 See the essays in Rosecrance and Stein, eds., *The Domestic Bases of Grand Strategy* on British, Soviet, and Japanese grand strategies. Also, Edward Luttwak, *The Grand Strategy of the Soviet Union* (New York: St. Martin's Press, 1983) and his *The Grand Strategy of the Roman Empire: From the First Century AD to the Third* (Baltimore: Johns Hopkins University Press, 1976), Paul Kennedy, ed., *Grand Strategy in War and Peace* (New Haven: Yale University Press, 1991), James Ramsey Montagu, ed., *Grand Strategy* (London: HMSO, 1956-76), Jack Snyder, *Myths of Empire: Domestic Politics and International Ambition* (Ithaca: Cornell University Press, 1991), and Barry Posen, *The Sources of Military Doctrine: Britain, France and Germany Between the World Wars* (Ithaca: Cornell University Press, 1984).

5 See Kanti Bajpai and Varun Sahni, *Secure and Solvent: Thinking About An Affordable Defence for India,* RGICS Paper No. 11, May 1994, pp. 34-40.

6 Bajpai and Sahni, *Secure and Solvent,* pp. 34-40.

# INDIAN STRATEGIC THOUGHT
## An Interpretive Essay

GEORGE K TANHAM

### INFLUENCES ON INDIAN STRATEGIC THINKING

Since it gained independence from Britain in August 1947 and began to assume a more prominent place in the international community, India has groped to define and articulate a coherent strategic identity. Deeply embedded habits of thought related to India's geography, history, culture and British rule exert a powerful influence on the character and directions of the modern Indian state; they will in the foreseeable future help to shape its strategic thinking and its strategy.

Now on its own for the first time in centuries, India is undergoing a wrenching transition between its traditional culture and practices and influences of the modern world. The crosscurrents of India's past continually converge on the present. An Indian intellectual remarked that one can stand in New Delhi and observe the simultaneous existence of many centuries of Indian history. One cannot, however, foresee which elements of the past will persist and which new characteristics will penetrate the national ethos.

Ethnic, linguistic, religious, caste and internal regional rivalries on a scale unimaginable to most Americans seem at times to prevail over national concerns and to threaten India's fragile coherence and national integration. At the same time, Indians appear consumed by personal and regional competition for political power—competition that diminishes India's claims to greatness, and ambitions to play a larger international role.

The extraordinary diversity, the size of the country and the dynamics of change sometimes make consensus over major issues difficult to achieve, and perhaps even more difficult to predict. Nevertheless, although the process is discontinous and uneven, rapid economic, technological, and social innovations are changing the fabric of Indian society and its ways of thinking.

After a word on methodology, the remainder of this section discusses the four factors—geography, history, culture, and British rule or Raj—that have most influenced the character and direction of modern Indian strategy and what thinking has been undertaken. Section 2 deals with Indian strategy as the Indians view it, and Section 3 analyses the basis for India's relative lack of strategic thinking. Sections 4 and 5 touch briefly on the role of the Indian Army and India's nuclear ambitions.

The analysis is based on interviews and discussions with Indian intellectuals, government officials and military strategists; observation of Indian actions in foreign policy and strategic affairs; and Indian historical and philosophical writings and the published sources listed in the Bibliography.

This is an unusual project for RAND in that it attempts to investigate and report on how another people—the Indians—think about their own strategic matters. Literature on the subject is meagre, and few persons inside or outside India have studied it or thought much about it. I began the research for this project by reading widely about India. Over the past four years, I made four trips to India, each over a month in length, during which I conducted a few structured interviews, but mostly engaged in informal conversations. These talks allowed Indians to express themselves easily and voluntarily on various subjects relevant to this study.

I called on many officials, including former foreign ministers, chiefs of the military services, and secretaries of defence and external affairs. I also spoke with academics, policy researchers, media personnel, businessmen, retired officials and military officers, and some average Indians. Most of the research was done in New Delhi, some in Bangalore, Madras and Calcutta.

The report reflects primarily the viewpoints of what I call *the Delhi nationalist elite*, which I believe is the primary (though not the only) group concerned with strategy in India. The report does not fully represent the views of all of India, including the powerful regional personalities and pressures that can and do influence strategy and foreign policy.

I do not presume to understand India, but hope that I have acquired some limited insights into an understanding of Indian society and how it thinks about strategy and military matters. The results of my research follow.

*Geography*

Geography has profoundly affected India's history and culture, and therefore its strategic thinking and strategy. Perhaps even more important than geography itself has been the conscious and often unconscious attitudes and thought processes that geography has induced in the formulation of Indian strategy. India's strategic location, size, and tremendous population have contributed to Indian leaders' belief in its greatness, its pre-eminence in the Indian Ocean region and its global importance.

The Himalayas and the Hindu Kush mountains in the north, the Bay of Bengal in the east, and the Arabian Sea in the west have created a giant natural entity often referred to as the Indian subcontinent (Figure 1). This diamond-shaped landmass stretches over 3000 kilometres from the southernmost trip of India north to the Himalayas and roughly the same distance from east to west. India, by far the largest part of the subcontinent, covers over 3 million square kilometres. It is the second largest nation in the world in population, with about 850 million people.

On a map of the eastern hemisphere (Figure 2), India appears to lie at the intersection of imaginary lines stretching from southern Africa to far north-eastern Russia and from Austalia to the United Kingdom. Thus, Indians have the impression that India is the middle of this great region, though in most ways it is not. India does, however, occupy a strategic position in relation to all the trade between Australia and Europe and between the Far East and the Middle East and Europe.[1]

Geography, especially rivers and mountains, has divided as well as unified the Indian subcontinent. The Vindhya range forms a north–south divide (Figure 1). To the north of it lies the great plain of the Indus and Ganges (Ganga) rivers, its fertile soil watered by the monsoons. These great rivers rushing out of the Himalayas make the northern plain the heartland of India. This rich agricultural area allowed the development of large kingdoms and often led to the dominations of part of the more fragmented south.[2]

Over the centuries, invaders from the north, attracted by the riches of India, brought new cultures which added to and gradually adapted to Indian thought and society. Most of the invaders came

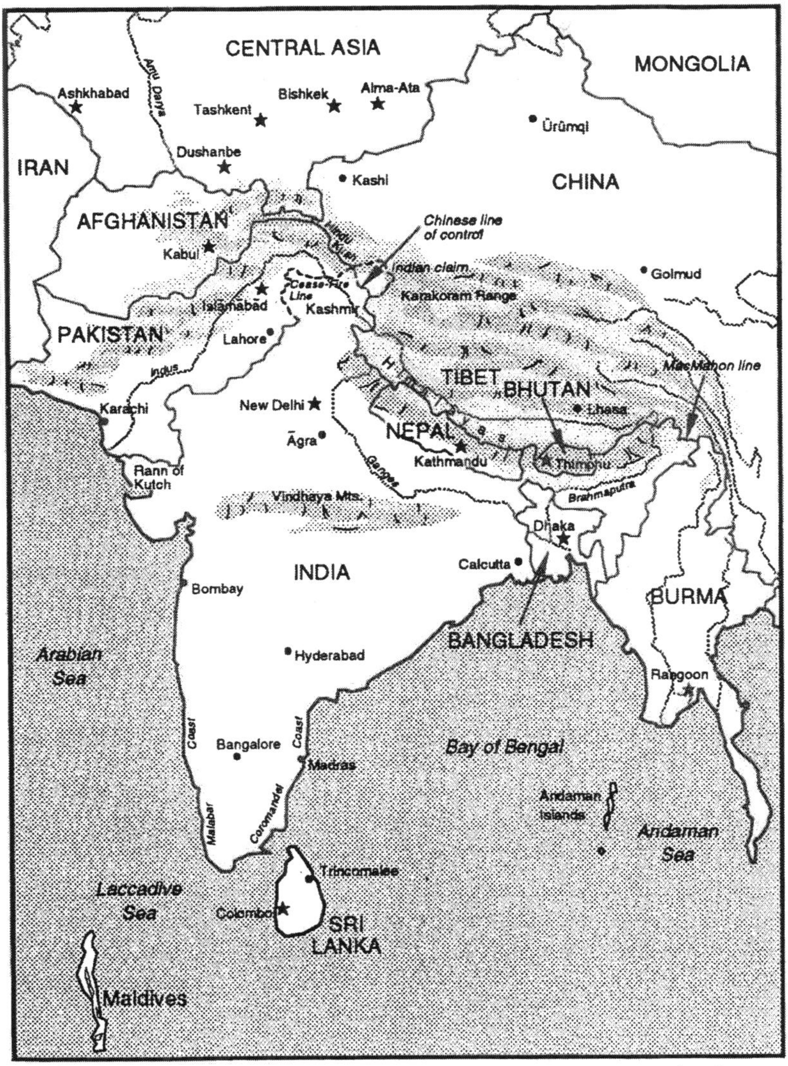


The external boundaries of India depicted in this map are neither correct nor authentic.

FIGURE 1: THE INDIAN SUBCONTINENT

from lands untouched by the sea, giving the dominant north a strong strategic land orientation with little attention to the ocean.

The south, occupied largely by peoples driven out of the Indian plain, was somewhat insulated from invaders and, thus, has retained more of its original Dravidian language and culture. Although the south is also agricultural, it has a much richer maritime tradition than the north. Parts of southern India, especially along the Malabar and Coromandel coasts, participated in the important commerce of the Indian Ocean, interacting by sea with the Arabs and Europeans to the west and the South-East Asians and Chinese to east (Figure 2).

These factors have contributed to a southern regionalism and a strategic outlook somewhat different from that of the north. Whereas northern India sees the threat from the northwest (today, Pakistan) and the north (China), the south resents the dominant northerners in India and looks seaward in its strategic approach.

Smaller rivers and lesser mountains have further divided India, especially in the south, and have created small geographical areas that developed separate entities with their own language, history and local variation of the great Indian culture. Thus, geography has simultaneously unified and divided India, leading to its claim of unity with diversity and creating some of the tensions that plague India today.

Indians have long regarded the mountains and seas as protective barriers against outside interference and invasion. In fact, however, the passes in the north-west have allowed invaders over the centuries to overun much of India. In World War II, the Japanese threatened India from the north-east, through Burma, and in 1962 the Chinese attacked across the mountains in the north-west and the north-east.

This dichotomy—the simultaneous sense of security based on geography and the realisation that geography has failed to keep India secure—is partially offset by India's ability to accommodate the invaders in various ways, thus creating and strengthening an evolving culture that plays a crucial role in modern India's identity. The dichotomy has, however, led to feelings of pride and confidence intermingled with feelings of insecurity and risk.

These same geographic barriers have played an even more important role in keeping Indians inside the subcontinent and allowing India to develop its own unique culture. In the view of

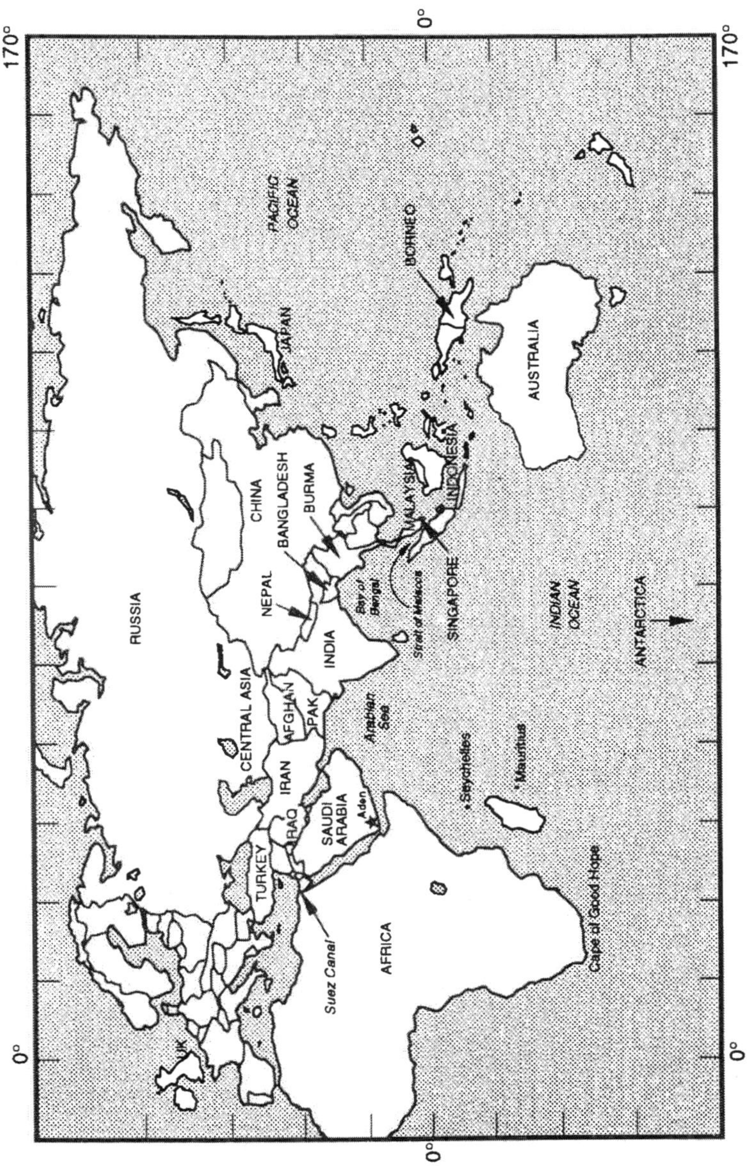


The external boundaries of India depicted in this map are neither correct nor authentic.

FIGURE 2: INDIA IN THE EASTERN HEMISPHERE

Jawaharlal Nehru, India's first prime minister, India's 'isolated evolution' is unique in the history of Indo-European peoples, although he acknowledges India's widespread contact and relations with most of the external world while retaining its unique culture.[3]

Foreign visitors and scholars from both the East and the West have left useful accounts of early India. Traders from the Middle East, Europe and China used India as a central staging area for their commerce. Until recent times, however, India has shown little interest in the outside world. Few historical accounts exist of Indians travelling abroad, and news of the outer world came mostly through foreigners. Thus, geography has strongly influenced Indian history and culture, both of which have centred on the subcontinent without great outside contact.

### *History*

Indians' attempts in the nineteenth century to discover their history as a whole coincided with the growth of nationalism. Although this European concept was quite foreign to Indian views of political entities, its appearance at that particular time led many Indians to search for and interpret their history through the prism of nationalism.

Until the mid-nineteenth century, while Indians knew their own local history, they knew little of the history of India as a whole and seemed largely uninterested in it. In fact, some scholars have claimed that Indians were not interested in their history at all.[4] However, as discussed below, the Indian views of life and time are not conducive to a sense of history, at least in the Western style.[5]

In the eighteenth and nineteenth centuries, however, British administrators, Jesuits and other Europeans became curious about the origins and history of the region referred to as India. Some of them learned Sanskrit and studied the sacred Vedic literature of the Aryans, the basis of at least Brahmanic Hinduism.[6] As Europeans uncovered and pieced together India's history and culture, they developed great respect for it. Indians also began to appreciate it, as they had never before viewed India from a complex perspective.

A renaissance of Hinduism, due in part to these historical discoveries, developed and blended with new-found nationalism, leading some Indians to develop a Hindu nationalism. However, Nehru and most Congress leaders preferred a secular nationalism and a secular state.

Because nationalism demanded deep historical roots, the Indian nationalists were among those most interested in the history of all of India, and they began to look for characteristics of the European nation state in their own history.[7] They were forced to go all the way back to the Mauryan empire of the fourth and third centuries BC to find a suitable example of an India governed by a central, indigenous ruling authority. The Mauryan empire, which covered almost all of India, had a vast and effective administrative structure that supported central authority and enhanced and encouraged loyalty to the emperor, though not to the state. The Mauryan empire was the exception, however, and did not establish a lasting precedent for Indian political unity.

The example of Ashoka, the great Mauryan emperor and a peaceful and moral leader, had a great effect on modern India. Indians pride themselves on the strong spiritual aspects and moral values of their society, and many nationalists found such qualities in Ashoka. When Ashoka, fighting for his empire, defeated his last adversary in the Battle of Kalinga, he was so appalled by the slaughter that he decided to give up war.[8]

Ashoka later preached non-violence, urged tolerance among groups, and tried to provide for the welfare of his subjects. Stone columns bearing inscriptions of exhortation and guidance for his subjects were discovered in the eighteenth century, but were not deciphered until the nineteenth. Ashoka himself was not positively identified as the great king until about 1915, but because he combined the attributes of strong leadership and high morality, he is now recognised as one of the India's greatest national leaders. The Ashoka wheel of *dharma* (moral law) is now invested in the centre of the Indian flag.

The search for other periods of political unity and great national leaders proved less fruitful. The Gupta dynasty of the fourth and fifth centuries AD produced able rulers who governed most of northern India, but their rule was less efficient and more limited in expanse than that of the Mauryan emperors.[9] Their reign is regarded as a golden age of Hinduism when art, literature, and philosophy flourished. Though perhaps not as great as the Mauryan emperors, the Guptas are exteremely important to those who consider Hinduism the essential element of Indian nationalism.[10]

Some 600 years later, beginning in the late tenth century, Muslim Turks from Afghanistan began to make raids into India. Only in the early sixteenth century, however, did the Muslim Mughals, under Babur, begin to recreate a unified imperial state in South Asia. This new stability and order not only influenced India's own cultural development, but also led to Indian contributions to Islamic thought.[11] The Muslims brought new military technologies, a new theology, and new political ideas, but they did not destroy Indian civilisation as they had destroyed pre-Islamic Persian culture, nor did the Hindus completely absorb them. Islam in a sense became a second culture, though it did not entirely escape Indian influence.

Akbar, perhaps the greatest of the Mughal rulers, seeing the need to integrate the various communal divisions of India, tried, albeit unsuccessfully, to synthesise Hinduism and Islam. He lifted the taxes and restrictions laid on the Hindus by more zealous Muslim predecessors, consulted not only Hindus but Jews and Christians, and reportedly had Hindu, Jewish and Christian wives. Many Hindus served as military officers and administrators. Aurangzeb, Akbar's grandson and a more devout and strict Muslim, however, showed less tolerance and conciliation, thereby weakening the Mughal empire and arousing communal passions that still exist in India today.[12]

Not accidentally, many Indian leaders pursued tolerance through intermarriage or conversion. India is a dazzlingly diverse country, and no ruler or dynasty has been able to impose a single doctrine or ideology on its population. Chandra Gupta, the founder of the Mauryan dynasty, was a Hindu; his grandson Ashoka converted to Buddhism; the Guptas were Hindus; and the Mughals were Muslims. Strikingly, Ashoka and Akbar—two non-Hindus—saw the need for tolerance and understanding among communal groups, though Hindus are noted for their tolerance.

Most of the modern Indian nationalist movement, especially the dominant Congress Party, accepted Hindu, Buddhist and Muslim rulers as 'Indians'. That Indian nationalists accepted both Ashoka and Akbar is a tribute to their tolerance, pragmatism and appreciation of greatness and also to their tradition of accepting and assimilating newcomers. Some nationalists, including Nehru, realised that the problems of integration that these emperors faced had continued into the twentieth century. For this reason, they opted for an independent secular state in which the different communal groups would be treated equally.

Two important dissents from this tradition of tolerance came during the period leading to independence. A segment of the Indian Muslim community felt that they could not live as a permanent minority in a predominantly Hindu state. This view eventually led to the movement for Pakistan. At the same time, a militant orthodox Hindu movement sought to make India a Hindu state. The Bharatiya Janata Party (BJP) holds this position today and did well in the election of June 1991.

The nationalist searching for cohesion in India's past discovered, in addition to the short periods of national unity, the long periods of disunity. Geography had divided the country into small units, and these developed their own language and subculture, as well as traditions of political unity and separate identity. The modern nationalists saw throughout Indian history a tension between the factors working for unity and those perpetuating regionalism and disunity. Most of the time, the centrifugal forces seemed to dominate, at least in the political sphere. This powerful tradition of regionalism remains a formidable force to this day.

Thus, the discovery of India's political past, even through nationalist eyes, did not suffice to satisfy the needs of a vital nationalism. The infrequency of India's great and glorious empires only dramatised the absence of lasting political unity. The nationalists therefore turned to the one continuous, powerful element in Indian history: its Hindu culture. The more deeply they delved into it, the prouder they became.[13]

Over several millennia, the Brahmanic tradition, with its sophisticated thought, its wide appeal and its pervasiveness in Indian society, provided important cohesiveness to India's cultural continuity. For the Hindu nationalists, India had existed for several thousand years. Nehru movingly summarises some of these thoughts and reflects his pride and excitement in *The Discovery of India*:

> The diversity of India is tremendous; it is obvious; it lies on the surface and nobody can see it. Yet, with all these differences, there is no mistaking the impress of India on the Pathan, as this is obvious on the Tamil.... Ancient India, like ancient China, was a world in itself, a culture and a civilization which gave shape to all things. Foreign influences poured in and often influenced that culture and were absorbed. Disruptive tendencies gave rise immediately to an attempt to find a synthesis. Some kind of a dream of unity has occupied the mind of India since the dawn of civilization. That unity was not conceived as something imposed from

outside.... It was sometimes deeper and, within its fold, the widest tolerance of belief and custom was practised and every variety acknowledged and even encouraged.[14]

This concept of national unity has translated into a special feeling of transcendent *Indianness*. Indianness implies more than political nationalism; it is an emotion or belief based on cultural identity; it is the deep, intense feeling of being an Indian.[15]

Asked the meaning of Indianness, Indians give various answers, all based on culture. Some say that they can go to a different region of India with a different language and feel at home because they will find their caste and feel compatible, knowing its rites and social mores, even though they cannot speak to its local members. Others claim that Hinduism provides a bond despite its diversity, that most Hindus know and revere certain gods, ceremonies, holy days and sacred places.

Non-Hindus feel Indian, it is said, because India became a secular state and because they see that its great history includes many non-Hindu leaders and achievements. Indians living abroad share this Indianness, which is now based partly on a thriving popular culture, the promulgation of secular holidays and the emergence of glamorous film, sport and political personalities.[16]

Indians also express pride in the spread of their culture and note that they have had the greatest influence abroad through ideas rather than through military or political coercion. Although Hinduism spread to South-East Asia in the early Christian period, it did not diffuse easily, as it was based on the caste system and the associated belief in transmigration.

Buddhism, which originated in India, spread to East Asia, including China, and to Ceylon (now Sri Lanka) and South-East Asia. Ironically, Buddhism almost disappeared in India while spreading abroad. Angkor Wat in Cambodia (now Kampuchea) and Borobadura in Indonesia remain as monuments to Indian cultural expansion in South-East Asia, where Chinese and Indian ideas and influence have long competed.[17]

Indian political-military history does not provide the cohesive element that culture does. In the first place, the Indians did most of their fighting inside India, only rarely undertaking military ventures outside the subcontinent. They made a few incursions north into Afghanistan and Persia (now Iran), and these were often defensive (Figure 3). They invaded Ceylon, but that island off the southern tip of India may be considered part of the region. In the south, they (notably the Cholas) made a few naval expeditions to South-East Asia, but these brief adventures occurred nearly 1000 years ago.[18]

In only a few instances in India history were foreign incursions into India through the north-west passes stopped or defeated. Although a few Indian leaders appreciated the need for a forward strategy, such as the control of Afghanistan, they seldom had such strategies. As a result, Indian forces were compelled to fight on the defensive, on Indian soil, after the invaders had already gained access to the rich north Indian plain. In addition, the many Indian states seemed unable or unwilling to unite their forces against the invaders, thus enabling the aggressors to defeat the Indians piecemeal.

These military failures indicate that only infrequently did Indians give much thought or attach much importance to the strategic defence of India as a whole. The small states were concerned about themselves, not the larger entity. This point has not been lost on modern Indian leaders.

Indian campaigns against the assaults from the north also reveal that Indian military technology through the ages lagged badly. For example, the Central Asians invented the saddle and stirrup and later used horse-mounted archers, developed tactics and manoeuvres and their employment. Little evidence exists that the Indians ever adopted these improvements.[19] Until the British period, Indian armies clung to largely static warfare based on a corps of elephants, with some cavalry and masses of infantry.

Only the Chola kingdom and a few southern states appear to have maintained significant ocean-going navies.[20] The great Indian states in the north had little interest in navies. The Mughals' disastrous failure to perceive the need for a navy enabled Europeans to land unopposed on Indian shores.

Contemporary Indian naval planners have learned the lessons of India's severely limited naval tradition, and they are not unaware that most of India's trade was carried in foreign bottoms and protected by the the Royal Navy during and briefly after the British Raj. Although the Indians engaged in extensive international commercial activities, they themselves seldom sailed the ships.[21] After independence, according to one observer, 'a new tradition had to be created'.[22]

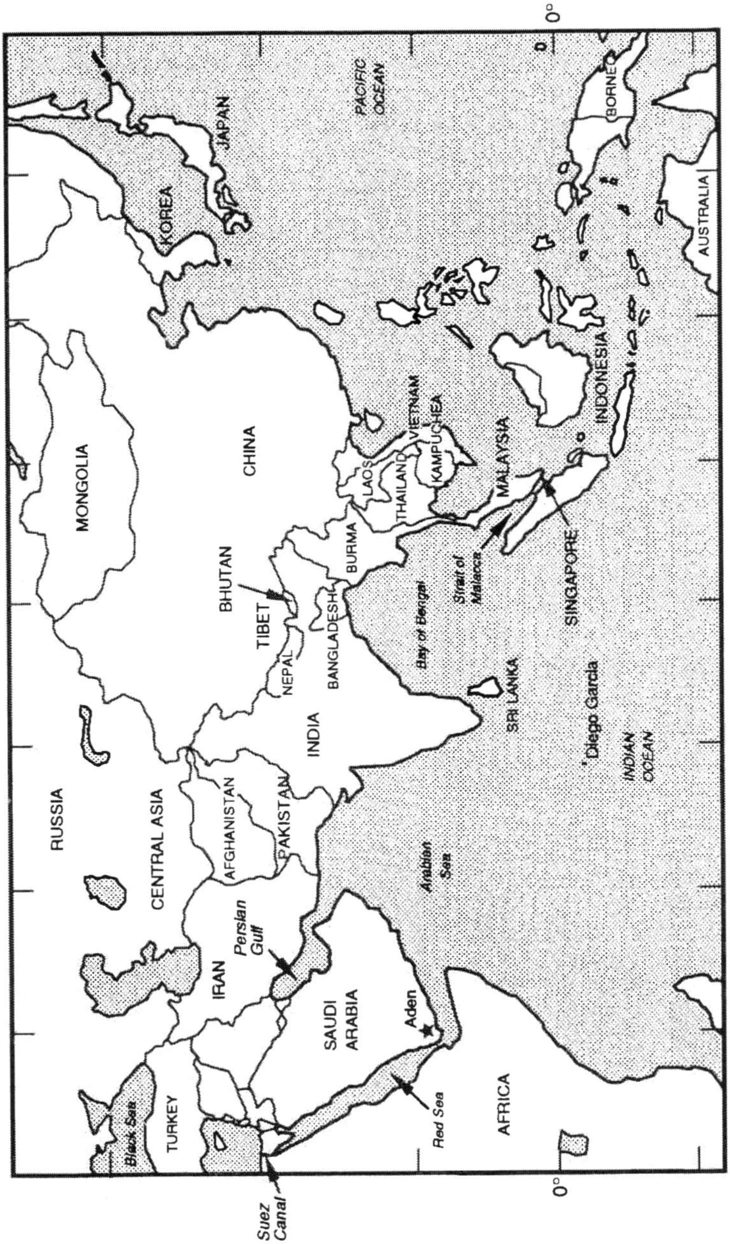


The external boundaries of India depicted in this map are neither correct nor authentic.

FIGURE 3: INDIA BETWEEN SOUTH-EAST AND SOUTH-WEST ASIA

*Culture*

Contemporary Indian society is built on a great civilisation that extends back more than 2500 years. Although the caste system and India's extensive linguistic and cultural diversity have changed over the centuries, the basis social and cultural patterns described by early Greek and Chinese travellers portray an India that is recognisable today.

Asked whether India will break up, as many countries are now doing, Indians usually answer that Indian culture is the binding force that will keep India united despite the strong regional subcultures and quarreling states that seem to threaten its existence. Many say also that democracy is a pillar of a unified India. Some add that the young and growing middle class is strengthening India and will support the Indian union.

The widely held perception that culture is a central feature of Indian life may be a greater force than the culture itself, which is slowly changing. Not surprisingly, Indian strategic thinking reflects and takes direction from this culture. The Brahmanic tradition, based on the ancient Indian epics, has a few generally accepted tenets and characteristics that seem to have influenced Indian strategic thinking, or the absence of it.

Hinduism, the basic element of Indian culture, is an amorphous body of beliefs resting on a few basic tenets. It has no 'book', no accepted creed or god, no organised church and no prophet. Ranging from the lofty intelletual concepts of the Brahman to the very personal, emotional beliefs of the devotees of the gods Vishnu and Shiva, and to the superstitions of the uneducated villagers, Hinduism is not a religion in the Western sense; it is more nearly a comprehensive way of life. It has adjusted to most invaders and penetrated the lives of Muslims, Christians and Jews living in India.

The caste system, an integral and pervasive part of Brahmanic Hinduism and one that developed several centuries before Christ, has survived to this day. According to Brahman belief, the caste system is divinely ordained and hence unchangeable by man. The system probably originated in occcupational classifications and evolved into its present form after the system of the four major classes or *varna*, emerged about 500 BC.[23] The Brahmans were the teachers and priests, the Kshatriyas were the warrior-rulers, the Vaishyas were merchants and businessmen, and, at the bottom, the Shudras were workers and farmers. Outside the system were the so-called untouchables, now called Harijans (children of God).

Membership in one of the tens of thousands of castes, which are subdivisions of the classes, is based on birth and circumscribed by endogamy, the largest group within which a person may marry.[24] Some castes are found throughout India, while others are local. Although new castes may be formed and castes may move up and down the social ladder, the caste system has been much criticised because of its hierarchical nature and denial of individual liberties.[25] It has, nevertheless, been the bedrock of an amazingly stable society and a rich and lasting culture.

Caste and family have built up powerful loyalties that may compete with national allegiance. Moreover, the caste system has given Indians a hierarchical view not only of India but of the world; they rank nations by size, culture and power. The caste system also suggests a stability and immutability in society and tends to foster a conservative and non-innovative mind-set—characteristics that describe many military establishments. However, this situation is changing, and wealth and education increasingly are slowly replacing caste as a measure of social status, especially in urban areas.

*Dharma, karma* and transmigration are other powerful, generally accepted concepts of Hinduism. *Dharma* is natural law or social order or duty that is incumbent on every member of a caste. *Karma* describes an individual's actions and efforts, the results of which will determine his future incarnation through transmigration. How one acts in this life is thought to determine how one will improve or worsen in one's next. Many Indians say that their guidance for life comes from the *Gita*, which emphasises the importance of an individual's performing his duty (*dharma*) and leading a moral life.[26]

To Indians, life is much more complex and less optimistic than in prevailing Western thought. They accept logic as one influence on life, but only one. Other influences include emotion, tradition, intuition and fate. Accordingly, life is unknowable, but man must strive to follow his *dharma*. Fate is something to be dealt with, but also to be accepted.

The Indian view may be seen as a realistic and pragmatic approach to life, but it also can lead to a passive, almost fatalistic, acceptance of life. Many argue, however, that *dharma* requires that an individual strive to fulfil his moral obligations. Although most Indians deny that they are fatalists, the acceptance of life as it comes carries considerable weight among believers.

This complex view of life makes the future appear uncertain and less subject to human manipulation than it does to a Westerner. Rational analysis, so vital to Western societies, has less influence in Indian society as so many other factors play important or dominant roles.[27] The acceptance of life as a mystery and the inability to manipulate events impedes preparation for the future in all areas of life, including the strategic.

The Indian belief in life cycles and repetitions, in particular, limits planning in the Western sense. To Indians, cycles constitute the basis of life and stand in stark contrast to the Western linear view of time.[28] An Indian is said to pass through four phases in life: student, homemaker, near hermit, and wanderer forsaking family and society until death. According to his actions (*karma*), he is reincarnated in another form, depending on the status he has earned, and begins the cycle over again.

Similarly, in the Indian view, the cosmos also goes through repeated cycles of creation, decay, destruction and recreation. Unlike human cycles, cosmic cycles take millions or billions of years. Indian history also appears as a cycle of unity, decay, disunity and reunification. A cyclical view suggests no past and no future, just a continuing series of cycles.[29]

The inherent pessimism and passivism of the cyclical view suggests little likelihood of major improvement in life, though *dharma* demands that one strive to lead a moral life. Even doing good deeds and leading the good life do not end the cycle. Only through renunciation of all desires, many Indians believe, can one break the cycle and join the Infinite in final peace and unity. That is, each individual has *atman*, or inner truth, which is one and the same as *Brahma*, the world spirit, the universal truth. *Atman* never ends; once free of the body, it soars and rejoins *Brahma*.

Thus, prevailing Indian beliefs, although changing in many ways, differ fundamentally from Western views, which assume a faith in logic and human progress, the efficacy of individual efforts, a sense of history and continuity, and a future to be shaped and worked for. The more educated Indians, however, especially those versed in technology and economics, are coming to recognise the need for planning and an integrated conception of social and economic development. These tensions find expression in many contemporary policy dilemmas, including those associated with strategic concerns.

*The British Raj*

The British East India Company used the Mughal's imperial administrative structure for its own purposes as it spread over India. Following the Indian Revolt of 1857, the British government took over from the company, and Queen Victoria supplanted the Mughal emperor. Using the Mughal structure as a starting point, the British began to mould India into a single administrative entity.

The British brought modern technology, railroads and the telegraph, thereby improving transportation and providing modern nation-wide communications, important parts of the necessary infrastructure of a modern state. They introduced English as a common language for education and government, and organised a more modern educational system, open to a wider range of Indians, than was available under the Mughals. The British also instituted a single legal system with courts for all. The Indian Civil Service, though predominantly British until the 1940s, was one of the world's best civil bureaucracies, and many of its skills were ultimately transferred to India.

All of these measures contributed to the development of a modern Indian nation-state with a unified administration, individual rights, and representative government in the form of a parliamentary system. Some have argued that administrative unity produces the state, then nationalism develops.[30] India, however, was simultaneously exposed to and influenced by the powerful nationalism at work at the time in Europe. As one scholar observed:

> European history glorified the nineteenth century flowering of nationalism as a spiritual renewal and political endeavour and posited the nation state as the highest and natural form of politics.[31]

British nationalism and pride, which the Indians easily sensed from their contacts with the British, especially aroused Indian nationalism.

Thus, British efforts to develop a unified colony laid the foundations for Indian unity, and the British concept of nationalism nurtured Indian nationalism. Indians realised, however, that the English applied their ideas of democracy and equality to themselves but not to Indians. Because of this racism, the English became the focus of nationalist resentment, thus adding a third powerful factor to the developing Indian nationalism.[32]

More important for this study, the British began to consider the strategic defence of a unified India.[33] Because they had arrived by sea, the British perceived the need to protect India from future naval attacks, especially from their European rivals. Accordingly, they evolved an Indian maritime strategy subsumed under a British global strategy to gain and maintain supremacy of all the oceans and to control the world's major choke points, especially those leading to the Indian Ocean.

The British gained control of the Suez Canal and established a base at Aden, which together gave them control of the most direct route from Europe, the most likely source of naval threat to India (Figure 2). In addition, the British gained suzerainty over Malaya and established Singapore in the early nineteenth century. This gave them control of the Strait of Malacca, the most important passage into the Indian Ocean from the Far East (Figure 3). The British also dominated the waters off the Cape of Good Hope in southern Africa, thus denying to hostile powers the use of the original European route to India.[34] British domination of the high seas turned the Indian Ocean into a British lake.

The British did not develop an Indian navy.[35] In World War II, a small Indian naval force served with the Royal Navy, but it lacked the necessary support elements to rank as an independent navy. Indian officers, being junior, gained only limited experience. The Indians inherited a small navy at independence but paid little attention to it.

As British naval power declined after World War II and withdrew from east of Suez in 1967, Indians realised the extent of their dependence on the British and began to organise their own navy. The lack of a naval tradition, the possession of only a few old Royal Navy vessels, and the general lack of an interest in naval matters meant that the Indians had to start almost from a scratch in the 1960s.

The land defence of India presented a more familiar but still difficult problem. While the moutains served as barriers in most places, several passes in the north-west had served for centuries as the main invasion routes. The rugged terrain and independent tribesmen found in these areas added to the difficulties. Furthermore, in the nineteenth century Russia was expanding into

Central Asia and looking southward, and the British began to view Russia as the primary land threat in the northwest.

However, neither Russia nor a weakened China threatened India from the northern and north-eastern frontiers. Nevertheless, by the middle of the nineteenth century, the British had taken Burma, which they governed from India, as a defence against China. Although China also claimed Tibet, the British kept it in their sphere of influence.

In the north-west, the British tried to develop a layered defence using diplomatic as well as military means. They first sought to establish a buffer system as far out from India as possible. This meant keeping Afghanistan and Iran friendly and out of the Russian sphere of influence. It also meant keeping Tibet out of Chinese and Russian control in the north. The second layer of the plan called for employing the northwest tribesmen as a defence screening force. The British, as the Mughals had before them, gained the tribesmen's support with subsidies. Neither layer of the strategy worked perfectly, as the Afghan wars and the constant skirmishes among or with the tribesmen attest.

Finally, the British planned for the defence of India itself if these other efforts failed. This eventuality materialised only in World War II. The British vacillated between a policy of forward employment of some army troops in the buffer areas and keeping them back in India for the direct defence of India.

The British empire at the end of the nineteenth century and the first half of the twentieth had become a status quo power. Its main purpose was to protect what it had. Consequently, British strategy was defensive in general, and particularly so for India. The 1907 Russo-British Agreement divided Iran into spheres of influence and reduced the problems of the northwest considerably. Unfortunately, the tribesmen were generally at war or ignored the agreement, and to this day unruly groups continue to operate in Pakistan. By World War I, the British had recognised Chinese suzerainty over Tibet but still advocated its independence.

London decided the imperial policy and goals, but Indian security strategy was formulated largely in India and was developed from an Indian perspective. The British formed the large, all-volunteer Indian Army with a large contingent of British troops and British officers. This force was organised to protect Britain's most important colony and to provide for internal security. It also helped to protect other parts of the British empire and fought in both world wars.

India inherited about two-thirds of the Indian Army, minus the British troops and officers, at independence. The Indian Army, at the request of the new civil leaders, played a role in persuading reluctant leaders in Hyderabad and Kashmir to join in the formation of the Indian union. It fought to defend Kashmir from tribal and Pakistani attack in 1947-8. The Indian government has subsequently called on the Army to quell intermittent internal disturbances. It has acted as a strong factor for Indian unity.

After World War II, the world around India changed. India and Pakistan became independent, China grew more powerful than it had been, and England began to lose interest. The defensive apparatus of an empire that had protected India so well in the past no longer existed for India. The gradual reduction of the British Navy opened India's seaward front. On land, Pakistan, now independent, began to challenge India, starting in 1947 in Kashmir. A strong and ambitious communist government took over China in 1949 after a long civil war, and soon seemed to confront India on its borders.

At the time of independence, India possessed very limited resources for defence and no experience in strategic planning. It inherited much from the British Raj, but it had to develop its own strategy and means of defence for the second half of the twentieth century. Neither effort has been completed, but strategic ideas are emerging, and considerable effort and progress has been made in creating military forces.

## INDIAN SECURITY STRATEGY: THE VIEW FROM DELHI

This section examines India's security strategy in a way favoured by many Indians: as a series of circles or rings (*mandala*).[36] The first circle is India itself. The second circle encompasses India's smaller contiguous neighbours: Sri Lanka, Nepal, Bangladesh and the Maldives (Figure 1, Section 1).

The third circle includes Pakistan, the only subcontinental state that has dared to challenge Indian regional military power; China, India's giant Asian rival; and the erstwhile Soviet Union that was India's best friend and partner in the geopolitical sphere of Asia, and perhaps the world. The Indian Ocean region as a whole forms a fourth ring, which Indians believe contains both opportunities and threats (Figure 3, Section 1). The final circle includes the more distant great powers and the rest of the world.

Delhi's strategic community places the entire subcontinent in the first circle, believing that it constitutes a single strategic unit defined by geography and culture.[37] Pakistan, Nepal, Bhutan, Bangladesh and Sri Lanka are seen as basically of Indian culture, though differences have obviously existed in the past and more have developed since their independence.

The British evolved the concept of the subcontinent as a strategic unit out of imperial necessity, and they went to great lengths to protect this most valuable part of their empire. But they did not share the fundamental belief, deeply embedded in the Indian psyche, that the unity of the subcontinent reflects the integrity and dreams of a people and constitutes an integral part of their social fabric.

The strategy of defending the subcontinental land border may seem like an offensive strategy, given the subcontinent's political makeup today. But Indians regard the strategy as purely defensive, just as having the navy keep hostile powers far from India' shores is seen as defensive. Given the political configuration of South Asia today, this image of the unity of the subcontinent raises two separate but closely related security problems for India:

- The internal unity of India itself.
- The security of India and its small, contiguous neighbours, now politically independent, but in Indian eyes still an integral part of India's strategic defence.

Indians do not readily admit publicly that they hold this concept of the strategic unity of the subcontinent. However, to understand India's security actions and policies relating to its close neighbours and Indians' extreme sensitivities about other nations intruding or trying to gain influence in this region, the observer must recognise that Indians do indeed regard security in terms of the strategic unity of the subcontinent.

### *India: The Regional Core*

India's most pressing strategic security concern is its own internal unity. In looking back on their country's history, Indian nationalists, though highlighting the periods of unity and splendour, have expressed concern about the much longer periods of conflict and disunity. Today, they are confronted by the same ethnic, linguistic, regional and communal factors, one or more of which have torn India asunder after each brief period of unity.

The nationalists have also noted the numerous successful invasions of India, mostly through the northwest passes, now controlled by a hostile Pakistan. In the past, India failed to defeat most of these invaders because of both internal disunity and technological backwardness. Indians thus see a close relationship between internal security and outside aggression. They know that without internal unity, external defence will remain difficult and hazardous.

Kashmir illustrates the conjunction of the dual threats stemming from weak internal security and outside aggression: The Kashmiris are revolting inside India, and the Pakistanis are supporting them from the outside. It explains why much of Delhi's strategic community refuses to compromise on this issue. To do so would be a major and potentially catastrophic compromise of India's most vital interest—its own internal security and unity as well as its belief in a secular state.

To understand better India's obsession with internal unity and integrity, it is useful to look again at its history. All periods of unity were based on empires assembled and held together by force. These emerged from smaller Indian states, or they were formed by foreign invaders who settled in India and became Indian. The last two empires, however, were built by foreigners, the Mughals and the British, who assimilated to a lesser degree than earlier outsiders, the former accommodating with the Hindus, the latter hardly at all.

The Mughal and British empires, also put together by force, were never real unions, but collections of states, many with long histories, their own language and culture, and a tradition of independence. The smaller states disliked being ruled by either Indian or foreign emperors and constantly revolted. They were in the process of overthowing the Mughal empire when the British arrived.

The various emperors seldom succeeded in developing strong imperial or Indian loyalties, much less in integrating the various states they had conquered into a union. Even the British directly ruled only a part of India. The so-called princely states retained their own rulers and not insignificant powers of self-rule until independence. Each ruler was concerned with his own state and distrusted the other states; none cared about Indian unity.

On arriving in India, the British observed that the idea of an empire was fairly popular, and they quietly worked under the Mughal imperial umbrella. After Indian soldiers—both Hindu and Muslim—revolted against the British in 1857, often called the Great Mutiny by the British and the First War of Independence by the Indians, the British abolished the Mughal empire and made it a part of the British empire; thus, India became an empire within an empire. While the ruling elite changed from Mughal to British, much continued as before.

The British expanded the Mughal empire and continued their centralising efforts. As noted in Section 1, they provided efficient administration, a common law and language, and modern technology, railroads, and telegraph that pulled the empire together. Many Indians give the British credit for creating modern India even as they criticise the British for retarding the growth of the Indian state, plundering India economically and delaying independence.

The British treated India as a separate empire. For example, London gave the British rulers in India considerable autonomy, allowing them to look at the strategic defence of India from an Indian perspective. London, of course, continued to view defence from the perspective of the larger British empire.

The Indian nationalists of the late nineteenth and early twentieth centuries led the independence movement and adopted the European ideas of nationalism and the nation-state. They were too few in number to win independence by themselves, but Gandhi rallied the masses around these ideas, though they may not have fully understood them.

Although the new nationalism propelled India toward independence, it has not supplanted regional traditions and loyalties. Within India, the various states retain their identities and subcultures, and several would, if independent, rank among the largest states in the world. Uttar Pradesh, for example, has over 150 million people, and Andhra Pradesh, in the south, over 60 million.

Many leading Indian strategists recall that their grandparents had identified themselves by caste, locality and language rather than as Indians or Hindus, thus suggesting that at independence the new nationalism had by no means replaced the old loyalties.

On the eve of independence, India remained a collection of states with a broad common culture but many subcultures, differing from each other in language and tradition, and held together politically by strong British rule.

When India became independent on 15 August 1947, nationalist euphoria ran high, but beneath the surface not a great deal had changed. Most princely states opted to join India; several preferred to remain independent, but were not allowed to. The fissiparous forces that Nehru had strongly warned against were very much alive, and the new Indian unity was a fragile one.

The new Indian ruling elite, many of whom were Brahmans, tended to rule from Delhi as masters, somewhat like the British. Their first challenge was the integration of the Indian princely states into a new republic.[38] This required the use of force, and of the new Indian Army, on several occasions. The task was accomplished largely by Sardar Patel, Nehru's conservative and practical *alter ego*, and the Indian Army. Nehru's consuming involvement in international affairs and world statesmanship led him to pay less attention to the internal problems that he had earlier written about so eloquently, though he pushed hard for Indian unity and economic development necessary for a free country.

Since 1947, successive Indian governments have relied on a mix of force and inducement to deal with problems of integration and unity. The various police and paramilitary forces that were raised to suppress separatist movements throughout the country and to maintain order now approach the regular armed forces in size. The Indian constitution also permits the central government to take over state governments and rule them by presidential decree from Delhi. An emergency was declared from 1975 to 1977 over all of India, and civil rights and freedoms have at other times been curtailed in many regions of the country.

The central government has also frequently called on the Army to maintain order and to suppress insurgencies and revolts. In several cases (such as those involving the Nagas and the Mizos in north-east India) military pressure was followed by economic and political inducements, and many separatist groups have laid down their arms. Yet these are tactics, or perhaps a strategy for dealing with internal revolts, but they are not a strategy of national integration.

Some Indian strategists argue that these periods of separatist, ethnic and communal unrest are cyclical and simply a part of the Indian way of life. Others see gradual progress and are more optimistic about the future. Thus far, however, few efforts have led to a long-term, constructive strategy entailing mass literary programmes, national educational standards, linguistic unification and other measures of national integration. The apparent neglect of national integration efforts contrasts sharply with specific actions undertaken by other ethnically diverse Asian societies, such as Indonesia.[39]

### *The Small Neighbours: Points of Vulnerability*

None of its smaller neighbours—except perhaps Pakistan—poses a serious military threat to India.[40] However, India sees these neighbours as threatening in other ways.

- First, with the exception of Sri Lanka, India's neighbours have been ruled predominantly by non-democratic governments.

Until recently Pakistan and Bangladesh were ruled by the military; Nepal and Bhutan are kingdoms; and all four are seen as inherently unstable. Indians believe that most South Asian peoples, as opposed to governments, share their view of the cultural unity of the region and its common security problems. If these states had democratic regimes, Indians argue, accommodationist views would surface and support Indian positions on regional security and integrity; in other words, stabler governments would collaborate more actively with India. This view is now being put to the test as Pakistan, Bangladesh and Nepal all have fledgling democracies. Pakistan, however, remains a special case.

- Second, these states have ethnic and communal problems similar to those of India, and some of these problems spill over present political boundaries, creating security problems for India.

Examples include Kashmiris in India and Pakistan; Tamils in Sri Lanka and Tamil Nadu (southern India); Bengalis in Bangladesh, West Bengal and western India; and tribal problems in north-east India, often involving Myanmar and China. The increase in national consciousness has made ethnic movements a threat to the integrity of all nations in the region, as politicians often use ethnic groups in all the states to further their own particular goals. Ethnic problems seem to be increasing, and they are likely to continue to create difficulties for India as well as other governments of the region.

- Third, these small states have often sought support and aid from powers outside the immediate region so as to balance India's preponderance of power.

While the smaller states see the search for balance as a natural and almost necessary step, New Delhi considers it a betrayal of regional integrity. Sri Lanka's flirtation with the United States and others, as well as Nepal's and Bangladesh's opening to China, have created anxiety in India that has led India to try to counteract all such activities. Indeed, Kautilya long ago warned against the intrigue of foreign kings 'as a threat to one's own security', even as he accepted intrigue and the use of internal spies as legitimate self-defence measures.[41]

- Fourth, Indians suffer from a pervasive fear of the 'foreign hand' at work among India's unstable neighbours and in India.

Although the Indians seldom name these foreigners, they are perceived to be the Chinese, sponsors of revolutionary wars and tribal unrest; the Americans in the form of the ubiquitous CIA; and the Pakistanis.[42] On the one hand, foreigners undoubtedly have at times intrigued and interfered in India's domestic affairs and those of its neighbours. On the other hand, the Indians sometimes blame the foreigners to such an extent that they overlook the inherent instability of some of their own region and of their neighbours.

Indians also fail to understand, or reluctantly accept, a neighbour's need to use foreigners to offset India's dominating influence as they do not see themselves as a threat to their neighbours. Moreover, India has engaged in such disruptive practices. In 1971, it interfered in East Pakistan and more recently in Sri Lanka. India's Research and Analysis Wing (RAW), its principal intelligence agency, is widely believed to have been involved in both cases.

Indians see these actions as less reprehensible than similar actions by the neighbours against them as Indians believe that their security: (1) must take priority in the region, and (2) that it generally benefits all of South Asia. Thus, India's regional strategy suggests two core perceptions:

- India will not allow a neighouring state to undertake any action in foreign affairs or defence policy that India deems potentially inimical to Indian security.
- India will not permit foreign governments to establish a presence or influence in neighbouring states that India views as unfriendly.

Some have described this as the 'Indira Doctrine', and it is not unlike the Monroe Doctrine. Indians believe, however, that their approach is firmly based on the cultural and geographical unity of the subcontinent. The Monroe Doctrine, in contrast, covered a vast area with no geographical unity and included countries with somewhat different cultures, languages and histories.

To advance this regional strategy, India built on earlier British treaties and agreements that restricted the freedom of its neighbours in their foreign and defence policies. Under treaties with Nepal and Bhutan, neither can take security actions of which India does not approve. The strategic location of Nepal and Bhutan atop the Himalayas constitutes a critical element in Indian defence against possible Chinese threats.

The 1972 Treaty of Friendship with Bangladesh, though less specific on security matters than the Himalayan nations treaties, sought to prevent Bangladesh from initiating unfriendly security policies. Similarly, a letter attachment to the 1987 accords between India and Sri Lanka limited the latter's freedom of action with respect to foreign use of the harbour of Trincomalee, its employment of security advisers from abroad and the establishment of foreign broadcasting facilities on its territory.

Delhi has also applied political and economic pressure to change the policies of its smaller neighbours. In mid-1970s, India supported groups in Sikkim that favoured union with India. When in the late 1980s Nepal and India disagreed over the renewal of their treaties covering trade and transit, India applied strong economic pressure to landlocked Nepal. The crisis was settled in 1990, after India yielded to Nepal on several key points; since then, however, internal changes in Nepal have brought to power a more pro-Indian government.[43]

India has intervened militarily in its smaller neighbours' affairs when it felt threatened by their internal discord. In 1970-1, Prime Minister Indira Gandhi regarded the disturbances in East Pakistan as a potential threat to all of eastern India, as masses of refugees were pouring over the border. The disturbances gave her the opportunity to cut Pakistan in two, an intervention that led to the partition of Pakistan and the creation of an initially friendly Bangladesh.

Again in 1987, Indira Gandhi's son and successor, Rajiv Gandhi, intervened in Sri Lanka to protect the Tamil minority to ensure the integrity of Sri Lanka and to help bring about a peaceful settlement of the Tamil insurgency on the island.[44] According to a Calcutta editor, 'thanks to him (Rajiv Gandhi), Pakistan is South Asia's only other truly independent nation'.[45]

The Maldive government in 1988 called on India for help during a coup attempt; India responded immediately, then promptly withdrew its troops after the crisis ended.[46] Even though many in the Indian Army in retrospect viewed the Sri Lankan intervention as a mistake, Indian hawks strongly defend the operation and assert that they would advocate similar operations in the future when important Indian interests are at stake.

These Indian interventions seem to conflict with the declared policy of Nehru and his successors that Delhi recognises its neighbours' sovereignty, territorial integrity and autonomy in their domestic matters. But the policy does not apply when matters of India's national interest are involved.[47] This may seem like a contradiction to Westerners, but it does not to the Indians. The situation decides the policy, and India's interests will always dominate in such circumstances. Where the subcontinent is concerned, pragmatism and self-interest prevail over morality and idealism.

The tension between India and its neighbours stems from (1) different concepts of regional security and (2) India's size. For Indians, the subcontinent's cultural and geographical unity implies a strategic unity, even if the region remains divided into various states. The subcontinent's smaller nations, in contrast, emphasise their political independence and seek to establish an identity of their own.

This tension is reflected in the South Asian Association for Regional Cooperation (SAARC). New Delhi fears that its neighbours will use SAARC to gang up on India, while its neighbours fear that large and powerful India will use SAARC as a forum to control them. India has always insisted on bilateral relations with these nations; but for them, fear and suspicion of

India lurks just beneath the surface. Their concern should not be surprising, given India's disportionate power and its willingness to intervene when it perceives threats to its own interests.

*Pakistan: The Regional Destabilizer*

Most Indian strategists consider Pakistan a unique case, threatening vital Indian interests in multiple ways:

- Pakistan's existence breaches the unity of the subcontinent and thus threatens its security.
- Geostrategically, Pakistan, a hostile power, sits astride the main land invasion routes into India.
- Pakistan's armed forces have remained a threat and have imposed a heavy defence burden on India, but they do not challenge India's survival.
- Pakistan's military power draws Indian power away from the defence of the subcontinent as a whole.
- Pakistan has developed a navy that could interfere with Indian access to Middle East oil and other Indian interests in that region.
- Pakistan has brought hostile outside powers into the subcontinent through its alliances; at various times these have included the United States, China and several Islamic states.
- Since 1947, Pakistan has aided and abetted separatists and other destabilising movements inside India, for example, in Punjab and Kashmir.[48]
- Finally, Pakistan's Islamic professions threaten Indian secularism; its ties to other Islamic nations are a source of financial and other support; and the spectre of Islamic fundamentalism surrounding India, in the view of Indians, amounts to encirclement by hostile elements. Pakistan even talks of an 'Islamic (nuclear) bomb'.

Indian politicians viewed the 1947 partition and creation of Pakistan as an unfortunate but temporary breach in the strategic unity of the subcontinent.[49] Kashmir also quickly became a bone of contention. The accession to India of the Hindu Maharaja of Kashmir with strong Indian support or pressure angered the Pakistanis, who viewed Kashmir as a Muslim state that should have belonged to Pakistan. The accession agreement provided for a popular vote on the issue, but the vote never took place.

Even before the Maharaja of Kashmir opted to join India, tribal elements, aided and abetted by Pakistan, had infiltrated the state; they were later joined by Pakistani army units. The fighting continued until 1 January 1949, when a cease-fire was drawn across the middle of Kashmir. Thus, from its inception, smaller Pakistan took the initiative and challenged India, its unity and its assumption of primacy in the region. Pakistan has generally kept India on the strategic defensive ever since.

Although Kashmir has been a continuing and visible source of serious conflict between the two countries, Indians regard Pakistan's refusal to accept the primacy of India in the region as the basic issue of contention betwen the two countries. Pakistan, about one-eighth the size of India, had been a part of Indian history for hundreds of years, and though it is Muslim, most Indians believe that it shares the same culture.[50]

Adding the threat of injury to insult, Pakistan has developed a military capability out of proportion to its size. It has gained the support of two great powers—the United States and China—and secured financial assistance from fellow Muslims in the Middle East. Few Indian strategists believe that Pakistan can destroy their country, but through propaganda, infiltration and subversion, and especially its encouragement of secessionist movements, Islamabad can create serious difficulties for Delhi.

India was America's first choice as a regional anti-communist ally, and Indian leaders hinted that the United States and India could forge a strategic partnership. For the American leadership of the 1940s and 1950s, however, Pakistan, though less attractive, was a more eager partner, as India preferred its policy of non-alignment.

Pakistan thus became a member of the two anti-communist treaty groups formed to contain the Soviets and the Chinese in Asia: the Central Treaty Organization (CENTO) and the South-East Asia Treaty Organization (SEATO). By 1958, American military aid had provided Pakistan with the foundation of a modern army, a development that further alienated the Indians. This led New Delhi to explore the possibilities of closer relations with the Soviet Union.

Delhi did not initially respond to the armament of Pakistan with a substantial buildup of its own. Nehru, determined to keep defence spending under control, counted on the United States to restrain Pakistan. Only after the Sino-Indian conflict of 1962 did India feel compelled to expand its military forces—with American, British and Soviet help. The Indian buildup, in turn, frightened Pakistan, which launched probing attacks in the Rann of Kutch in April 1965 and larger attacks on Indian Kashmir in September of that year. The Pakistani initiative in Kashmir failed, and the Soviet Union, trying its hand as regional peace-maker, arranged a cease-fire. The Tashkent agreement of January 1966 ended the war.

Pakistan then took other steps to improve its military position. It began to look to the Islamic Middle East for support and financial backing; it also received substantial military assistance from the People's Republic of China (PRC).

As India perceived the development of an 'Islamabad-Washington-Peking axis', it actively cultivated the Soviet Union to counter-balance both the PRC and the United States.[51] After deciding to attack East Pakistan, Prime Minister Indira Gandhi in August 1971 hastily signed the friendship treaty that India and the Soviet Union had been discussing since 1969. This move was deliberately calculated to neutralise the PRC when India became militarily involved in East Pakistan.

After Pakistan attacked India in the west (some believe that India provoked the attack), the Indian Army, in December 1971, quickly marched into East Pakistan and set up the government of Bangladesh. This initiative—the first against Pakistan—helped India regain its self-respect and status in the subcontinent after its 1962 defeat by China. However, the Indians deeply resented the dispatch of the *USS Enterprise* into the Bay of Bengal, a late and futile US gesture to support Pakistan. The Simla agreement of 1972, which ended the war, stated that all Indo-Pakistani differences should be settled by peaceful means.

To the chagrin and surprise of the Indian strategic community, Pakistan recovered from the 1971 defeat, and began work on its 'Islamic bomb'. By the 1980s, Pakistan was receiving considerable military assistance from several states and was on its way to becoming a powerful military, and possibly a nuclear, power.

Indians continue to take the Pakistani threat very seriously, and much of Delhi's diplomacy and strategic manoeuvring is devoted to balancing and countering Islamabad. In the region, India strongly opposes Pakistan's efforts to provide military assistance to India's regional neighbours, especially Sri Lanka, as India sees such aid as another effort to weaken it and challenge it in the region.

India's entire Afghanistan policy flows from the principle of 'my enemy's enemy is my friend', and Indian strategists often quoted Kautilya to justify their steady support of whatever regime rules in Kabul as long as that regime is hostile to Pakistan. India has tried to contest Pakistan's natural advantage in the Islamic world with the claim that it has more Muslims than Pakistan; it even declares that this large Muslim population makes it an 'Islamic' state.[52] This tactic backfired at the 1969 Rabat meeting of the Organization of the Islamic Conference, which refused India membership. India has also tried to counter Pakistan's efforts in the Middle East Islamic countries.[53]

Indian strategists remain perplexed and concerned about Pakistan. Activists argue that India should take such actions as the 1971 attack on East Pakistan more often and wrest the initiative from Pakistan. General Sundarji's bold 1987 *Brasstacks* exercise on the Pakistani border, while he was Chief of the Army Staff, was somewhat controversial, but no similar exercises have followed.

In sum, India has devised no overall strategy to deal with Pakistan. The government finds itself in an expensive arms race with a much smaller country that has parlayed its relations with outside powers to great advantage. More recently, India has been alarmed by Pakistan's nuclear programme, which threatens to reduce the strategic gap between the two. Pakistan is now believed to have nuclear weapons. Finally, Pakistan's alleged support of low-level terrorism and insurrection poses a threat to India's domestic security.

The perceived Pakistani threats are particularly dangerous as they strike India's most sensitive nerve—its fragile national unity. As long as Pakistan continues to challenge India's primacy in the region and create trouble inside India, the relationship will not improve though both sides seem to realise that war is not the answer.[54]

### *China: The Major Rival*

Because of its size, population and military might, including a nuclear capability, Indians consider China the major external military threat, though it has not proved as steadily and actively hostile to India as has Pakistan. In Indian eyes, however, China is at least a fitting and worthy opponent. Nehru wrote that, unlike some of India's smaller neighbours, India and China were the only states that embodied entire civilisations. The Chinese threat has three components:

- A direct challenge along the 4000-kilometre China-India border
- An indirect threat from Beijing's support of India's other neighbours, especially Pakistan
- A potential challege to Indian pre-eminence in South Asia.
- The two also compete in the Middle East and in South-East Asia.

The Sino-Indian border war of 1962 was India's greatest humiliation since independence. Nehru had expected the two states to cooperate and had gone out of his way to bring China into the family of nations. China's takeover of Tibet in 1950 disturbed some Indian strategists, but Nehru accepted it in the 1954 Sino-Indian Agreement.

In the preamble to that treaty, India and China agreed on Panchsheel (five principles): respect for each other's territorial integrity and sovereignty, mutual non-aggression, mutual non-interference in each other's internal affairs, equality and mutual benefit and peaceful coexistence. Nehru extended these five principles to relationships among all nations.

Border tensions and incidents nevertheless escalated, and the Chinese finally attacked India in 1962. The incursion shocked Nehru and, in the view of some, may have contributed to his death. Ostensibly a Chinese reaction to what it saw as Indian intrusion into Chinese territory along the border, the attack's broader purpose seems to have been to humble India and expose its weakness, as well as to prove that the PRC was a major player in South Asia.

Border disputes have remained a problem, with serious tension recurring in 1987. Indian passions have since subsided, and Rajiv Gandhi visited China in 1988. Subsequent low-level talks, conducted by the secretariat-level Joint Working Group, have met with little enthusiasm on either side for a definitive solution.

The solution will take time to work out, as the approaches to the problem differ. India bases its arguments on what it sees as historical facts while China seeks a political deal. After the 1962 war, the Indian government vowed not to give up any more Indian territory. Moreover, public opinion would probably not allow the

Indian government to give up any Indian territory at this time. More recently, Prime Ministers Rao and Li Peng agreed in December 1991 that the Joint Working Group should meet regularly and discuss specific solutions. The group met in February 1992 in New Delhi.

India for several reasons sees China's close and continuing relationship with Pakistan as a serious threat. China has provided military, perhaps even nuclear, aid to Pakistan. It might support Pakistan in times of crisis and, under certain scenarios, help with a second front against India. China's resentment of India's special relationship with the former Soviet Union exacerbates the situation, though improvements in Sino-Soviet relations in the 1980s diminished these concerns.

Because of the threat of a war with China and Pakistan, Indian strategists must plan for at least a two-front war. While interior lines confer certain advantages, the distances between the fronts are great and India's transportation system has a limited capacity for large-scale troop movement. One can only guess at India's strategic or operational plans for defeating a two-pronged threat.

India has most likely adopted a version of the famous Schlieffen Plan of World War I. India's position poses similar problems to those faced by Germany: a small-mobilising country on the west and a larger, but slower, country on the east. The plan would entail a quick defeat of Pakistan while the ten mountain divisions and the Indian Air Force hold the Chinese in check. Once Pakistan was defeated, the main elements of the Indian Army would move to the eastern front for the longer, larger struggle against the Chinese.

Those concerned with the Indian Navy also fear Chinese naval expansion and increased activity in the Indian Ocean. Chinese submarines have been reported in the Indian Ocean, and several Chinese naval vessels have visited Bangladesh and Pakistan. However, given China's ancient submarines and limited surface fleet, the threat is not considered serious at this time. China's naval capabilities may be more a rationalisation for India's naval development than an immediate and serious threat to its vital security objectives.

The border dispute in northernmost India (Figure 1) is the most obvious issue between the two powers, but the basic problem is the role and place of each in the region. India had hoped to play the leading role in South Asia, but China, with its 1962 intrusion, has indicated that it too wants an important place. India and China have competed for the most part peacefully in South-East Asia over the centuries, but the existing rivalry could become more serious as both grow stronger and seek spheres of influence.

India also feels threatened by Chinese efforts in the Middle East. It is especially concerned over China supplying missiles and other military hardware to Saudi Arabia and its help to other Middle East nations.

India has based its strategy for dealing with the Chinese threat on a combination of military and diplomatic approaches. It has directly addressed the threat by forming and training ten mountain divisions for high-altitude warfare against the Chinese, and it has trained its Air Force, which was not ready in 1962, for operating at high land altitudes. The Air Force can play a key role against extended Chinese supply routes. These forces, however, can only delay a major Chinese attack.

On the diplomatic front, India developed closer relations with the Soviet Union to balance China's relationship with Pakistan. The Treaty of Friendship in 1971 called for consultation between India and the Soviet Union in a crisis and generally accomplished India's aim of neutralising China. The treaty, renewed in 1991, now applies to Russia.[55]

Thanks to the end of the cold war and the changed world situation, India faces new and complex problems, but also the possibility of restoring relations with China. Somewhat improved Russo-Chinese interaction might weaken Russian support for India, but the opportunity for better Indian relations with China might reduce India's need for Russian support. In fact, Moscow has encouraged India to improve ties with China.

Prime Minister Li Peng's six-day visit to New Delhi in December 1991, the first by a Chinese prime minster in 31 years, seemed to herald the new interaction. While no major issues were resolved, the friendly and constructive approach on both sides should help with the problems and obstacles separating the two nations. Li Peng agreed that India and China should work together for regional peace, stability and development. The two sides reiterated their adherence to the five principles agreed to in 1954 and expressed the hope that the meeting would usher in a new era in their relationship.

Great differences remain, however, in the ideology and the goals of Beijing and New Delhi in South Asia, and both must overcome a long period of mistrust.[56] China's unilateral declaration of sovereignty over the islands of the South and East China seas, its activities in Myanmar, and its nuclear explosion in June 1992 did nothing to reassure India.

### *The Soviet Union*

Generally hostile relations between India and China since the late 1950s, and the latter's increasing support to Pakistan, caused India to turn more and more to the Soviet Union for friendship and aid. India's relationship with the USSR came easily and naturally, as Nehru and other early Indian leaders had long admired the Soviets and their way to development as a model for other undeveloped nations, though many did not wholly approve of the Soviet political system.

The USSR and China developed a rift in the 1950s and Pakistan became involved in the US anti-Soviet network of alliances. The Soviets supported India's takeover of Goa in 1961, the Indian position on Kashmir and its opposition to the transfer of US arms to Pakistan.

In 1968, the Soviets indicated their willingness to sign a formal treaty of friendship with India, and a draft treaty was negotiated by late 1970. India was reluctant to sign, however, partially because it feared that doing so might jeopardise its non-aligned foreign policy. Moreover, the Indian public was not ready for such a move.

Pakistani-Chinese relations became increasingly close in the late 1960s, and the internal situation in East Pakistan worsened during the same period as the government of Yahya Khan in Karachi cracked down on the independence fighters in the east and hundreds of thousands of East Pakistanis (Bengalis) fled to West Bengal. In early 1971, Indira Gandhi decided to intervene in East Pakistan in support of the guerilla independence movement. At the same time, India turned increasingly to the Soviet Union because of (1) the approaching crisis in East Pakistan, (2) Henry Kissinger's visit to Beijing in July 1971, which Pakistan helped to facilitate and which suggested closer US-PRC ties, and (3) the possibility of US and Chinese aid to Pakistan.

The Soviet Union, however, declined to back India on the East Pakistan issue and urged a peaceful settlement. Mrs Gandhi—either to improve relations with China so as to forestall its possible support of Pakistan, or to gain Soviet support—made some friendly gestures to Beijing that the latter did not reciprocate. The gestures sufficed, however, to make the Soviets choose India over Pakistan. India and the USSR finally signed a Treaty of Peace, Friendship and Copperation on 9 August 1971 in New Delhi, about a month after Kissinger's trip to China.

The Soviet Union stopped sending arms to Pakistan and warned China that it would not tolerate any intervention on behalf of Pakistan in East Pakistan. At the same time, Soviet submarines in the Indian Ocean reminded the Americans of the Soviet friendship with India. The Soviets saw the treaty as a first step toward Brezhnev's goal of a cooperative security pact with Asia. The Soviets also believed that India could be a helpful friend in world councils, particularly at the UN and in the non-aligned movement.

The Soviet-Indian treaty was not, however, an alliance; in fact, over the next 20 years, each government interpreted the treaty to serve its own interests at any given time, emphasising the treaty's economic, political or security aspects as it suited them. Indian friendship with the Soviet Union, begun even before the treaty consolidated it, lasted for over 30 years and will doubtless continue with Russia and the Central Asian republics.

India and the Soviets did not agree on all matters. India, for example, albeit rather quietly, opposed the Soviet invasion of Hungary in 1956 and of Afghanistan in 1979. India only mildly disapproved the presence of the Soviet fleet in the Indian Ocean, but loudly protested that of the US fleet. It never accepted Brezhnev's or Gorbachev's ideas of a collective security pact in Asia.

As trade between the USSR and India increased and the former suplied arms to the latter, relations grew closer. India nevertheless has maintained its independence, never allowing Soviet military personnel on its military bases. And despite Moscow's urging, it has refused to sign the non-proliferation treaty.

The two nations have, however, shared many of the same interests and goals, and were circumspect when they did not. Both opposed colonialism and, as they saw it, the American version of it. Both have been seriously concerned about China as a security threat (though at brief intervals seeking better relations with the Chinese), and have developed close and mutually beneficial trade relations. Some agreements on ideological considerations (i.e. socialism) and cultural and other exchanges have contributed to a continuing friendly relationship.

The sudden disintegration of the Soviet Union shocked Indians and in some ways left them feeling unprotected.[57] Althought the Soviet-Indian friendship treaty was not an alliance, India considered the Soviet nuclear capability a protection against the Chinese and the Americans. India now seeks to improve relations with both the United States and, though not at the same pace, with China. It is also reaching out for broader contacts throughout the world, including Turkey, South-East Asia and Israel.

India has not forsaken Russia, which it sees as largely replacing the Soviet Union, and they have renewed the friendship treaty. India gave a million tons of grain to help the Soviet Union, and Indians still talk of their long and fruitful friendship with the Soviets. India wants to continue its relationship with Russia as well as with other parts of the former Soviet Union, especially the Central Asian republics. It sees Russia as an important country and one that still has nuclear weapons. Indians believe that Russia will eventually be able to help counter the unipolarity of the world, which Indians abhor, and they intend to continue to cultivate their relationship with Russia.[58]

### *Beyond South Asia: The Indian Oean Region*

India sees the Ocean as a vital frontier, along with the north-west and north-east land boundaries (Figure 3). Until the late 1960s, the Royal Navy defended India from the sea. Its departure in 1967, when Britain withdrew from east of Suez, left the Indians feeling vulnerable and unprotected. They felt even more so when the United States gained a base at Diego Garcia (Figure 3) and both superpowers sent naval ships into the Indian Ocean.

Indian admirals like to remind the government that Britain—the one power to subjugate India from afar—had come by sea and that such an invasion should not be allowed to happen again. India now believes that it should have defensive forces in the Indian Ocean to keep hostile powers at bay and protect its maritime interests. India would like a 360-degree *cordon sanitaire*.

India has many specific concerns about the Indian Ocean region, including its strategic competition with Pakistan and China discussed earlier. This competition extends to both the Middle

East and South-East Asia, and even to Africa and the Indian Ocean island states. New Delhi raised an alarm when China sold IRBM missiles to Saudi Arabia, arguing that this represented a further encirclement of India by Beijing.

Other concerns stem from Indian fears, partially a legacy of the colonial era but also a result of post-independence experience, that powerful outside states will establish a presence in the Indian Ocean area, perhaps in collusion with weaker regional states.

In the seventies and eighties, India feared that the United States, usually seen as unfriendly to India, was becoming a major hostile power in the area by virtue of the US acquisition of a base on Diego Garcia and the presence in the Indian Ocean of large elements of the US fleet.[59] Soviet naval deployments seemed to suggest a superpower confrontation in the region and possible military activities. With the end of the cold war, both powers have reduced their presence and the threat of superpower conflict has almost disappeared.

Now, however, the relative military superiority of the United States in the area, as demonstrated by Operation Desert Storm, worries the Indians. Though the Indian government has voiced no strong objections, as it feels an improving relationship with the United States lessens the American threat, some Indians are nevertheless wary of an American presence: In the first place, they distrust Washington's uneven record of support of New Delhi; second, they have consistently opposed an American presence in the Indian Ocean region. Anti-American feeling remains widespread in India, though the government seems eager to improve relations.[60]

Indians also worry about the arrival of foreign navies in the Indian Ocean at some future time. Indian naval advocates especially fear a Chinese naval presence in the area and, in the more distant future, the possible return of Japanese forces. India would much prefer a *Pax Indica* in the Indian Ocean, with little or no outside naval presence.

India has special interests in the Middle East and West Asia, especially in the Persian Gulf region, as well as security concerns:

- New Delhi hopes to become a source of finished products, goods, and advanced engineering and construction services, not merely a source of cheap labour or a subcontractor to Western multinationals.

- India depends on the Middle East for a large percentage of its oil. However, many likely oil suppliers are orthodox Islamic states that have regularly criticised New Delhi for its treatment of Indian Muslims and for India's control over part of Kashmir. Only Iraq supported India on Kashmir.
- Several Islamic fundamentalist Arab states have funded militant Indian Muslim groups.

Members of the Indian strategic community often express a sense of being surrounded by a sea of Islamic fanatics and argue that India and the United States have a common interest in containing militant Islam. There seems to be no real Muslim strategic threat to Indian security, but psychologically the Muslim presence revives Indian feelings of being encircled by hostile, Islamic, forces.[61]

The Indian government, in a change of policy, normalised its relationship with Israel in 1992, and the two countries have exchanged ambassadors. India has not, however, severed ties with the Palestine Liberation Organization (PLO) and Iraq.

The overseas Indian communities, which stretch from Fiji in the east to South Africa in the west, have concerned both Indian politicians and the Indian public. India has vigorously opposed *apartheid* in South Africa. Only in recent years, however, has India even come close to acquiring the military capability to think about protecting such communities. The persecution of Indian minorities in Sri Lanka and Fiji, a powerful human rights issue throughout India, could well serve as a stimulus for sustaining power-projection capabilities.

India feels that it has good relations with the nations of South-East Asia and points with pride to the influence of Indian culture on the area. It also has an interest in the Strait of Malacca, which Indonesia, Malaysia and Singapore dominate (Figure 3). Some Indians speak of an informal coalition of India, Indonesia and Vietnam to keep peace in the region and, not incidentally, to contain China's ambitions in the area.

India admires and envies the tremendous economic growth of the ASEAN states as well as the ASEAN cooperative mechanism. But while India is giving these neighbours somewhat more attention than formerly, they do not loom large in Indian thinking.

Among the South-East Asian states, however, Myanmar (what was formerly Burma) deserves special mention. It is the only South-

East Asian state to have a land border with India, though the border is a long distance and a difficult journey from central India, and some Burmese tribes inhabit both sides of the border. The British conquered Myanmar in the nineteenth century with the essential help of Indian troops. The British brought in Indian labour and administrators, and Indians soon became a powerful factor in the Burmese economy.

The Burmese rioted against the Indians in the 1930s and anti-Indian feelings have been high at times. In 1961, General Ne Win of Burma expelled 200,000 natives of the subcontinent (they had lived in Burma since before the partition, so they were neither Indian nor Pakistani) and confiscated their properties. The Burmese permitted cross-border aid to the Nagas and other tribes rebelling against the Indian government in north-eastern India and allowed the rebels sanctuary in Burma.

India, for its part, has opposed the State Law and Order Restoration Council (SLORC), the military regime that took over the Burmese government in 1988. India broadcast anti-SLORC programmes on All-India Radio, a practice that SLORC much resented. India also openly support the democratic opposition.

All nations but China have cut off aid to this repressive military regime. The Chinese, with the agreement of the Burmese, have opened the Sino-Burmese border in the north to the free flow of goods. Having also provided considerable aid and a billion dollars' worth of military assistance to northern Myanmar, China has essentially established economic hegemony in that part of the country, increased its influence over the Myanmar government, and established close relations with the Myanmar military.

The Chinese are rumoured to be seeking better access to the Bay of Bengal by improving roads from the north of Rangoon, and they have offered to improve harbour facilities in the city. Pakistan, China's long-time friend, is also believed to be providing unspecified assistance to the military regime in Myanmar.

The Thais are concerned about the expanded Chinese influence in Myanmar, traditionally a nation of special interest to Thailand. At Emperor Hirohito's funeral in February 1989, Thai Prime Minister Chatchai called on President Bush to expand relations with Vietnam and Myanmar as he feared too much Chinese influence was developing in the latter.

All of these changes disturb India, and one Indian has written that it is part of an encirclement of India led by the Chinese.[62] Other than to protest and to wage psychological operations against the SLORC, India probably cannot do much. The friendly visit of Chinese Prime Minister Li Peng to India in December 1991 contrasts with China's unfriendly behaviour elsewhere in India's neighbourhood.

The other South-East Asian states do not see the situation exactly as the Indians do, but rather share some of the concerns and anxieties of India's closer neighbour. Some wonder about Indian intentions in the Andaman Islands (Figure 1), what actions India might undertake with a large navy, and how India would behave, should the United States withdraw from the region.[63] Several local states want to obtain surveillance aircraft for use in the Indian Ocean.

Indians speak of their country's peaceful cultural influence in South-East Asia, but India's military buildup raises suspicions that India's interests may not be peaceful. Indians living in these states might also attract the attention of India if they were perceived as being mistreated. On the surface, relations between India and South-East Asia generally appear good, but the smaller states are genuinely concerned about India's military power and what it proposes to do with that power.[64]

Strategically, India aspires to serve as a friendly regional peace-keeper. It sees itself as a benevolent nation and a friendly policeman that seeks peace and stability for the entire Indian Ocean region. It denies any hegemonic designs or territorial ambitions. It vehemently rejects and resents charges of being a regional bully. It wants not only to play the role of friendly peace-keeper but also to be acknowledged and endorsed in that role by others, especially the great powers.

In sum, while they may disagree on particulars, virtually the entire Indian strategic community is united in the belief that others have not recognised New Delhi's legitimate regional role. India sees itself as the pre-eminent power in the region, though not an authoritarian one. At the same time, New Delhi has never fully articulated its strategy or policies for the region. Indians were pleased at American support for their operation in Sri Lanka and the Maldives, but wonder about the firmness of such support for India's longer-term regional role and aspirations.

*India and the World*

The Indian strategic community is one of the few in the world that aspires to a global role. As best expressed in Nehru's writings, Indians have always seen their country as an international player and contributor to a new world order. This broader vision is a major factor in shaping Indian relations with the United States and other major powers.

Shortly after independence, Nehru wrote: 'India is going to be and is bound to be a country that counts in world affairs, not I hope in a military sense, but in many other senses, which are more important and effective in the end.'[65] Indians today still emphasise the idea that although they have no territorial ambitions, a state as large and important as India should be heard and respected in world councils.

Nehru recognised the linkage between domestic weakness and a global role in the 1950, observing that 'any part we want to play in world affairs depends entirely on internal strength, unity and conditions of our country'.[66] He understood that others would pay attention to India in proportion to its strength—and not necessarily its military strength; his policies of self-reliance clearly indicate this awareness, as did his early concentration on developing a sound economy.

Indian nationalists believe that India has always been a great country, even though it has rarely been united or militarily powerful. Since the late nineteenth century, they have argued that India's size, population, strategic location and culture constitute an obvious basis for India's standing as a great world nation.[32] Nehru could not imagine that the world would not accord India its rightful position.

But the world has not accorded India its rightful position in the eyes of most of the Indian political and strategic community. Indians brush aside the typical foreign view—that India lacks historical and political continuity and coherence, and that it is a land of poverty—as stemming from ignorance of the powerful unity produced by India's rich culture.

At independence, most Indians saw the beginning of a new and glorious period for their country. Nehru's famous speech of 14 August 1947, 'A Tryst with Destiny', reflected this pride and expectation.[68] Even recent critics of Nehru (who believe he was too soft on Pakistan and China) argue that India was fortunate to have had such a world-renowned leader. They appreciate the way he applied India's spiritual and moral tradition to world affairs.

Nehru believed that a nation's foreign policy had to reflect and express its values, and that pluralistic, democratic and secular India was destined to play a principled, moral role in world affairs. Nehru asserted this belief in his espousal of Pan-Asianism and non-alignment, his frequent criticism of the use of force to settle disputes between nations, and his strong support for the United Nations, at least in its early years.

Non-alignment became the essential basis of Nehru's foreign policy. This policy, though much misunderstood and maligned, has served India well. It avoided entangling alliances and joining either bloc. It rested on neither neutrality nor passivity, nor did it place India equidistant between the blocs, as President Eisenhower mistakenly believed. Nehru detested the cold war and what he called the 'bloc mentality'. His was essentially a policy of independence, of doing what he thought was best for India, of keeping India free of dependence on any other authority. It was, in many ways, a pragmatic policy.

Nehru conceived of Indian interests in the context of world peace. Understanding that the first duty of a country is to protect itself, he put India's interests first. However, his pursuit of India's interests—for example, his China policy—was sometimes unrealistic. He is best remembered for his eloquent espousal of the idealistic goals of peace, world cooperation, anti-colonialism, racial equality and Pan-Asianism.

No other newly independent nation arrived on the world scene with the likes of Nehru to lead it. His wise and realistic policy of independent action, or non-alignment, proved to be exactly what this great, but young and militarily weak, nation needed. He gave India a stature in the world that it has not enjoyed since his death.[69]

After World War II, all of the colonies in Asia began to achieve independence, a shared goal after the shared experience of colonialism for most. Nehru believed in and tried to lead a Pan-Asian movement. Asia, he said, had come alive. He held conferences and meetings and talked about the 'new spirit of Asia', Asian sentiment, and Asian cooperation. Unfortunately, the euphoria of Indian independence blinded him to the great differences in ethnic composition, culture, history, geographical position and interests of the various new Asian nations.

Furthermore, many in India and elsewhere did not share Nehru's broad vision of Asia. This vision was shaken by the Chinese takeover of Tibet in 1950 and abruptly destroyed by the Chinese invasion of India in 1962. Asians turned out not to be one homogeneous group, all believing in peace and cooperation. Pan-Asianism was not a practical concept. To Nehru's credit, he learned his lesson: He realised, though somewhat late, that India must have powerful defence forces and began their development after 1962.

Indian strategists disagree as to exactly what role India should play in the world and how to reach such a goal. Senior members of the Indian strategic community, including several who worked with Nehru, insist that India's claim to world leadership must be based on moral and spiritual values. Others do not believe that a moral basis alone will enable India to achieve a world position. They argue that India must have military power, and indeed must become a world military power.

Naval and nuclear advocates, especially, argue that India must have a nuclear capability and a navy able to project power.[70] The frustrations and ambitions of the nuclear hawks can be summed up by the comment of a Calcutta publisher: 'Moscow and Washington can nuke Delhi, so why shouldn't Delhi have the capability to nuke them.'[71] However, some Indian thinkers appear to have come full circle and have reasserted Nehru's principle that the real basis for power in the contemporary world is economic rather than military strength.[72]

Despite the range of Indians' views on the proper global role for India, most agree that India has not received the attention or recognition it deserves. Indians strongly believe that India's size, population, history, culture and recent achievements make India a world nation. They resent the fact that their country is not yet considered a world power, even a regional power. For many, the indifference of the world is worse than hostility. They feel a real need for world position and for the world's recognition of that position.[73]

## PROPOSITIONS

### *The Absence of Strategic Thinking*

Although India has, over time, developed elements of a defence strategy, as discussed in Section 2, it has produced little formal strategic thinking and planning. Air Chief Marshal Suri, who headed the Indian Air Force till recently, accurately reflected the Indian approach to strategy and planning when he characterised the Air Force as 'reactive', rather than 'active', adding that India had no territorial ambitions. He expressed little concen over Pakistani efforts to acquire an advanced early warning (AEW) system: 'We will see how to counter it if Pakistan acquires the new capability'.[74]

The lacunae in strategy and planning derive largely from India's historical and cultural development:

- First, because India lacked political unity throughout most of its history, Indians have not thought in terms of national defence planning. The few brief periods of imperial unity depended on the will and power of a great leader, and the unity did not lead to a modern nation-state.[75] At other times, the smaller individual Indian states saw to their own local defences.
- Second, the Hindu concept of time, or rather the lack of a sense of time—Indians view life as an eternal present, with neither history nor future—discourages planning.
- Third, Hindus consider life a mystery, largely unknowable and not entirely under man's control. In this view, fate, intuition, tradition and emotions play important roles, but how, how much, and when is never clearly known. Man's control over his life is thus limited in Hindu eyes, and he cannot forecast or plan with any confidence.[76]

Aside from the Mauryan, Gupta and Mughal empires, little historical evidence exists to suggest an Indian political entity. One finds temporary alliances of various Indian states to gain an advantage in war, but these were local agreements and in no way concerned with a greater India. The fact that Indian states almost never banded together to fight invaders suggests that they had no sense of a defence for India as a whole, only for their individual states. Many Indians told the author that their forbearers identified themselves by caste, locality and language, rather than as Indian or Hindu, which, they maintained, were Western terms.

The seeming lack of efforts toward and feelings of Indian political unity suggests that there was little thought of India even as a collection of states that might gain from some form of cooperative action or agreed-on interstate norms.[77] Broad cultural unity, however, has long existed and continues to flourish in India, though it did not, before the nationalist movement, have political attributes.

The major component of Indian unity—Hinduism—is so amorphous that Westerners have difficulty understanding how it can serve as a bond for Indians. Yet Indians consider Hinduism the primary basis for the concept of an age-old India and for the political nation of India today. Cultural history, however, is not the same as a political history, and cultural unity differs from political unity. Neither the ideal of an enduring India nor an ancient culture has had to face the myriad socio-economic, foreign policy and strategic problems that a political state must confront.

The British developed strategic ideas for the defence of India, but they kept the Indians out of discussions and decisions in matters of strategy. British strategic policy for the defence of India evolved over the years, and was often debated between Whitehall and Delhi, but neither drew up a complete strategic plan. Indians thus had no experience with the formulation of modern strategy. As in most democracies, the British government kept a rather tight rein on the military, not allowing them to participate in the highest levels of government where strategy was sometimes considered.

The India of today, though based on culture, is a new and fragile political union. Large and complex problems confront it in every sphere. It cannot solve these problems without some careful planning. While Indian culture helped make this union possible, it handicaps the union's progress by its views of time and life. Strategic thinking about this new political entity is thus a new problem.

Most Indians assert that no military or government leaders and few civil servants are directly concerned with strategic planning. India's early prime ministers, particularly Nehru and his daughter, Indira Gandhi, thought out and managed foreign policies and strategies on their own, or with a small coterie of advisers. No serious strategic planning institutions, if they ever existed, have survived in independent India, and none exists today. The recent creation of the National Security Council (NSC) acknowledges the need for strategic planning, but many Indians consider the NSC stillborn, while others believe that it will not begin to function, at least for some time.

The powerful hold of India's culture notwithstanding, Indians pragmatically recognise that Western ideas are bringing changes.

India will adjust to this conflict in its own way and its own speed. With their talent for analysis and conceptualisation, Indians seem admirably equipped for strategic thinking. Furthermore, Indians do think strategically and have developed some strategic concepts, but like the British before them, they have developed these concepts in an informal and haphazard way. For example, India has never issued a white paper on defence strategy and does not appear inclined to do so.

Thus the forces of culture and history and the attitude and policies of the independent Indian government have worked against the concept of strategic thinking and planning. As India's need for strategic planning increases, a structure for planning is likely to develop slowly.

### *India on the Strategic Defensive*

Throughout most of its history, India has been on the strategic defensive. Over the centuries, armies from Central Asia and Persia have invaded the subcontinent by land, and Europeans, for a shorter period, have invaded by sea. Rarely did the Indians succeed in repulsing invaders, and they seemed not to learn from past experiences how to change this. The small Indian states concentrated more on fighting each other or assisting the invader against a rival than in turning back the invaders collectively. Indian armies seldom attempted a forward strategy against the invaders, and thus most of the fighting took place on Indian territory.

At the height of the Indian nationalists' campaign for independence in the late nineteenth and early twentieth centuries, when their sensitivities were most acute, British India began to adopt a more passive defensive posture. Until that time, it had followed a policy ranging from offensive expansion to aggressive defence. Thus, the events of their own lifetime tended to reinforce the nationalists' perception that India historically had maintained a defensive posture and fought defensive wars.[78]

India arrived on the world scene as an independent nation and status quo power with considerable resources. The new nation inherited most of the land and resources of the subcontinent and much of the British governmental apparatus. Its goal was to hold and defend what it had. Pakistan, a much smaller nation with fewer resources, was born with an inferiority complex and with a grievance over what it considered was an unfair distribution of

British assets. It was particularly upset over the loss of part of Kashmir at independence.

While India hoped that Pakistan and India would reunite, thus restoring a cultural unity and a defensible India, Pakistan preferred independence. It did not want India to enjoy its assumed superior status. Pakistan accepted the 1948 United Nations arrangement for a cease-fire line that cut Kashmir in half. India, in a defensive move, made its half an integral state of the Indian union. Pakistan took a somewhat more offensive stand: It kept its share as a territory, hoping someday to unite all of Kashmir by force or other means and to create a single Kashmiri state in Pakistan.

Since 1947, India and Pakistan have confronted each other in an almost continuous state of tension and have fought three wars. India believes that Pakistan has been the aggressor in these wars and that Islamabad continues to take the offensive with its assistance to separatist groups inside India. India considers itself constantly on the defensive and believes that it must keep fending off Pakistani attacks of one variety or another.[79]

Since Indian independence, China has also put India on the defensive. China seized Tibet in 1950, a move the British had worked for years to prevent . Nehru, however, did not oppose the seizure. He seemed to think that China had a right to Tibet, and he hesitated to violate the spirit of Pan-Asianism, which he held so strongly. In 1962, China revealed its hostility to India, its desire for a position in South Asia, and its willingness to take action against a fellow Asian nation by attacking India. India was not prepared and again seemed to be on the defensive.

India and China, at least for the moment, accept the present status quo on the border and are conducting low-level talks. India seems satisfied to hold land up to the MacMahon Line, a position it has always taken in the north-east (Figure 1, Section 1). The Chinese hold the Aksai Chin salient, very important strategically to them in the north-west, but both claim the other's present holdings. India has lived with the Chinese nuclear capability for some years, seemingly without much concern.

China in many ways has behaved less provocatively than Pakistan *vis-à-vis* India. Furthermore, China lies outside the subcontinent and though it is India's most powerful rival, it is psychologically less of a threat to India's vital interests than Pakistan, which lies within the subcontinent. However, India has not forgotten the

Chinese attack in 1962 and has prepared forces to deter, and if necessary to oppose, any renewed Chinese aggression.

*The Lack of an Expansionist Military Tradition*

Largely because of its geography, India has a long history of non-aggression and non-expansion outside the subcontinent. Had the Indians sought to expand to the west, north or east, they would have faced a long, cold trek through the mountains to lands that are relatively poor and barren. Thanks to India's relative riches, however, Indians lacked an incentive to expand.

As India developed within its own boundaries, its people, especially those in the fertile northern Indo-Gangetic plain, became increasingly involved in their own internal affairs. In a few cases, they were building great empires; in others, they were conducting interstate rivalries and small wars. At the same time, they were producing a rich and unique culture. Self-sufficient in the necessities of life, they were largely oblivious to the outside world.

The south, although often dominated by the north, was less influenced by Aryan cultural restraints and more exposed to the sea; as a result, early in Indian history it developed a significant maritime tradition. Several southern dynasties, including the Cholas, pursued an expansionist policy, particularly in South-East Asia. The Cholas, whose short-lived empire existed nearly a thousand years ago, were the last, however, to establish colonies in what is now Malaysia and Indonesia and to fight with the local states for control of the east-west trade with China. Little maritime activity has taken place since then, until the recent naval buildup.

Independent India sees itself as continuing the tradition of non-aggression and non-expansion outside the subcontinent. Nehru's foreign policy rested on these principles, and subsequent leaders have followed suit. The tradition of non-aggression, however, has never applied internally. Warfare within the subcontinent has been the norm for centuries. States fought to gain power and wealth, to establish empires, or to destroy them.

This seeming paradox with regard to non-aggression arises from the Indian view of the subcontinent as a single strategic area that coincides with Indian national interests. This belief justified India's taking much more active measures—some say aggressive measures—to protect its interests in the subcontinent; for example, India:

- Took over Portuguese Goa in 1962 in an effort to rid itself of the last vestiges of colonialism.[80]
- Peacefully, though exerting some pressure, absorbed Sikkim in 1975.
- Actively supported the separatists in East Pakistan in 1971.
- Sent the Indian Army to defeat the Pakistani forces and to establish the new nation of Bangladesh in 1971.
- Dispatched a 50,000-man 'peace-keeping force' to Sri Lanka in 1987 (but subsequently withdrew it)
- Sent forces to the Maldives (at their request) in 1988.

Most Indians see these not as aggressive moves, but rather as defensive actions to preserve India's internal security. India's neighbours, of course, take the diametrically opposite view of India's posture and actions in the subcontinent.

### *The Army, Land Warfare and Primary Strategic Concerns*

India continues to rely heavily on its Army, despite recent attention to the buildup of the Indian Navy. The Army remains the dominant military service and receives most of the defence resources.

The British, when they ruled India, developed a land-oriented defence strategy for the country. Their control of the world seas protected India from seaborne attack, but on land they were forced to contend with the Russians and Chinese for the control of Afghanistan, Iran, Central Asia and Burma.[81]

From London, the British government, basing its power on the Royal Navy, took a global strategic view. India represented only a part of what the British empire had to protect. The Indian government, in contrast, developed a regional land-oriented strategic view: From its perspective, the land approach presented the greatest threat.

The Indian government continues to focus on land, rather than naval, warfare. During World War II, Japan threatened India overland in the north-east. Since independence, India has fought three wars with Pakistan, primarily on the land, and one with China along the vast land border stretching from Pakistan in the west to Myanmar in the east. The border problems with China remain unresolved, and the Pakistanis continue to aid and abet the dissidents in Punjab and Kashmir.

In addition to protecting India's borders, the Army plays an increasingly important role in internal security. Neither the Air Force nor the Navy can contribute to this mission. In many cases, the domestic problems have exceeded the capabilities of the Indian government's civil forces to deal with them, and the government had no alternative but to call in the Army; for example, to deal with the current difficulties in Kashmir, Punjab and Assam.

The Army does not consider these internal operations its primary responsibility, as they divert it from preparing for a real war. Army leaders believe, however, that they must respond to civil direction. Despite the Army's attitude, some Indians are concerned that the Army may have to take control of the country if the internal disorders worsen.

The Army has evolved as an important agency of the Indian government. As an institution, it is heavily entrenched, with a momentum of its own, and it plays a powerful role in the allocation of resources. While the Navy has attracted more attention recently, the Army and the land threat will remain the pre-eminent concern of India in the foreseeable future, though India's new economic policies will make trade and the seas more important to India.

### *Self-Reliance and Independence*

The drive for self-reliance has become an important element in the Indian strategy for attaining security, true independence and international stature. Nehru early on came out in favour of strategic self-reliance and independence:

> In our external and internal domestic policy, in our political policy, or economic policy, we do not propose to accept anything that involves in the slighest degree dependence on any other authority.[82]

Nehru's primary foreign policy doctrine of non-alignment was intended to steer an independent course between the two superpowers. Rather than neutralism, it represented India's right to take positions in India's interest.

To ensure India's independence, Nehru emphasised the need for economic and industrial self-reliance. Even if the process proved slower and more expensive than dependence on foreign products, he believed that India must develop its own capabilities.

Just before the Chinese attack in 1962, however, Nehru brought VK Krishna Menon into the government as minister of defence, in part to speed up the process of achieving military self-reliance. The trickle of aid from the United Kingdom and the United States did not meet India's needs in the critical days of late 1962. Moreover, no foreign power was going to send 40 wings to defend India, as Nehru requested President Kennedy to do. Clearly, India needed to mobilise its own forces for action, preferably armed with Indian-made weapons.

After the Chinese attack, the Indian government initiated a vigorous military research and development programme, stepped up the construction of military industries and re-equipped the Army and the Air Force. Discarding long-held ideas that military expenditures degraded economic developement, the government opted for a new policy of joint military and economic development that it hoped would produce synergistic effects.

India subsequently built tanks, airplanes and ships, developed missiles and conducted a peaceful nuclear explosion. Although much of the dual-use technology, serving both civilian and military needs, has been of good quality, India has had only limited success in producing advanced weapon systems.[83]

While seeking military and economic self-reliance, India has had to rely on outside suppliers for the most modern technology. The military demanded the best weapons and their acquisition as soon as possible. As a developing nation, India could in no way satisfy all the needs of its military for modern technology at this point in time.

In the 1960s, India in vain sought weapons from the United States and the United Kingdom. Unable to obtain them, it turned to the Soviet Union. In the 1970s and 1980s, India purchased and, through licensing agreements, built many Soviet weapons. It also diversified its purchases so as to avoid complete dependence on any one foreign source, buying aircrafts from both France and the United Kingdom, naval vessels from Germany, and some US equipment.

India continued to depend on the Soviet Union for spare parts and for some of its new weapons and equipment. Even before the Soviet Union broke up at the end of 1991, however, it was slow to fill India's orders. Indians do not know what to expect in the future from what was the erstwhile Soviet Union.

Delhi also continues to depend on outside suppliers for many advanced-technology items, including components of the proposed light combat aircraft. It needs computers and other sophisticated equipment from the United States, but it hopes to attain soon the capability to produce complete naval ships and other weapons with the most sophisticated and advanced components.

While Indian leaders often decry the international munitions trade, they talk of exporting weapons to spread the cost of research and development across a larger number of consumers as well as to reduce the production costs by turning out more weapons. The demands of the Indian military itself do not justify keeping open enough production lines to keep India self-reliant.[84]

India will not give up its two goals of true independence and unity unless critically important circumstances require outside support. One unknown Indian politician is reported to have said he would rather fail going it alone than survive with outside help. Self-reliance in weaponry provides the independence Indians so cherish, and thus affects strategy. By reducing reliance on foreign countries, India hopes to free itself to act independently on the world scene. However, the new economic policies and military needs for high technology are undermining, though by no means destroying, this policy.

### *Passivity in Military Affairs*

In addition to the factors listed at the beginning of this section—India's historical lack of political unity and the Hindu concepts of time and the mystery of life—that have contributed to the passive or reactive tendencies in Indian military matters, three others merit mention. These include the agricultural basis of Indian culture, the rigid structure of Indian society and the bureaucracy of the Indian administrative services.

India, being predominantly an agricultural country, has largely a rural population. Like most rural people, Indian farmers have no tradition or understanding of long-range planning. For them, nature has determined the important—and unchanging—sequence of when to plant, when to harvest, etc. However, determined efforts to irrigate, fertilise and improve seeds have created a revolution in Indian agriculture. The success of this green revolution is partially changing peasants' views. The peasant psyche remains important, however, as many of today's leaders come from the rural areas of India.[85]

Moreover, the fairly rigid and hierarchical structure of Indian society, while it does not completely stifle initiative, makes changes and individual initiative difficult. Individuals have few incentives to test the system, as failure or loss of caste is considered a calamity. Caste and family are critical, and an individual is lost outside of them. Urbanisation and other modern institutions are breaking down castes, but the caste riots in 1990 showed that the system retains much vitality, though it is changing and adjusting as India grapples with the problem of the development of democracy.

Finally, the Indian administrative services, especially powerful in the absence of stable political leadership at the centre, react rather than initiate. Their training, their social background, and the influence of Fabian and socialist thought does not encourage individual initiative. Strategic innovation will not come from within the traditional government bureaucracy.

*Status and Symbolism*

Status and symbolism matter greatly in Indian society, particularly in India's strategic calculations and military perceptions. Indians consider specific military capabilities—e.g. nuclear weapons, long-range missiles and aircraft, a large blue-water navy and a strong military-industrial base—symbols of great-power status, and India therefore must have them.

Indian policymakers sometimes have difficulty explaining their intentions and plans for new weapons, especially missiles, and for expanding the Navy. This situation suggests that either they hope to obscure their long-term strategic designs or, more likely, the new weapons have not been integrated into a carefully developed strategic plan.[86] The admirals, for example, may need no further justification or rationale than that India's greatness mandates a powerful Navy. Being sensitive to status and symbols, many Indians may assume that if India had these symbols of great power it would be recognised as such.[87]

Gaining recognition of India's status in the region and in the world also plays a pivotal role in Indian strategic thought. Indeed, external recognition and validation of India's place is almost as important as actually having that status. For example, India unquestionably dominates the Indian Ocean region, but Indians are greatly frustrated by the failure of external powers to acknowledge this fact.

While the Indian government showed considerable embarrassment over the international attention to its naval buildup and insisted that it had no offensive designs in the region, some Indians were gratified that outsiders were beginning to pay attention to India's regional status. Outside approval of Indian actions in the Maldives and Sri Lanka especially pleased the Indians, since it implied recognition and endorsement of India's peacekeeping role and its status in the region.

Indians often question why India is not a permanent member of the United Nations Security Council. At the time of independence, Nehru believed that the United States, the Soviet Union, China and India would be the four great world states. Three of the four have permanent seats, but India does not. This clear symbol of great-power status eludes India, even though India is much larger than France and the United Kingdom and is soon to surpass them in such measures of national power as industrial, military and economic capabilities.

Some Indian strategists now mention the possibility of cooperation with the United States in peacekeeping roles. Despite the profound differences between the two countries in economic and military strength, the strategists insist that any cooperation with the United States must be based on absolute equality. They refuse to serve under the United States. The point here is not to argue whether or not the United States and India are really equal in practical terms, but to emphasise how strongly India feels about equal status with the great powers.

### *The Effect of Modern Weapons on Indian Strategic Thinking*

In the absence of a strategic plan, modern military technology is beginning to shape India's strategic policy. Weapon programmes are driven by technological opportunism and the institutional interests of the defence science community, not by specific strategic requirements. Indian policymakers are becoming aware of the implications of these emerging technologies and see a greater need for mechanisms to develop a strategy.

Several factors in addition to its own inner dynamics are spurring India's drive toward modern military technology. First, the indigenous production of the advanced weapons systems of the great powers, Indians believe, would partially fulfil Indian ambitions for regional and world status. India seeks to keep up with Pakistan, China and other neighbours, who are ahead in, or moving faster into, the world of advanced military technology.

Second, India's perceptions of its own historical inferiority in weapons feeds a 'never again' attitude. India's increasing maritime interests and the need to protect them require a modern Navy. India wants to be modern and militarily strong and considers these attributes its destiny.

Third, the speed, range, precision and devastation of modern weapons systems are rapidly changing the nature of war and making the traditional Indian strategic posture less effective. The Gulf War showed clearly the enormous power of offensive weapons. Advanced armour, precision guided missiles, long-range missiles and modern aircraft will require New Delhi to revise its defensive concepts.[88] The Indians, already alert to the need for modern weapons, see this need even more clearly now.

India has three options for defence against its main threat, Pakistan:

- First, it can pursue its traditional defensive strategy of guarding the border with mobile reserves.
- Second, it can develop forces strong enough to deter a Pakistani attack.
- Third, it can preempt.

Under the first option, Pakistan might plan a quick surprise blitz with immediate territorial gains, hoping that world opinion would soon halt the war, with Pakistan holding the gains. These would be powerful bargaining chips for subsequent peace negotiations. In a longer war, India's greater staying power and mobile reserves would probably prevail. Because this second possibility is less likely, India would have to develop a more effective and immediate defence.

The second option would require forces strong enough to deter any Pakistani attack. To be credible in Pakistan, these forces must convince the Pakistanis that they would lose any war that they started. Deterrence, however, is delicate; it can change rapidly with the introduction of new weapons, shifts in alliances, and the perceived change of will on the part of Indian or Pakistani leaders.

The third and boldest option would involve preemption. In this case, India would attack Pakistani forces before they could launch an attack. The decision to preempt depends on reliable intelligence and the capability for rapid execution. Whether General

Sundarji's Operation *Brasstacks* manoeuvres in 1987 constituted a bold exercise or the beginning of a preemptive attack on Pakistan was not clear at the time. Few in the Indian Army are as bold as Sundarji, but technolgy is driving the Indians to review their strategic posture and it will likely lead to a more active defence posture in the future.

It is not a great leap from an offensive defence or preemption to thinking offensively. This is not to suggest that India has any specific offensive intentions or goals, but some modern weapons encourage offensive thinking. Irrespective of whether the Indian leadership is thinking offensively, India is developing a capacity to execute offensive military actions.

India has twice (the second time in June 1992) successfully launched the Agni intermediate-range ballistic missile (IRBM), which has a range of about 1500 miles and could reach the Middle East, China and South-East Asia.[89] If produced and deployed, Agni would give India the capability for deterrence or for a preemptive first strike in a large radius around India. In addition, technological advances in naval platforms and weapons have extended India's reach into the Indian Ocean for both forward defence and limited power projection.

The Indian Air Force has transport aircraft that can rapidly move a battalion or more. Furthermore, India carried out an amazingly effective airlift early in the Gulf crisis, when aircraft of the civilian A320 Airbus fleet airlifted about 150,000 Indians out of the Middle East in about three weeks, approximately the same as the number of troops that the United States was flying in.

Both India and Pakistan seem close to attaining a nuclear weapons capability. In fact, Pakistan claims that it has such a capability. Although China already produces these weapons, India seems less concerned at the moment about China's intentions than about Pakistan's.[90] The latter's acquisition of a nuclear weapons capability will almost surely trigger an overt Indian programme, if it has not already done so. The possibility of acquiring nuclear weapons is already stimulating debates on nuclear strategies for South Asia. Participants in these debates often cite the long peace between the super-powers—peace that they attribute to nuclear balance—as a reason for India and Pakistan to have nuclear capability. Whether nuclear weapons would stabilise or destabilise is a major unanswered question.[91]

*The Navy*

The role and objectives of the Indian Navy are eliciting considerable discussion inside and outside India.[92] Most Indians consider the Indian Ocean India's third important frontier (the north-east and the northern being the first and the second), and they argue that India needs its Navy to protect itself from outside aggression. Indians also see the need to safeguard India's increasing maritime interests, including:

- Its trade routes and ships
- Its access to Middle East oil
- Its extended economic zone
- Its pioneer status under the Law of the Seas for the potential mineral exploration of a large area in the Indian Ocean and similar interest in the Antarctic region.
- Its islands in the Bay of Bengal and the Arabian Sea
- Its close relations with Mauritius and the Seychelles (Figure 2, Section 1)
- Its considerable interest in the choke points of the Indian Ocean, including the Red Sea, the Strait of Malacca and the Madagascar region (Figure 3, Section 1).

Indian naval proponents hesitate to discuss specific threats; instead, they emphasise the broad range of India's maritime interests as adequate justification for a large navy. They note also that a great India requires a large navy to carry out its regional responsibilites.[93]

Naval proponents do, however, discuss threats in a general way. They point out the high mobility of navies and note that a hostile threat may develop in the Indian Ocean with little warning. Smaller states, including Pakistan, can and do, without informing India, invite the great powers to send naval ships into the Indian Ocean so as to counter Indian power. Future threats that may arise from China, Japan and other nations, naval proponents say, must be anticipated now, as it takes a long time to build ships and develop the infrastructure to support them.

The presence of naval ships of the great powers, especially the American naval buildup in the Indian Ocean and the acquisition of a base at Diego Garcia, aroused Indian fears in the 1970s, though neither was directed against India. In late 1971, however, the foray of the *USS Enterprise* into the Bay of Bengal to show support for Pakistan after India's victory reminded Indians of the threat from the sea. As a result, the Indian government has paid greater attention to the Navy, instituting a programme for its modernisation and expansion.

The Navy at present has 2 old carriers, 19 conventional submarines (the leased nuclear submarine was returned to the Soviet Union), 25 destroyers and frigates, 27 patrol and coastal ships, and 41 combat aircraft including Sea Harriers and TU-142 Bear F surveillance aircraft.[94] This fleet dwarfs the navies of the other 40-odd states on the Indian Ocean periphery and appears to dominate the region, except for the presence of the great-power naval forces.

The Indian Navy also attracts the attention of India's neighbours, who see it as an instrument of Indian power projection and ambition to dominate the Indian Ocean region. However, a careful look at the Navy—the carriers for instance—reveals a limited power-projection capability against even modest opposition. In January 1990, the then Secretary of Defence Naresh Chandra said that he was lucky to have one of these old carriers operational on any given day.[95] The carriers' small complement of Harriers and helicopters—six to eight of each—gives the carriers only a short power-projection range, and problems of logistic support limit the time on station away from port.[96]

Now that the cold war is over and the United States is reducing its presence in the Indian Ocean, the Indians see new problems. The US withdrawal will likely create a vacuum that will add to India's uncertainties. They wonder whether other outside powers will move into the region, or whether other regional powers will develop navies to fill the vaccum. India, as the great and democratic nation of the region, considers itself bound by duty and responsibility to fill this vacuum.

India's new and wider-ranging maritime interests, as well as the protection of India itself, pose new challenges for the Navy in the modern technological age. The rapidly changing political world also poses new challenges and opportunities. In a sense, the Navy is constrained by neither the conservative traditions of land defence nor the restrictions that land frontiers impose on the Army.[97] The Navy, having come of age as major technological advances were made in naval warfare, is more likely than the Army to meet modern problems with modern technology and to face future challenges with greater boldness.

This is not to suggest that naval officers have shed all their culture, for they have not; however, the pragmatic side of the Indian psyche often comes to the fore in such situations. Naval officers may have a greater appreciaton of modern weapons than the officers of the other services, but the Gulf War has made all military officers more aware of the importance and power of modern weapons. This awareness will undoubtedly initiate serious rethinking of strategy.[98]

No authoritative government statement exists on Indian naval strategy. Several regional states attribute to India a desire for regional hegemony; some Indians would also state this as their goal and would seek to acquire power-projection capabilities for the Navy.[99] Yet most members of the Indian strategic community contend that the Navy is only one part of India's defensive posture in the region. Given India's budgetary problems, the government is unlikely to increase the size of the Navy as planned. The Navy will, however, remain a dominant force in the region.

### *The Complexities and Paradoxes of Indian Strategic Thinking*

In this effort to identify and distill the main characteristics of India's strategy and strategic thinking, I have had to resort to considerable simplification. Complexity, not simplicity, however, is the norm for India. I shall therefore review briefly, again oversimplifying, the major complexities and contradictions that characterise Indian strategy and strategic thinking.

- No formal efforts or institutions of the government exist to develop strategies for India, but on an *ad hoc* and pragmatic basis, Indians have produced the strategies and policies discussed above.
- Military and economic power exist side by side with widespread and abject poverty. Indians see poverty as a condition of life and maintain that it has nothing to do with military might. However, Indians are increasingly concerned with the poor and the down-trodden.
- Indians are often assertive in their views and positions; at the same time their strategic thinking tends to be defensive.

- Although the Indian government denies that it is seeking power in the international hierarchy, many of its actions are seen as contributing to the aggrandisement of its power.
- India argues for the legal and moral equality of all nations, yet it looks down on smaller states and seeks a permanent seat on the UN Security Council.
- Indians are proud and extremely sensitive. They believe that India merits international status by virtue of its culture, size, population, achievements since independence, and especially its democracy; and they resent being ignored and undervalued by the important nations of the world despite these attributes. Yet Indians appear insensitive of the feelings of their smaller neighbours and seem to ignore the simple fact that the size of their country alone elicits feelings of insecurity in the region.
- Indians tend to be suspicious, fearful of betrayal, and envious of their neighbours; yet they value truth and spiritual morality.
- Indians esteem their past empires, and the Indian elite is alleged to have inherited the 'imperial' mind-set of the British. India nevertheless ranks among the world's most strident anti-imperialists, as it decries the oppressiveness and evil of Western colonialism.
- Indians can be expedient and pragmatic in their foreign policies and strategies, but they like to emphasise the moral and spiritual aspects of India.
- Hinduism is one of the most tolerant and encompassing beliefs in the world, yet today one finds so-called fundamentalist—or, more accurately, militant and fanatical—Hindus. Westerners have difficulty understanding how adherents of this tolerant, diverse religion can adopt fundamentalist positions, and most Indians believe that the word 'fundamentalism' does not apply to Hindus.
- India is culturally old but politically young. It reveres its old, unifying culture; at the same time, it is struggling with serious separatist problems.
- India would like to be the friendly peace-keeper of the Indian Ocean, but it is building up its military power to dominate the region.
- Indians feel proud and strong yet insecure and encircled by

hostile forces. India's growing strength reassures them, but they fear the spreading Islamic fundamentalism that surrounds them and the uncertainty of the post-cold-war world.

- Indians are fiercely independent, but their fear of encirclement almost demands that they have powerful friends, such as the British and the Soviets. They seem somewhat lost without the Soviets, but they are trying to maintain good relations with Russia and are courting the United States.
- Much is changing in India, but much remains the same. Indians are quick to accept the modern materialistic life, but deep within they retain many old and basic beliefs. They consider culture the basis for modern Indian national political identity, but giving it up, yet retaining Indian identity poses serious problems and tensions.

## THE ROLE OF THE MILITARY

Since independence, the Indian government has exercised extremely tight civilian control over the military.[100] Most democracies follow this policy, including the British, who ruled India and commanded the Indian Army before independence. India has pursued the policy to a point where the military have almost no input at all in the formulation of higher defence policy and national strategy.

Nehru had a rather strong anti-military attitude, most likely based, first and foremost, on his respect and affection for Gandhi and his successful non-violent independence campaign. Other factors probably included Nehru's contacts with Fabian socialists, most of whom were pacifists; his great admiration for the pacifist emperor Ashoka; and the fact that the Army did not take part in the nationalist movement. Nehru gave top priority to peaceful coexistence and non-alignment to ensure world peace; he wanted India to pursue economic development with all its effort and resources. He neglected the military, giving it few resources, and downgraded its top leadership in the Warrant of Precedence, while increasing the status and pay of both the civil servants and the police.

As a matter of fact, the Army believed that it had contributed to independence. Immediately after World War II, the Army experienced several revolts. In the view of the military, the revolts suggested to the British that some of the unrest in India had seeped into the military. The realisation that they might not be able to count on the Indian Army thus weakened the British resolve to fight to keep India.[101] The Army also liked to point out that it had played a role in persuading the few recalcitrant princely states to join the Indian union in 1947-8, had successfully defended Kashmir from the Pakistanis, and had helped the thousands of refugees after partition. It considered itself a loyal participant in the new Indian union.

Nevertheless, Nehru often refused to accept advice or counsel from the military leadership, sometimes rather dramatically. In 1951, General Cariappa, then commander in chief of the Indian Army, warned the minister of defence of a possible Chinese threat to India after the Chinese had taken over Tibet; Cariappa urged that defensive actions be taken in the north-east. On the defence minister's recommendation, Cariappa also briefed the prime minister on these recommended defensive measures. Nehru asked why these measures were needed; Cariappa replied that the Chinese might have designs on this region of India. At this point, Nehru said:

> It is not the business of the Commander in Chief to tell the Prime Minister who is going to attack us where. In fact, the Chinese will defend our Eastern frontier. You mind only Kashmir and Pakistan.[102]

Few senior officers would be willing to confront the prime minister again.

Cariappa's was not the only warning that Nehru had ignored. On 7 November 1950, Sardar Patel, a Congress leader, had written Nehru a carefully thought-out letter telling him of the Chinese threat. Although Nehru did not take the note seriously, the General Himmatsinghji Committee was established in February 1951 to look into the defence of the North East Frontier Agency.[103] The committee produced an extensive report outlining the military shortcomings in the area and making a series of recommendations, few of which were ever implemented. Paucity of funds, difficult terrain and the lack of a sense of urgency probably explain this failure. The Border Roads Organization, which the committee recommended, was set up only in 1960.

Nehru continued to believe that the Chinese would not attack, though by the late 1950s he had come to realise that the PRC was a 'hostile' state.[104] Still, he did not change his mind about the military.

The nadir for the military services, particularly the Army, came during Krishna Menon's tenure as defence minister (1957-62). The year 1957 seemed to start off well for the Army: The able and well-liked General Thimayya became Chief of the Army Staff, and Nehru's close confidante and favourite, Krishna Menon, was made minister of defence. It seemed like a good team, and perhaps Menon's appointment meant greater attention to the military. Menon, however, had no knowledge of military matters, was accused of pro-communist and pro-Chinese sympathies, and shared Nehru's anti-militarism.

General Thimayya warned Indian leaders of the Chinese threat and the weaknesses of the Indian Army, but they ignored him and his relations with the defence minister deteriorated. Thimayya offered his resignation when his relations with Menon developed almost into open hostility. The timing was unfortunate. The next day, General Ayub Khan, the president of Pakistan, was to discuss joint defence policy with the Indians. Nehru talked Thimayya out of resigning. Thimayya hoped that the prime minister might chasten Menon; instead Nehru ridiculed Thimayya in public. Thimayya lost his credibility with his fellow officers and Menon totally ignored him.

Menon wreaked havoc with the Army and caused mistrust and suspicion among the services and between them and the ministry.[105] He was openly contemptuous of and rude to senior Army officers; he often seemed to try to humiliate them; he encouraged cliques, sought to turn juniors against seniors, sowed distrust among the officer corps and promoted his own favourites. He chose General PN Thapar over the Army choice, General Thorat, as Chief of the Army Staff and made his favourite, General BM Kaul, Chief of the General Staff of the Army.

Menon politicised the Army, a fate it had carefully tried to avoid. It was increasingly demoralised and largelly unprepared for the Chinese attack in 1962, which Menon said would not take place. Once the war began, Nehru and Menon tried to micromanage it from New Delhi, though neither had any military experience.[106]

The Indian defeat and humiliation awakened Nehru and India to the fact that the country needed a strong military force. Nehru reluctantly fired Menon, though under him not all had been bad. The Army had established important new schools, one for jungle warfare and one for high-altitude combat. The National Defence College was established in New Delhi. Menon had established new factories for the production of weapons and begun to improve military facilities, such as barracks.

After Menon's departure in 1963, the military budget doubled. The Army began a rapid expansion, the Air Force received increased support, and even the Navy received more attention and funds. General Chaudhuri, the new Chief of the Army Staff, was an able and impressive leader who improved Army morale and supervised the Army's expansion. He was supported by a helpful and sympathetic defence minister, YB Chavan. India has held to a fairly steady expenditure of between 3 to 4 per cent of its GNP on the military since that time.

Prime Minister Indira Gandhi understood the need for the military and how to use it. She gave the services ample time to prepare for the campaign against East Pakistan to set up Bangladesh. General Manekshaw, Chief of the Army Staff, included the other two service chiefs in his plans. Interservice coordination worked well and contributed to the 1971 victory. This triumph restored the confidence of the military and revealed the progress that it had made, and India could hold its head high again.[107] But even after the victory, the military leaders were again lowered in status in the Warrant of Precedence, possibly because Mrs Gandhi did not want them to become too popular or too powerful.

Civilians have feared a military coup since independence. It is not entirely clear why this is so, as the Indian Army had rarely challenged civilian control under the British and never since independence. The Army may have been considered too pro-British, not in tune with the nationalist times, and hence not entirely reliable. Also, armies of other newly independent and developing countries caused some of the alarm, as most had become deeply involved in their own domestic politics. Even the Pakistani and Burmese armies, with the same British background as the Indian Army, played decisive political roles in these two countries. In fact, General Cariappa, early on, told the Army sternly to remain out of and above politics. Other Army leaders reiterated this theme.

The fear of a coup has led to extremely close control of the military services at the highest level of the government: The

Cabinet Committee on Political Affairs (CCPA), rather than the military, makes the major strategy and military decisions.[108] The civilian minister of defence and his civilian staff receive recommendations from the services, make decisions and pass on the important issues to the CCPA. A section of the Ministry of Finance with an office in the Ministry of Defence has a near veto on all expenditures proposed by the services, and an input to recommendations to the Ministry of Defence.

The control of unusual major troop movements or other military forces in peacetime resides with the minister. The Ministry of Defence in essence serves as a higher headquarters that makes all decisions; the service chiefs have no statutory power to make government decisions.[109] They are limited to operations and operational plans.

Many of the civilians in Defence and Finance have little knowledge of military affairs and may be rotated in and out, thus providing little continuity or expertise. The military resent the fact that these largely uninformed and inexperienced civilians make all the major decisions.[110] In addition, civilians control the development and production of indigenous weapons in government-owned laboratories and factories operated by the Department of Defence Production. The Department of Atomic Energy, a civilian agency, undertakes all nuclear developments, while the civilian Space Department develops all missiles. The government maintains that both are civilian efforts directed to peaceful purposes; however, it is unlikely that vast sums are spent in these two areas for civilian uses only.[111]

In effect, the services have been down-graded in status, taken out of the national security decision-making process, and for the most part kept ignorant of nuclear developments, while the Ministry of Defence civilian staff has grown in prestige and power and controls almost all military activities and programmes. At the same time, civilians and police leaders have been upgraded and their pay increased.

The fear of a coup, along with bureaucratic opposition, has prevented the formation of much needed institutions for the coordination of the military services, as well as the development of a national strategy. Civilians, bureaucrats and policians alike have consistently opposed creating the position of Chief of the Defence Staff and a joint staff, which most modern nations have and which India needs. The Navy and Air Force fear that an Army general would hold the new position, giving the Army even greater power; many naval and Air Force officers, however, understand the need for the position, which they believe should rotate. The civilian elite are concerned that the position of Chief of the Defence Staff would give an individual a dangerous amount of power and encourage unhealthy ambitions.

The chairman of the Joint Chiefs of Staff Committee, made up of the various chiefs, with the senior one as chairman, is the normal forum for coordinating the activities of the chiefs. It works well when they get along; their cooperation in 1971 shows how well it can work. Service rivalries and strong personalities, however, do not always promote cooperation. In any case, modern warfare requires much more staff work than the chiefs can themselves conduct; they cannot get into the detailed staff work needed for joint planning and operations. The Defence Planning Committee is intended to fill that need.

Serving officers cannot talk about the operations of the Defence Planning Committee, and outsiders therefore have some difficulty determining what it actually does on a continuing basis.[112] By most accounts, this staff develops plans for the procurement of weapons and equipment and, on an *ad hoc* basis, works out strategy and plans papers that are sent to the Ministry of External Affairs and the intelligence community for coordination; once a paper is agreed on, it is sent to the defence minister. Most of the push for joint planning comes from the lower and younger levels of the services.

The Defence Planning Committee is extremely small and inter-service feelings are strong, all of which limits what it can do even under the best circumstances. Some observers consider it simply a forum for talk; others believe that it undertakes some planning. Most would agree that the present system does not meet the needs of modern warfare, particularly for a country the size of India. India thus has no effective means at present for inter-service coordination in peace time, for the formulation of national strategies and policies, and for the higher direction of war, should it come. The decision to create a National Security Council, made during the VP Singh government in 1990, has not been implemented as of mid-1992.

The Army takes pride in its apolitical stand and its support of the civil government and India's internal security. However, the pressure of continual use for internal security and stability is beginning to take its toll.[113] The Army is not trained for police action; it does not want to oppose its own people; and it feels deprived of valuable training for war, its primary mission. Army personnel increasingly believe that the Army is doing too much large-scale internal security, such as in Punjab and Kashmir. In April 1992, to the displeasure of some opposition politicians, Army Chief of Staff General Rodrigues said that the poor economy and poor civil governance had led to this state of affairs.[114]

Despite the Army's concern over its internal security operations, its conviction that it must do the bidding of its civiliam masters, distasteful though at times it may be, seemingly has not weakened. One finds no hint of a challenge to civilian control. However, some observers, including Americans, worry that continual use of the Army for internal security missions could lead to greater dissatisfaction and frustration in the Army and the possibility that it might decide to take matters into its own hands.[115] This seems unlikely in the immediate future, as the apolitical status of the Army and its belief in civilian control remain a strong part of the military culture.

Some army leaders have been concerned about the present condition of the Army Officer Corps. General Sundarji, when he took over as Chief of the Army Staff in 1986, sent a long letter to all officers in which he complained of poor morale and low self-esteem; he attributed these to the influence of opportunistic, sycophantic and corrupt officers who thought only of themselves and their careers. He also complained of too great an emphasis on officer privileges and comfort.

Other officers have complained that the downgrading of the services has led to the recruitment of less qualified officers and, consequently, a lowering of professionalism.[116] Some admit that the top Army leadership has failed to maintain high standards. Many officers feel that the leadership should have fought harder to keep a higher place in the Warrant of Precedence and that it failed to adequately warn the government of the danger to the country of constantly downgrading the military.

Despite the perceived slights, the services today seem to have good morale, self-confidence, and professional pride. The Army remains the dominant service and takes particular satisfaction in its long history. Most officers will quickly and proudly talk of their regiment, its age and its achievements, even though many of these were accomplished under British rule.

The Army fought to support the British empire in many parts of the world and in both world wars participated in combat with great distinction. Since independence, the Army has helped to keep the country together and served as a symbol of national unity. It participated in UN peace-keeping missions in Korea, Gaza, Indochina, Lebanon and the Congo, all with great distinction and credit to India. It is probably the most experienced army in the world in missions that contribute to international peace.

The Indian Army has continued such British traditions as great loyalty to the regiments, a high sense of professionalism, and families having served the Army for many generations.[117] The Air Force and the Navy are developing their own traditions, and both new services have confidence in their abilities. They are also less restrained by tradition and often more open to leadership and social change in their composition.

The services seem to have taken the lead in closer relations with the United States, a significant policy decision not normally made by the services. Officials of the Ministry of External Affairs claim that this could not have been done without their support. The civilians in the Ministry of Defence, it is alleged, at least in the beginning did not support this initiative, but they have now come around: witness the visit of Minister of Defence Pawar to the United States in April 1992.[118]

These actions raise the question of the military's seeking a greater role in policy matters. However, Indo-American relations have been improving in many other areas of government; thus, the military did not really make a major policy decision. Furthermore, civilians still hold tight reins on the military.[119]

The military plays only a minimal role in decision-making on matters of national security. If allowed, many well-educated and thoughtful military officers could contribute, under civil direction, to the formulation of national strategy and defence plans. The services remain apolitical and adhere strongly to the principle of civilian control.

The need for inter-service coordination and the development of a national strategy remains great but unfulfilled. As the world grows more complicated and India plays a greater role, the requirements will become ever more pressing. Past government progress in addressing these problems is not encouraging, though now, as in the case of economic and financial reform, attention to strategic needs may also increase.

## A NOTE ON NUCLEAR STRATEGY

Strategies for the use of nuclear weapons—not addressed in this study—will undoubtedly influence India's strategic thinking as time goes on. They may have already done so, but the Indian government has neither announced nor revealed a nuclear strategy, and it continues to pursue a policy of ambiguity about its nuclear capability.

All nuclear developments are carried out by the Department of Atomic Energy, a civilian agency, which maintains that it works only for peaceful purposes. Nevertheless, it exercises tight control over all information on nuclear matters. Up to now, the military have been excluded from the programme and therefore do not talk about it. However, a very few military officers apparently are now involved one way or another in the programme.

One may reasonably conclude that, given India's peaceful nuclear explosion in 1974, China's nuclear capability, and Pakistan's long-time and well-known desire for a nuclear capability, India has not neglected the military aspects of its nuclear programme. Its missile programme, again conducted by civilians, has produced the Agni IRBM and other missiles, indicating that relatively long-range missile delivery systems are being developed. Officially, these too are for peaceful purposes.[120] Officials sometimes say unofficially that the Agni, if used for military purposes, will carry only conventional warheads, a contention hard to believe, given the cost of the missile and the limited lethal range of conventional weapons.

Pakistan's admitted nuclear capability now has probably increased India's efforts. Mrs Gandhi took the position that India must respond accordingly to any Pakistani developments. VP Singh warned in April 1991 that 'Pakistan will have to pay a heavy cost' if it gets the bomb.[121] Prime Minister Rao indicated that India would take care of itself.

One hears limited but increasing public discussion on the nuclear issue, and most of it concerns whether Pakistan has the bomb and whether India should have one.[122] Many Indians oppose having a nuclear capability on moral and other grounds. A few, however, maintain that India should develop a nuclear capability, arguing that it must have nuclear weapons to deter Pakistan and China and to free itself from blackmail by either. Moreover, they say, it must prepare to use them in war if necessary. They also argue that until India has the bomb, other nations will not recognise it as the great nation that Indians believe it to be.

Some say that the military are not interested in nuclear weapons, that they are content with their conventional superiority over Pakistan; others suggest the services might consider tactical nuclear weapons. In any case, either the active military are specifically prohibited from discussing nuclear matters, or they have an understanding with the civilians that they will not speak out on them.

The Indian military simply cannot be unaware of the problem of nuclear war or of the considerable information about nuclear weapons in the world. They have read the enormous open literature on the subject of nuclear weapons, and they have attended military schools in the United States, the UK, and the Soviet Union where these matters are discussed. The fact that the Pakistanis say they have the bomb must make the Indian military think about nuclear matters, at least privately, even if they are prohibited from official discussions.

Retired officers, including General Sundarji, have strongly advocated that India obtain a nuclear capability. At the same time, Sundarji believes that even if Pakistan has the bomb and uses it, India can still absorb the attack and win the war with conventional weapons. According to one Army officer, when General Sundarji was chief, the Army had already begun to develop defensive tactics against nuclear attacks.

In contrast, K Subrahmanyam, who has written extensively about nuclear weapons, sees the serious dangers of asymmetry in nuclear capabilities.[123] If a neighbour were to gain a nuclear capability, Subrahmanyam argues, Indian civilian and military morale would both suffer, though this did not seem to be the case after the public announcement that Pakistan had the bomb.[124]

A nuclear capability, Subrahmanyam said, allows the state that has it to concentrate its forces against a non-nuclear state, which would have to disperse its forces. He further suggested that psychological operations could cause panic in the non-nuclear country, creating huge refugee problems and impeding military operations. These psychological operations, in his view, might succeed so well that the aggressor would not have to use the bomb.

There has been some limited discussion in India of well-known nuclear issues, such as minimum deterrence, a counter-force strategy, and the value of a second-strike capability, but there have been no major studies, at least none that have been made public. The present diffused public discussion does not help much in understanding Indian nuclear strategy, or ascertaining if it has one.

The PRC has had a nuclear capability for three decades, but this has not caused the Indians to worry greatly.[125] Foreign Secretary JN Dixit, on a visit to Washington in March 1992, calmly stated that the PRC had tactical nuclear weapons in Tibet. The Indians, he said, have lived with this threat for years. China's huge explosion in June 1992 may change the Indians' casual attitude.

Indians view Pakistan's nuclear capability in an entirely different light from the way they view China's. But even in the case of Pakistan the public has not panicked. Indians have openly discussed this situation, and the public seems assured that the Indian government has it under control.

While some fear the asymmetry problems raised above, others like General Sundarji say that this really does not matter so much, though they still urge India to get the bomb. Some argue that it would be better for both India and Pakistan to announce that they have the bomb, as that would create a more stable situation; others argue the opposite, especailly in Pakistan, where the generals control the bomb, unlike in India, where civilians control it.

Based on this analysis of Indian strategic thinking, one might conclude that the Indians may not address the problems seriously until a real crisis arises. On the other hand, if the Indians seriously want a nuclear capability, they must develop a strategy for the employment of nuclear weapons. Some say that a small group of civilians is developing this prerequisite, but the leadership has remained silent on the matter. One might also surmise that Indians may be considering reactive or defensive strategy and tactics to deter an opponent, to stop a major enemy breakthrough, to cut the passes in the Himalayas, or to assist in an Indian counter-attack.

The military have not participated in policy-making, but some military commanders evidently may now have instructions on the use of nuclear weapons in war under certain circumstances, though these are sealed until ordered to be opened by the civilian government. This presents an awkward situation, as the military maintain that they are unaware of the programme, can make no plans, have received no general guidance for the use of weapons, and no command and control system appears to exist.

The present governmental secrecy, the Indian inclination not to plan ahead, and the deliberate policy of ambiguity make an accurate analysis of the effect of nuclear weapons on Indian strategic thinking and strategy difficult and unreliable at this time, at least to any outsider without intelligence information. In the next year or so, however, the government will probably take some action and perhaps even issue some policy statements. Certainly, there will be more public study and discussion of nuclear strategy, and the United States will want to follow these developments.

## NOTES

1 Given India's strategic position astride some of the world's major trade routes and its long coastline, one would have expected an extensive history of maritime and naval operations. Although India has participated actively in international trade and commerce for centuries, it has not played a major role in the purely maritime aspects of trade, i.e. sailing the ships.

2 See Romila Thapar, *A History of India*, Vol. 1, Penguin Books, London, 1987, p. 21, for a brief but interesting discussion of the influences of geography on the north and south.

3 Jawaharlal Nehru, *The Discovery of India*, Oxford University Press, New Delhi, 1982, p. 88. According to Amaury de Riencourt, *The Soul of India*, rev., Honeyglen, UK, 1962, p. 152, 'the sea played no part in the building of India' and India had 'no organized relations with the oceans as' for example, South-East Asia had'.

4 De Riencourt (p. 15) says of Indians that 'of all the people on earth they are the least interested in history'. This statement applied less, as nationalism developed. See also NK Sinha and Nisith R Ray, *A History of India*, Orient Longman, Hyderabad, 1973, who maintain that Indians revere the past but know little of it (p. 10).

5 India has few historical records and nothing comparable to the works of Herodotus or Thucydides in Greece in the fifth century BC. The Indian epics are great and moving accounts of certain historical events, but they are more mythology than history.

6 Brahman here refers to the upper caste, rather than to Brahman,

the world spirit. The Brahmans' more intellectual approach to Hinduism is called the Great Tradition; the less structured, more emotional, and more diverse approach is known as the Lesser Tradition. The Brahmans have carefully maintained the Great Tradition, which the English discovered before they encountered the Lesser Tradition. The latter, because it had innumerable variations and evolved orally, left a less clear and more diverse record.

7 For a moving and inspirational example of one man's discovery of Indian history, see Nehru, 1982.

8 Some cynics have argued that there was no one left to fight, but this seems doubtful: Local kings fought and eventually contributed to the end of the Mauryan empire.

9 Samudragupta (AD 320-80), probably the greatest Gupta emperor, has been called the 'Indian Napoleon'. See Lt. Col HC Kar, *Military History of India,* Firma KLM Private Ltd., Calcutta, 1980, p. 69.

10 The Indian nationalist movement in fact lost its cultural moorings and began 'to coalesce with old Hindu xenophobia which had appeared before the Muslim conquest and became hardened under Muslim rule'. See Nirad C Chaudhuri, *Thy Hand, Great Anarch!* The Hogarth Press, London, 1987, p. 33.

11 Many Middle Eastern fundamentalist groups have been influenced by the thought and writings of Abul Ala Maududi, who died in 1979 in Pakistan. Many ideas of the present Islamic revival came from India, and one of the most active *dahwah* (missionary) groups, the Indian Jamaat Tabligh, operates in parts of South-East Asia, thus in sense renewing Indian cultural ties to that area.

12 Hindus see Aurangzeb as a fanatic and zealot, but Muslims insist that he was a stricter and more devout Muslim than Akbar.

13 Some Indians have dismissed the nationalist leaders' knowledge of India and its cultural history. Chaudhuri (p. 33) wrote: 'From 1921 onwards the nationalist movement was carried on in a growing cultural void. The civilization of ancient India became a subject of chauvinstic bragging. Hinduism, which was certainly the most stable, deep-rooted and authentic cultural force among a great majority of Indians, became in the Westernized India a nationalistic myth.' The subsection immediately following, entitled 'Culture', presents a brief overview of Hinduism as it relates to strategy.

14 Jawaharlal Nehru, *The Discovery of India,* 4th ed., rev., Meridian Books, London, 1960, p. 49. Chaudhuri (p. 32) claims that Nehru knew little of India or its history.

15 Indians in the south feel their Indianness somewhat less intensely than those in the north. Southerners take pride in their own history and culture and in some ways feel superior to northerners, who had often been invaded by 'barbarians'. Bengalis are equally proud

and independent. Regional and state loyalties remain strong, as pressure for the devolution of power from the central government to the states suggests.

16 Nehru was proud of the vitality and success of Indians who went abroad, but worried about their mistreatment. He also recognised the limitation of what India could do for them in a foreign country. See Jawaharlal Nehru, *India's Foreign Policy,* Government of India, Ministry of Information and Broadcasting, New Delhi, 1983, p. 127.

17 Indians sometimes refer to this area as 'Greater India'. Sinha and Ray, p. 4.

18 The Chola King Rajendra's expeditions to South-East Asia were 'unique in the annals of India', according to AL Basham, *The Wonder That Was India*, Sidgwick & Jackson, London, 1967, p. 75. Kar (p. 110) states that Rajendra's 'naval expeditions form a glorious chapter of our own maritime history. No Indian monarch before and after him even attained such conspicuous success in this field'.

19 The Guptas briefly experimented with some innovations but soon returned to their conservative and familiar forms of war.

20 See note 18 above.

21 According to Thapar (p. 113), 'Indians preferred to allow sailors of other nations to transport their goods.'

22 KM Pannikar, *Problems of Indian Defence*, Asia Publishing House, New York, 1960, p. 60.

23 The idea of *varna* may have influenced Plato's philosophical ordering in *The Republic.*

24 The Sanskrit word for castes is *jati*; 'caste' is of Portuguese origin (*casta*), meaning tribe, clan or family. For the classic introduction to Indian civilisation, see Basham, p. 149.

25 It is difficult for an individual to move, as his caste is essential to his identity and place in society.

26 *The Bhagavad Gita* [Song of the Blessed One (Krishna)]. Although many Indians take seriously the duty to lead a moral life, some in the lower castes accept their fate, as they see little chance of changing it. Although today many Indians no longer think specifically of transmigration, the tenet lingers in their psyche.

27 One Indian told me that Indians had relied on intuition and emotion for a million years, so why should they give them up for logic, which is only a few thousand years old.

28 De Riencourt (pp. 45, 102-5) argues that Indians have a spatial rather than a temporal view of life and reality and that this leads to the related conclusion that time does not exist.

29 De Riencourt (p. 45) writes: 'Since the process of time has no meaning, since history has no goal, every individual is merely

reacting the same endless part, creating nothing new, making no original contribution to human progress.' De Riencourt is wrong, of course, as Indians over the years have made great contributions to human knowledge and understanding including the concept of zero and the nine so-called Arabic numerals, which the Arabs introduced to the West in the ninth century.

30 See Ainslie T Embree, *India's Search for National Identity*, Chanakya Publications, New Delhi, 1987, p. 2.

31 Judith M Brown, *Modern India: The Origins of an Asian Democracy*, Oxford University Pess, New Delhi, 1988, p. 147.

32 Some Indians have said that India would still be part of the British empire had it not been for British racism. According to others (for example, Chaudhuri, p. 31), nationalism developed as a negative movement against the British, and the lack of any positive goals greatly weakened it.

33 As noted above, Indians had been aware of invasions and threats, especially from the northwest, for centuries but had made few, if any, attempts at a unified or explict strategy. The states sought only to defend their own limited areas.

34 Given the disorganised expansion of the British empire in Asia, not all of these acquisitions were originally seen as part of India's defence, but all became incorporated in it. Although unable to control the straits in the Dutch East Indies empire, the British gained footholds in North Borneo and developed northern Australia to counter the Dutch.

35 See Pannikar, p. 59. A very small Indian Navy was created in 1924, but it was unable to defend even local waters.

36 The Indian government has never articulated its security strategy in any one place or time. The *mandala* concept is based on Kautilya's *mandala*, but applied more broadly here. According to the concept, a nation's contiguous neighours are always seen as enemies and their outer neighbours as friends, in a series of circles. See *Kautilya's Arthashastra*, translated by Dr R Shamasastry, Mysore Printing and Publishing House, Mysore, 1967, pp. 22-4. Kautilya, a Brahman adviser to the Mauryans, used the *mandala* concept in describing his work on the art of govenment.

37 The northern part, at least, of the Indian Ocean is included in this definition.

38 The Indian constitution approved in 1950 provides for a federal system that takes into account the divisions within India while trying to mould a union. In recent years, the central government has taken on more and more power, and the states have now begun to call for the devolution of authority to the local level.

39 Indonesia has adopted and educated its people in one national

language, promulgated five principles of national ideology, *Pancasila* and through socio-economic measures tried to demonstrate the opportunities and value of Indonesian unity.

40 Pakistan is discussed in the subsection immediately following.

41 Kautilya, often referred to as Chanakya, preceded Machiavelli in a cynical and amoral approach to strategy. See *Kautilya's Arthashastra*, pp. 22-4.

42 Even after considerable improvement in Indo-American relations, some Indians still blamed the CIA for Prime Minister Rajiv Gandhi's assassination in May 1991.

43 In May 1991, the Nepali Congress, backed by the Indian Congress, won the national election to form a new democratic government. However, the opposition in 1992 is threatening the pro-Indian government.

44 The Indian Army intervened ostensibly to protect the Tamils and ensure their welfare and to preserve the integrity of Sri Lanka. After the arrival of the Indian Peace-Keeping Force (IPKF), the Tamil Tigers, the most militant Tamil group, refused to accommodate, and the IPKF in effect began to fight the Tamil Tigers, but the Tigers and the Sri Lankan government remained far apart.

45 Sunanda K Datta-Ray , editor of the *Statesman* (Calcutta), 'India's Monroe Doctrirne', the *Sunday Statesman*, 2 August 1987, p. 1.

46 The Maldives purportedly turned first to Sri Lanka, the United States, and possibly Singapore for assistance, all of whom declined. However, American naval assets helped India track down and capture the fleeing mercenaries.

47 A few Indians contend that there are no fully sovereign states around India except Pakistan. Others disagree. The various treaties and restrictions on its neighbours suggest that the contention has some basis.

48 These low-level conflicts have repeatedly inflamed Indo-Pakistani relations as they threaten India's vital concern for its unity. Furthermore, Pakistan's tactics are difficult to counter, they represent a low-cost option for Pakistan but an expensive response for India.

49 Most Indians now accept Pakistan as permanent.

50 The two nations do in many ways have the same culture, as most Muslims are converted Indians who eat the same food (eschewing pork), enjoy the same music and share a long history.

51 India's friendship with the Soviet Union was a major break with the British policy of opposing Russia and denying it a meaningful role in the subcontinent.

52 India also tried to develop close ties to the new Iranian revolutionary government and sent a Muslim delegation to Tehran. The Iranians

were not cordial, perhaps remembering the willingness of India to become part of the Shah's regional strategic system.

53 India's relations with the Middle East are discussed under the heading 'Beyond South Asia: The Indian Ocean Region'.

54 Talks at the secretary level took place in 1991-2. The two sides have also agreed not to strike each other's nuclear installations. Tensions rise and fall, but calm heads have prevailed thus far, and they have not fought a war for over 20 years.

55 Indo-Soviet relations are discussed later in this section.

56 For an excellent summary of Indo-Chinese relations, see Surjit Mansingh, 'An Overview of India-China Relations: From When to Where', *Indian Defence Review*, 1992, pp. 70-8.

57 Having been ruled over and protected for so long by the Mughals and the British, Indians tend to feel insecure and surrounded by hostile states when they do not have a protector. The collapse of the Soviet Union raised fears and insecurity and accounts to some extent for India's rapproachement with the United States.

58 AP Venkateswaran, 'To End with a Whimper', *Indian Defence Review*, January 1992, p. 23. See also the report on Russo-Indian cooperation in manufacturing weapons, *Washington Times*, 17 June 1992, p. A2.

59 The Indians imposed limitation on Sri Lanka's use of Trincomalee harbour in the 1987 agreement out of fear that the United States might gain the use of it.

60 The United States has historically been India's largest aid donor and it provided some military and political support to New Delhi in the 1962 war with China. However, Washington gave aid to neither side during the 1965 India-Pakistan war, and it overtly opposed New Delhi in the 1971 war, which led to the creation of Bangladesh.

61 Some officials do not fear Muslim encirclement. For example, the then Foreign Secretary Dixit said on a visit to Washington in April 1992 that he did not consider the Muslims a threat.

62 Mansingh, 1992, p. 75.

63 Some Indians realize that South-East Asians, though otherwise friendly, are concerned about the Indian buildup. See Professor PK Singh 'Maritime Security of India', *USI Journal*, October-December 1990, p. 423.

64 Australia shares these concerns. Part of the problem stems from the failure of the Indian government to clearly state its naval strategy.

65 Nehru, 1983, p. 47.

66 Ibid., p. 70.

67 I use the term 'world nation' to mean a nation that counts importantly in the world, but does not rank as a world power and cannot project military power throughout the world.

68 See Nehru, 1983.

69 Robert Bradnock, *India's Foreign Policy Since 1971*, Chatham House Paper, Council on Foreign Relations Press, New York, 1990, p. 17.

70 Given India's present internal problems and severe budget constraints, these capabilities lie far in the future, but India has not given up its goals.

71 Interviewed by the author in Calcutta, January 1990.

72 The then Indian ambassador to the United States, Dr Abid Hussain, is a leading advocate of this position.

73 The desire for world power and power-projection capabilities raises some serious questions regarding India's true intentions. Questions about this generally receive evasive answers, but I believe that Indians really do not know precisely what they want, except, in general terms, world recognition.

74 See 'Pakistan Will be Better Armed', (interview aboard Indian Air Force plane, 17 February), *Times of India* (Bombay), 18 February, 1992, p. 10.

75 Interestingly, the great Indian empires are known by the name of the dynasty: Mauryan, Gupta and Mughal. This more personal, less national approach contrasts with that of the Roman empire, which was called the Roman empire no matter who ruled it.

76 The remark of one senior civil servant during a discussion of how to plan for the 1962 Chinese attack on India seems to epitomise the second and third points: 'Why all this [discussion]; we will see when it comes'. See Steven A Hoffman, *India and the China Crisis*, University of California Press, Berkeley, 1990, p. 254.

77 Indian history is devoid of ideas for an Indian federation comparable to Sully's Grand Design for the federation of the Christian states of Europe in the late sixteenth century. Moreover, despite the existence of some laws governing interstate and international relations, in Kautilya's view, mistrust, betrayal and the law of the jungle characterised relations among the Indian states. See *Kautilya*, passim. See also P Bandyopadhyay, *International Law and Custom in Ancient India*, Calcutta, 1920, SU Viswanatha, *International Law in Ancient India*, London, 1925, and VR Ramachandra Dikshitar, *War in Ancient India*, Motilal Banarsidass, New Delhi, 1987.

78 Some current military leaders complain of this defensive mentality and cite the reluctance of Indian Army leaders to develop a doctrine and tactics for armoured units as an example of this defensive psyche. See Maj Gen Rajendra Nath, *Military Leadership in India: Vedic Period to Indo-Pakistani Wars*, Lancer Books, New Delhi, 1990, p. 379.

79 At the same time, Pakistan alleges that India interferes in Sri Lanka

and in Pakistan. India also acted aggressively in 1971 to split Pakistan. India is also being accused of fomenting trouble in Sind Province, Pakistan.

80 Much of the motivation for this military move came from Defence Minister Krishna Menon's need to gain political support around Goa.

81 The Russian aspect of this contest was called the 'Great Game'.

82 Nehru, 1983, p. 38.

83 Much of the missile effort, for example, was carried out in the civil sector, although it has definite military uses.

84 According to the *Asian Pacific Defence Reporter*, April 1991, p. 22, 'The Indian Government has decided to liberalize the policy for defence exports under which exports of certain defence items will not require case by case clearance.' The government will also, the source reports, establish a committee to sort out problems of defence exports.

85 A large rural population is, of course, not unique to India, but this rural attitude accounts for, or reinforces, certain cultural beliefs noted above.

86 Some Indians frankly admit that they have not thought through a strategic framework for modern weapons.

87 I questioned several Indians about this proposition. They had not thought of it before, but after reflection some said it was probably correct.

88 Current technology developments will undoubtedly change both land and naval warfare drastically in the next few decades.

89 The Integrated Guided Missile Development Programme (IGMDP), building on an older civilian space programme, has developed a family of missiles that could cover the entire region and, of course, carry nuclear warheads. This indigenous missile programme has popular support. The Agni test is referred to officially as a technological demonstration.

90 China's large nuclear explosion in June 1992, while the President of India was visiting there, may change India's view of the Chinese.

91 The Lawrence Livermore National Laboratories in California are exploring this question. See also *Nuclear Proliferation in South Asia: The Prospects for Arms Control*, a report prepared for Los Alamos National Laboratory, edited by Stephen Philip Cohen, Westview Press, Boulder, Colorado, 1991.

92 The considerable literature on the Navy includes several articles by Ashley Tellis, 'Banking on Deterrence', *Naval Proceedings*, March 1988, pp. 148-52; 'India's Naval Expansion: Reflections on History and Strategy', *Comparative Strategy*, Vol. 8, No. 2, 1987, pp. 185-219; 'Securing the Barracks: The Logic, Structure and Objectives

of India's Naval Expansion', Department of Political Science, University of Chicago, unpublished and undated; 'New Acquisitions on the Indian Subcontinent', *Naval Forces*, Vol. 11, No. 1, 1990. Admiral RH Tahiliani: interview, *Indian Defence Review*, July 1988, pp. 16-21, and 'Maritime Strategy for the 90s', *Indian Defence Review*, July 1989, pp. 19-30. See also Admiral HN Kohli, 'The Geopolitical and Strategic Considerations that Necessitate the Expansion and Modernization of the Indian Navy', *Indian Defence Review*, January 1989, pp. 33-46; and Professor PK Singh, 'Martime Security of India', *USI Journal*, October-December 1990, pp. 414-25. KM Pannikar, *Problems of Indian Defence*, New York, 1985, pp. 105-14, an old but excellent discussion of India's defence problems. *Indian Defence Review*, July 1990, has several articles on the Navy.

93 Admiral JG Nadkarni, formerly Chief of the Naval Staff, and Eric Gonsalves, formerly Secretary of the External Affairs Ministry, have both made this point. See editorial *USI Journal*, October-December 1990, p. 413.

94 *Asian Pacific Defence Reporter*, 1991 Annual Reference Edition, December 1990-January 1991, pp. 146-7.

95 Interview, 18 January 1990, New Delhi. Chandra also said that he had heard much talk of blue-water but he would be happy to have a clear-water navy.

96 Talk of India's power projection seems exaggerated; however, neither the Indian Navy nor plans for its future should be underestimated.

97 The Indian admirals may silently remember the Royal Navy's contribution to British India's security through control of the seas, but they speak openly of the European arrival by sea and the subsequent 'enslavement' of India. Had the Mughals only recognized the naval threat and developed a Navy, they argue, India might have had quite a different history.

98 *USI Journal*, January-March 1991 is devoted largely to the need for new thinking and improved government capabilities.

99 The perception of a powerful and expanding Indian Navy could trigger a naval race in the region as the smaller states, especially in South-East Asia, try to develop defences against it. Several ASEAN states, for example, have asked that surveillance aircraft be used in the Indian Ocean, and have discussed new naval facilities in the area.

100 The military are also physically separated from civilian society and kept in cantonments away from the public eye. Even on internal security missions, they usually operate in the background, behind the police and paramilitary forces.

101 Rajesh Kadian, *India and its Army*, Vision Books, New Delhi, 1990, p. 41.
102 Major KC Praval, *The Indian Army After Independence*, rev. edn., Lancer International, New Delhi, 1990, p. 143.
103 Steven A Hoffman, *India and the China Crisis*, Universtity of California Press, Berkeley, 1990, p. 31. See also Praval, pp. 144-5.
104 Hoffman, pp. 55 and 221.
105 Kadian, p. 52. Major General Rajendra Nath, *Military Leadership in India: Vedic Period to the Indo-Pakistani Wars*, Lancer Books, New Delhi, 1990, pp. 299-303.
106 See Stephen P Cohen, *The Indian Army: Its Contribution to the Development of a Nation*, University of California Press, Berkeley, 1971, p. 176.
107 The progress was less than it seemed because Pakistani forces were woefully weak, as General Manekshaw knew and admitted. Kadian, p. 63.
108 This small committee, the pinnacle of government, is chaired by the prime minister and includes the ministers of defence, external affairs, home, transport and communication, and finance; others are invited as needed, including the service chiefs.
109 Conversation with K Subrahmanyam, Washington, DC, 29 April 1992.
110 General Nath wrote that 'a mere joint secretary' handed the order to the Chief of the Army Staff to evict China in 1962 (p. 368).
111 Raju GC Thomas, *Indian Security Policy*, Princeton University Press, Princeton, New Jersey, 1986, pp. 175, 177, 181.
112 Most information is tightly held, and even among those who know, opinions differ as to the committee's effectiveness.
113 See *Indian Defence Review*, January 1992, pp. 122-3 for current discussions of the repercussions of using the Army to aid the civil power.
114 See 'Storm in Teacup', *India Today*, 15 April 1992, p. 7, which indicated that many civilians had said that they agreed with Rodrigues but that he probably should not have said it.
115 See, for example, F Tomasson Jannuzzi, *India in Transition*, Westview Press, Boulder, Colorado, 1989, pp. 121-2.
116 See Nath, pp. 567-72, for a discussion of the present shortcomings of the Army.
117 See Kadian, pp. 127-42, for a discussion of retained British tradition.
118 Defence Secretary NN Vohra came to Washington with Pawar and then returned only two weeks later for the third Indo-American Strategic Symposium held at Airlie House, Virginia, 21-3 April 1992.
119 For example, the government keeps senior military officers under

surveillance to observe their actions.

120 The Agni tests were referred to as a 'technological demonstration', and the 1974 nuclear explosion was called 'the peaceful nuclear explosion' or PNE.

121 *Indian Express*, 11 April 1991.

122 India rejects both the Nuclear Proliferation Treaty and the proposed five-power talks, but shares the US opposition to proliferation. It resents the implication that the United States and the former Soviet Union acted responsibly but that India would not.

123 See K Subrahmanyam (ed.), *Nuclear Myths and Realities: India's Dilemma,* New Delhi, 1983-4, pp. 195-221, for a discussion of the implications of nuclear asymmetry. Former Minister of Defence KC Pant also warned of the dangers of asymmetry.

124 Foreign Secretary Dixit said at a breakfast in Washington, 11 March 1992, that India has known since 1987 that Pakistan had the capacity to make the bomb.

125 See IDR Research Team, 'Nuclear China: The Equation with India', *Indian Defence Review*, July 1989, for an interesting review of Chinese nuclear capabilities and intentions.

# INDIAN STRATEGY IN FLUX?

GEORGE K TANHAM

Many Indians consider 1991 a watershed year in the history of independent India. Two major events that year influenced Indian foreign and domestic policies: India's financial and economic crisis in the spring and the sudden collapse of the Soviet Union in the late summer. Two other developments also had important implications for India, though their effects were neither as clear nor as immediate as the effects of the first two: the Persian Gulf crisis and war in 1990-1 and the continuing rapid growth of the economy and military power of China. While it is too early to assess and understand the lasting effects of these developments, some short-term observations may be made.

Independence, internal security and territorial integrity have always been the overriding priorities in Indian strategy. Therefore, I shall first look at the recent internal developments in India, particularly the fiscal and economic problems and their possible strategic implications. Then I shall address the major foreign events and their influence on Indian strategy. Finally, I shall make some personal observations on the Indian reaction to these events.

## DOMESTIC PROBLEMS

India's perennial problems of caste, ethnicity and religion worsened as the present decade began. In 1990, Prime Minister VP Singh resurrected the ten-year-old Mandal Commission Report, which had recommended reservations for the other backward classes (OBCs). This led to violence, including self-immolation, on the part of some upper class youths who despaired of their future.

At the same time, the Bharatiya Janata Party (BJP), often referred to as a 'fundamentalist' Hindu party, raised the issue of the Babri Masjid, which had not been used for many years. The BJP claimed that nearly 500 years ago the Muslims had destroyed a Hindu temple at the site of Lord Rama's birthplace, and had erected the Babri Masjid in its place. LK Advani, president of the BJP, led a *yatra* (a march or procession) that travelled 10,000 miles around India urging each Hindu to bring a brick with which to rebuild the temple. Communal tensions turned to violence when BJP supporters destroyed the mosque in December 1992. The blame for allowing the mosque to be destroyed is still a matter of dispute.

Communal and caste problems surfaced again in early 1995, when activists of the banned Vishwa Hindu Parishad (VHP) started a campaign to 'liberate' the Gyanvapi Masjid in Varanasi. Caste politics is also causing unrest in the Hindi belt of northern India. In 1989, conflict had begun again in Kashmir and is still going on, and ethnic violence continues in the north-east.

Government weakness at the Centre, though endemic for some years, increased in 1989-91. During this brief period, India held two elections and had four governments, three of which were minority governments. While the transfer of power from one leader to another was peaceful and legal, the political fragility at the Centre was apparent. The Congress Party, which had ruled India since Independence, was growing weaker. The assassination of Rajiv Gandhi, its young leader, in May 1991 marked the end of the Nehru dynasty and created a deep sense of unease.

Gandhi's assassination seemed to help the Congress in the elections, but not enough for it to gain a clear majority of seats in the Lok Sabha. Narasimha Rao was asked to form a minority government, which he has finally built into a majority. Although he has undertaken major economic reforms, Indians feel that his leadership has lacked decisiveness. Weakness at the Centre continues to plague India, personal politics and corruption have seriously undermined the entire political structure, and in 1995 the governance of India is in trouble.

The fiscal and economic crisis, which came to a head in the spring of 1991, demanded decisive government action. While the Indian economy seemed reasonably healthy in the 1980s and showed a modest growth rate, it did not come close to matching the economic vigour of some South-East Asian nations, and Indians noted with some chagrin that they were falling behind these smaller countries.

The partial success of the Indian economy hid serious inherent weaknesses and a fiscal problem that had reached crisis proportions. The highly regulated economy was not producing the exports to match India's imports, and the unfavourable balance of trade was escalating. The government was also spending beyond its means, partially to provide agriculture subsidies and partially to cover losses of public sector enterprises. Rajiv Gandhi's increased spending on defence also contributed to the deficit. The government was forced to seek short-term loans which, in turn, made its debt repayments even larger and more of a drain on the exchequer. Inflation rose tangentially. By the spring of 1991, India's foreign reserves had sunk to a critical low of about one billion dollars, or about three weeks' requirement. This crisis demanded government action and major reforms in the Indian economy.

In this mixed but highly regulated and protected economy there were opportunities for small businesses and individually-led enterprises to develop outside, or inspite of, the government's economic system. The Indian entrepreneurial spirit (some have said inherent capitalist outlook) revealed itself, and the success of these small but growing endeavours helped to produce a young, dynamic and growing middle class. Professionals, including doctors, lawyers, engineers and other groups, added to the numbers of the aggressive and increasingly robust middle class. They were angry with and frustrated by the army of bureaucrats with their endless red tape and obstructionist tactics against any reform in the economy. These middle-class entrepreneurs demanded changes, and although the voice of the private sector had become more powerful by the 1970s, it could not overcome the pervasive political and bureaucratic stranglehold over the economy, or attract the attention and capital of the free world. By 1991, however, India was ready for liberalisation and reform.

Some Indian leaders had seen the need for economic reforms for years. Prime Minister Indira Gandhi, in the early 1970s, made attempts in this direction, offering tax incentives to attract foreign capital and touting India as a great market. However, the world saw India as too socialistic and a dubious nation for foreign investments. The departure of Coca Cola from India reinforced this idea abroad.[1] Mrs Gandhi's son, Rajiv, in the mid-1980s, made a serious effort to modernise India. He tried to loosen the regulatory shackles on Indian industry, to reduce the inefficiencies in the closely-controlled and vastly over-staffed economy, and to encourage exports and trade with the rest of the world. But he failed because of the bureaucracy, his inexperience in politics and the lack of adequate outside support.[2]

The crisis in the spring of 1991 accelerated and India was faced with the choice of bankruptcy, an unacceptable option for New Delhi, or borrowing from the World Bank and the International Monetary Fund (IMF), both of which insisted on fiscal reform and economic restructuring. Despite what some saw as infringements on India's fiercely guarded independence, the government chose the lesser of the two evils and accepted the conditions for a loan.

Prime Minister Narasimha Rao and Finance Minister Manmohan Singh saw the urgency and quickly addressed the problem. They devalued the rupee by about 20 per cent, and a new budget in July revealed the major thrust of the reforms. They tried to establish fiscal responsibility by cutting government expenditures, subsidies, grants to the states and capital expenditures, while at the same time seeking to increase revenues by tax reform and more efficient collection of taxes. Efforts were also made to reduce inflation. While there has been some progress in establishing fiscal stability by reducing the fiscal deficit, this has not gone as well as hoped for, despite the increased tax revenues. Inflation is rising as of early 1995. On the positive side, there has been a dramatic increase in India's foreign reserves from about one billion dollars in 1991 to nearly 20 billion in 1994. However, some of this was 'hot' money, i.e. investments in stock that could be withdrawn quickly with consequent loss of confidence in the government and possibly an economic crisis.

A major aspect of the reforms is the government's effort to encourage trade. India has reduced tariffs and encouraged exports. Imports grew about 23 per cent in 1994, while exports increased about 18 per cent. However, many of the imports were for capital goods and projects to enhance India's industrial base. While the Indian government is not particularly pleased with the trade imbalance, it believes that industrial production will continue to increase rapidly and that this increase will create jobs and increase exports, which in turn will improve the trade imbalance.

The government has also begun to decentralise, deregulate and liberalise the economy. Restrictions on industries have been reduced, inducements have been introduced to bring foreign capital into India and Non-Resident Indians (NRIs) are being encouraged to invest their funds in India. The policy thrust has shifted from self-sufficiency and import limitations to the encouragement of exports and free trade.

While the details of the reforms need not be covered here, their general thrust is important from the strategic point of view. Indians who support reform see that the outward-looking aspects of this economic policy will affect strategic and defence policies. India has long sought to be self-reliant in its military weapons and supplies.[3] India did not want to depend on any one source, but while it purchased weapons from the West, it in fact relied excessively on the Soviet Union, which provided about 70 per cent of its weapons and military equipment. Today the government is openly seeking outside support from a wide variety of sources for some of its military projects, such as the Light Combat Aircraft project. India hopes to become self-sufficient by increasing exports to pay for imported military equipment.

Foreign markets will become more important as India develops economically, and they will significantly influence what India considers its primary strategic interests abroad. Freedom of the seas and choke points will become more important as trade increases, and naval advocates assert that India needs a large navy to protect its interests abroad, particularly in the Indian Ocean.

The opening up of India's economy not only leads it to look abroad, but also attracts the attention of many other important countries, which see India as a huge potential market and a great area for investment. As the United States, several European nations, and probably Japan invest in India, India will become a much more important player in world affairs. A steadily growing economy will broaden India's strategic horizons and may help it to attain one of its most cherished strategic goals: to be, and to be seen to be, a major participant in global affairs.

## KEY NEW FOREIGN DEVELOPMENTS

The first external event to significantly affect India was the sudden collapse of the Soviet Union in the summer of 1991. The end of the cold war had a much less visible impact on India than it did on Europe and America, as Indians had regarded the cold war as an East-West confrontation taking place primarily in the upper northern hemisphere. Indians had been more than a little troubled, however, when the United States leased the island of Diego Garcia as a naval base. The problem of having the US fleet in the Indian Ocean was exacerbated when the Soviet Union acquired the naval base at Cam Ranh Bay, Vietnam, and Soviet submarines also came into the Indian Ocean. India was concerned that the cold war would turn into a hot one in the Indian Ocean. War did not break out, however, and in fact there were no publicly known confrontations at this time.

The cold war came closer to India when the Soviets invaded Afghanistan in December 1979. It was not in India's interest to have the Soviets in Afghanistan. Although the Indian government may have opposed the Soviet invasion, India did not publicly condemn the Soviet Union. The invasion brought renewed US assistance to Pakistan, which again became an active US ally against the Soviet Union, thereby upsetting the Indians.

The collapse of the Soviet Union was a traumatic shock for India. While India and most of the world had been aware of the Soviet Union's problems, no one expected its sudden collapse. Its disintegration was a severe blow to India's economy, especially at that particular time. The Soviet Union was India's largest mutually-beneficial trading partner, with India having the favourable balance of trade.[4] When Gorbachev visited India in 1988, he had talked about doubling trade with India; instead, in less than three years trade had become non-existent. Some Indians consider the economic *denouement* the most important consequence of the Soviet collapse.

The Soviet Union also supplied India with most of its arms and military equipment at low cost, good credit terms, and often with licensing privileges. The demise of the Soviet Union has created severe problems for the Indian military. Spare parts for India's ageing military equipment are difficult, if not impossible, to find. The problem is now exacerbated by Russia's demand for payment in hard currency. India's defence community sees the loss of its source of arms, and particularly spares, as the most important consequence to India of the Soviet Union's collapse.

From a strategic point of view, the collapse of the Soviet Union suddenly removed India's friend and her counter to an increasingly powerful China. With the United States as the sole superpower in a unipolar world, there appeared to be a strategic imbalance that was not in India's favour. Sensing this before it happened, India had already, prior to the end of the cold war, begun to improve relations with China, and Rajiv Gandhi worked hard to improve relations with both China and the United States. Prime Minister Rao's timely visits to China in 1993 and the United States in 1994 further contributed to better relations with both countries.

India has traditionally sought total independence, and many Indians believed that Mrs Gandhi had been disturbed by Clause 9 of the Friendship Treaty of 1971, which called for consultation between India and the Soviet Union in case of attack or threat of attack on one of the parties. Mrs Gandhi, it was said, thought this clause made India appear dependent on the Soviet Union, and that is why, as a sign of Indian independence, she had proceeded with the nuclear research programme and approved the 1974 peaceful nuclear explosion (PNE). Most Indians believed, however, that she pursued the nuclear option to divert attention from her serious domestic problems.

India's relations with the Soviet Union in the 1980s had begun to show subtle changes. India had not approved of the Soviet Union's invasion of Afghanistan and was pleased when it withdrew in 1989.[5] India's faith in the Soviet Union's support declined when it saw its former ally working closely with the United States at the UN on the Persian Gulf crisis. Many, but not all, Indians argue that there never had been a Soviet nuclear umbrella, but that the Soviets had served to counteract China and the United States. Soviet help became less necessary, they said, as Delhi improved its relations with China and the United States in the 1980s. One gets the impression, at least in discussions in 1995, that the relationship between India and the Soviet Union was becoming less close, though still important, by the end of the cold war.

Indians have pointed out that the Indo-Soviet relationship was primarily between governments and that it did not affect many Indians. Despite cultural exchanges, the Indians and the Russians seemed to remain far apart, and the lack of a common language hindered the development of closer relations between the two peoples. Young Indians maintain also that they have always looked to the West for cultural engagement, and increasingly to America, and that even during the cold war they preferred to go to the United States.

Many Indians would, nevertheless, maintain good relations with Russia. High-level goodwill visits, cooperation on weapon repairs and new equipment, and reviving trade suggest that India and Russia will continue to have a mutually beneficial relationship.[6] Both governments are working together toward this goal. But contrary to the situation in the cold war, this does not preclude India's having good relations with China and the United States.

The second event to significantly affect India was the Gulf crisis in 1990 and the war in 1991. India firmly rejected naked aggression and hence opposed Saddam Hussein's attack on, and takeover of, Kuwait in August 1990. Many Indians sympathised with Iraq, however, as India and Iraq had enjoyed good relations and Iraq was the only Arab state that had consistently supported India on the Kashmir issue. The fact that the Baathist regime in Iraq is essentially secular appealed to India, which is also a secular state.

Furthermore, India had many economic interests in Iraq. Thousands of Indian workers employed there and in the Gulf region sent home perhaps a billion dollars a year in remittances to their families. The crisis put these workers in jeopardy, and the Indian government, in a very efficient airlift operation, evacuated about 200,000 in just a few weeks. In addition, India received much of its oil from Iraq and from the Soviet Union through Iraq. This source was completely cut off at the time that the price of oil shot up in the world market because of the Gulf crisis. India and Iraq also had a profitable trade relationship, and Indian companies were engaged in construction and other work in Iraq. At the UN, India vacillated but finally supported the UN coalition. India allowed USAF aircraft to refuel on its territory, but for political reasons withdrew this permission just a few days before the end of the war. The period of the Gulf crisis and war was a difficult time for India.

The war highlighted if not the emergence of a unipolar world, at least a world in which the United States was the sole remaining superpower, one that had not been particularly friendly with India. It also revealed Arab disunity and the inability of the Organisation of Islamic Conference to play a meaningful role. The Non-Aligned Movement was unable to take effective action, thus raising questions about its relevance in the post-cold war world. India and a few other nations asserted that the United States had not explored all diplomatic opportunities, especially the French proposal that if Saddam Hussein evacuated Kuwait the coalition would withdraw its forces. India, in particular, felt that the United States overly dominated the UN and was using it as a cover for the US agenda.

The war clearly demonstrated the power of modern military technology. The United States used all its most-modern weapons and equipment to quickly defeat Iraq. The entire world saw the demonstration of its air power and high technology on television. As a result, India and other developing states are now seeking more modern military technology.

The Iraqis' Soviet-made weapons and equipment did not compare well with those of the United States, though Iraqi training, or the lack of it, and poor morale may have had something to do with Iraq's poor performance. To all non-nuclear powers, including India, the war seemed to have revealed the importance of having nuclear weapons. In the view of many non-Americans, the United States probably would not have confronted Saddam in the way it did if Iraq had in fact had nuclear weapons. Finally, the war also revealed how expensive modern warfare can be, as even the United States had to ask for, and received, substantial contributions from many other countries.

The end of the cold war, the collapse of the Soviet Union, and the Gulf war to a lesser extent, have changed the world enormously. The superpower confrontation made the major problems of the world relatively predictable, but the feared conflagration did not occur. Local and regional conflicts, and ethnic and communal violence had been more or less forcibly controlled by the superpowers in their respective spheres of influence, and to a lesser extent in the non-aligned world. As superpower pressure disappeared, small, old conflicts emerged more clearly and new ones arose. The world did not become more peaceful; instead it became more complex and contentious, and many feel infinitely more dangerous.

With only one superpower, many turned to the UN as the arbiter of world affairs and the primary organisation to deal with the smaller, though intense, crises and conflicts. Many Indians resent what they see as US domination of the UN and would prefer that the UN be more independent of any one power and deal with the numerous world conflicts collectively.[7] India believes that an enlarged Security Council with more permanent members, including itself, would be a step in the right direction. As constituted now, the UN has tried, but with modest success, to grapple with the world's problems. However, it is not properly organised to operate peace-keeping missions or command military forces, as has been demonstrated so clearly in Bosnia and elsewhere.

India, with its extensive experience in peace-keeping under UN auspices, seeks to play a greater role in this field. Since its participation in the Congo in the 1960s, India has sent forces and observers to participate in UN peace-keeping missions around the world. Today it has military forces and civilian observers in Latin America, Africa, Asia and Europe. It is justly proud of its record.

## EVOLVING STRATEGIES

Perhaps India's major strategic change as a result of the end of the cold war has been its decision to work more closely with the United States. In fact, Indo-American relations had already begun to improve even before the cold war ended. The Reagan administration initially ignored India, but later adopted a policy of trying to wean India away from the Soviet Union. President Reagan's good relationship with Prime Minister Indira Gandhi and later with Rajiv Gandhi, when he became the prime minister, contributed to the success of this policy. Discussions led to a Memorandum of Understanding on the transfer of technology to India, agreed upon in 1984. While not giving India all it wanted, the agreement provided considerable modern technology and seemed to be a positive step in the relationship. Although by 1988 relations between the two countries had improved considerably, substantive differences and mutual distrust and suspicion remained in the background. The relationship might not have become closer had it not been for the end of the cold war.

The military in both countries quickly saw the opening provided by the cold war's demise and began to develop closer relations in 1992, when General Kicklighter, the US Army component commander in the Pacific, brought to India a list of specific proposals for closer relations. This has led to visits of high-level officers of each country, greater attendance at each other's schools, and a strong 'getting-to-know-you' effort. In January 1995, Secretary of Defence Perry's visit to India gave the stamp of approval to these military-to-military relations and provided for closer civilian relationships on defence policies and technology. Perry also advocated closer cooperation on peace-keeping efforts. However, India wants greater progress in technology talks, but sees the US as dragging its feet. This is partially true as the US is concerned about verification measures. India has not signed the MTCR, which includes verification measures. India has also made clear that there will be no transparency in strategic issues. It seems that progress on the technology front is necessary before closer relationships can be developed.

The economic relationship, however, is the driving force in improving Indo-American relations. India's decision to reform and liberalise its economy, to encourage foreign investments and to open the potentially huge Indian market has attracted the attention of the US business community. The Clinton administration has gone further than most American governments in helping American industry abroad.

The Indo-American relationship obviously is not entirely without problems. The Indians are highly emotional about the Clinton administration's attempt to renew the NPT, as they believe it discriminates unfairly against non-nuclear powers and is racist. Moreover, Paragraph 301 of the US Omnibus Trade Competitiveness Act (ACTA) of 1988 hangs ominously over the relationship, as does the Intellectual Property Rights issue. India complains that the United States is trying to keep her weak, that it still does not recognise India's rightful place in the world and that it equates Pakistan and India, while favouring Pakistan. One hears criticism in India of the US stands on human rights and environmental issues. In 1995, the suspicions and distrust still exist on both sides. However, there is a desire on both sides to broaden and improve the relationship.

India has also made a strategic move to recognise Israel, even at the risk of some Arab displeasure. The United States supports this action. Israel, which has access to US high technology, could become an important source of this technology for India. Israel was a primary bidder in the competition to upgrade the MIG-21-bis and is anxious to do both military and civilian business with India. Furthermore, Israel shares India's deep concern about Islamic fundamentalism. Relations seem to be progressing well and to the benefit of both countries.

## MUCH REMAINS THE SAME

In many ways, Indian strategic problems remain unchanged, though they have been modified by world developments. New Delhi continues to see as its top strategic priority the unity and territorial integrity of India itself. The end of the cold war has not changed this view, and increased internal stresses, some aided and abetted from outside, have only strengthened this focus. Various internal problems—religion, caste and ethnicity—continue to plague India, and the government has not yet developed an overall strategy to deal with them. The current economic reforms could add a new dimension to these divisive factors as some states are moving ahead rapidly in their economic development while others are falling further behind. The gap between the rich and the poor is also widening. This situation could raise wide-spread social problems and unrest if not properly addressed. Internal security remains a top priority for India.

Pakistan's involvement in the low-level conflicts in India only makes them more costly and more complicated to deal with. While India does not appear to have developed an overall strategy for internal security, she has developed counter-insurgency tactics. The continued use of the army because of the inadequacy of the police and para-military forces, however, distract it from its primary mission of defending the nation from outside attack.

India has noted that, as time has elapsed, its close neighbours, Bhutan and Nepal, have been working hard on developing their separate identities and are anxious to act more independently, particularly with control over their foreign policies. The new communist government in Nepal has made clear that it wants to review and renegotiate its 1950 treaty with India, especially its security provisions. Nepal and Bhutan are special cases, as India still feels that their northern borders are also its border, and it will continue to try to keep them within its security orbit. India realises, however, that changes are taking place, and it has shown a willingness to discuss differences with its neighbours.

Bangladesh and Sri Lanka, though never tied to India by treaty, still have often had to take India's wishes into account in their foreign policies. Sri Lanka has allowed the Voice of America (VOA) to establish a station there, a move that India had consistently opposed. While India does not intend to make a public issue over Colombo's action, partially because of improved Indo-American relations, it is not happy with Sri Lanka's decision. Colombo's Foreign Minister, Lakshman Kadirgamar, publicly stated in early February 1995 that he hoped that India would not 'impede' Colombo's negotiations with the Liberation Tigers of Tamil Eelam (LTTE), an indication that there is still anxiety there about possible Indian interference. On the other hand, Sri Lanka's president, Mrs Chandrika Bandaranaike Kumaratunga, visited India in April 1995 and made clear her desire for closer and more friendly relations between the two nations, a view Prime Minister Rao shared with her. Bangladesh is not entirely happy with India, as it feels that it has not received a fair deal over water allocations, and it wants to review its agreement with India on this issue. Refugee problems also continue to irritate the relationship. The increasing independence of its neighbours and India's own internal problems seem likely to modify its view of the subcontinent as its own strategic area.

Two other close neighbours, Afghanistan and Myanmar, always an important part of India's strategic interests, are also of increasing concern to New Delhi. Until about 18 months ago, India opposed the State Law and Order Restoration Council (SLORC), the undemocratic military government of Myanmar, and had beamed radio programmes in support of Aung San Suu Kyi and the democratic elements in the country. But the reported extensive activities of the Chinese have caused apprehension in the Indian government, which has decided it must work with the SLORC to counter the increasingly strong Chinese influence in the country. Northern Myanmar has close economic ties with China. The Chinese appear to be building and improving Myanmar's roads and harbours; these are dual-purpose projects, as they help the economy but can also be used by military forces. The roads could give China access to the Indian Ocean.[8] Reports of a listening station on Cocos Island are more disturbing, as such a post could track and observe Indian missiles launched from Orissa. That China has reportedly supplied Myanmar with over a billion dollars' worth of military equipment adds to India's concern.

Myanmar has borders with India which insurgents and dissidents can easily traverse, as border surveillance in both countries is poor. Given India's unrest in the north-east, this border problem is potentially a serious one, and one that India would like to tackle cooperatively with Myanmar. Border control, the right of hot pursuit, and the return of 'wanted' insurgents are all issues that India needs to discuss and work out with the SLORC. For these reasons, Myanmar under Chinese influence, and perhaps unfriendly to India, would certainly not be in India's interests. New Delhi will continue and probably increase its efforts to court Myanmar.

Afghanistan's instability is also causing concern in New Delhi. India has traditionally tried to stay on friendly terms with Afghanistan so as to prevent undue Pakistani influence there and to act as a restraint on Pakistan from its rear. The Soviet withdrawal has not brought peace to Afghanistan as rival forces continue to fight each other and the government in Kabul is weak. Recently, the possibility that a new and powerful militant Islamic group, the Taliban, allegedly recruited and trained by the Pakistan Inter-Service Intelligence (ISI), might take over Afghanistan is even more disturbing. An unstable Afghanistan could cause serious problems in the region as Pakistan and Iran compete for influence. At the moment, there is little New Delhi can do to influence the situation, though it is trying to develop better relations with Iran.

Prime Minister Rao's new Look-East policy is driven primarily by the desire to reach out to the fast-growing economies of East and South-East Asia and to develop closer trade and investment relations with them. In addition to improved economic relations with South-East Asia, it seems likely that security matters will become increasingly important as the small nations there are concerned about the growing giant that is China. Peaceful though China's intentions may be today, they could quickly change. In recent history, China has taught both India and Vietnam 'lessons' that neither country has forgotten. India shares these concerns about China, and this could be a basis for forging closer security relationships.

Despite geographic difficulties, India is interested in developing economic opportunities and cultivating the new republics of Central Asia. Prime Minister Rao visited Uzbekistan and Kazakhstan on 23-26 May 1993, and felt that he laid the basis for good relations with them. However, the Himalayan mountains between them and India are a serious barrier, as are the geographic positions of Afghanistan and Pakistan. The Indian government is considering working with Iran on the development of direct links between Central Asia, Iran and the Indian Ocean—links that India could use. This would be a long-term venture, as all roads from

Central Asia now lead to Moscow, and constructing new routes into Iran and the Indian Ocean would take time and money. However, it may be worthwhile in the long term as these countries possess huge supplies of oil and minerals that would be of value to India.

## SOME THREATS AND ASPIRATIONS REMAIN

Of all its external threats, India still sees its traditional adversaries, China and Pakistan, as the most critical. China's strategic position seems to be improving since the end of the cold war and the demise of its old threat, the Soviet Union.[9] The United States is slowly withdrawing from East Asia and thus does not constitute a military challenge. China has no active border disputes with India, having come to an agreement in 1994 to reduce tensions along the common border. China still has unresolved border disputes with Russia, but these are dormant at the moment. China's long-standing relationship with Pakistan in the west and an increasingly close relationship with Myanmar in the east could be seen as a strategic flanking of India.

Sino-Indian rivalries in many areas are likely to continue, with some periods of good relations and some of tension. In early 1995, relations seem to be reasonably good. Whether this continues depends to some extent on post-Deng Chinese leaders, and whether they want peace and cooperation or whether they choose expansion and aggression. India's present China strategy seems to be to maintain its military forces, but to discuss their border problem and reduce tensions. Progress has been made in agreeing to contact points on the border and establishing communication between the forces on both sides. India's overall policy is to try to improve relations with China and to work out differences peacefully.

In addition to its unsettled borders with some of its neighbours, China has an on-going controversy with five ASEAN nations over the Spratley Islands and the South China Sea. China claims sovereignty over this entire area and has stated categorically that it will defend it by force if necessary. It does not, however, view its position as 'expansionist', but rather as the reaffirmation of its historic claim to the entire South China Sea. Informal talks with the five other nations involved have not made great progress. China has offered to participate in various joint economic ventures with these smaller nations, but has remained adamant on its claim of sovereignty over the entire region.[10] China would, it is generally believed, prefer peace in the foreseeable future so as to continue its economic liberalisation and the modernisation of its military forces. Its long-term intentions, however, are difficult to fathom, and experts disagree on them.

China has embarked on an extensive modernisation of its military forces. Some observers believe that it is more than just modernisation: that it is an upgrading of its forces to project power in East Asia and eventually in the world. Long-range aircraft and air-refueling capability, a submarine launched ballistic missile (SLBM) capability, and talk of a carrier would suggest that the Chinese want to have this power projection capability. Because of the complexity of the actual spending in various government agencies and a lack of transparency in China's defence budget accounting, it is impossible to estimate exactly how much China is spending on its armed forces. Some observers have put the figures as high as 20-35 billion dollars.

A large portion of China's defence budget is allocated to research and development as it seeks to improve its technological base and capability to produce the most modern weapons. It continues to test nuclear weapons despite the *de facto* agreement among the nuclear powers not to do so. It is reportedly also developing a neutron bomb and laser weapons. Considerable attention has been paid to the navy and the air force, and the army is being converted from a huge, largely guerrilla force into a modern conventional force with young leadership. The growing Chinese economy is able to sustain a high level of military spending, which in the not-too-distant future will make China a world superpower and give it the option of continuing to coexist peacefully or taking a much tougher position. Intentions can change quickly, but it takes years to acquire modern military forces, as Nehru learned in 1962.

In addition to building up its own military forces, China is helping many of India's neighbours militarily as well as economically. The long-existing Chinese-Pakistan relationship is likely to continue into the future. The two countries are cooperating on developing and producing such weapons as the K-8 aircraft, and China has contributed to Pakistan's technological modernisation. Many reports have suggested that China has supplied the M-11 missile to Pakistan and helped with its nuclear programme. China has also reportedly supplied weapons to Bangladesh and Myanmar, two more of India's important neighbours. India is concerned that it is being surrounded by nations that are helped by its rival, China.

Pakistan, though not a threat to India's territorial integrity or sovereignty, is seen as a continuing and high-profile adversary. Kashmir has been festering on and off for nearly 48 years, and no solution seems to be in sight. The Indians claim that the Pakistanis are providing arms and training for the insurgency in Kashmir. However, the real issues between India and Pakistan are, first, Pakistan's need for the rivalry in order to keep it united and to prevent it from being swallowed up economically and culturally by India; the conflict in a sense helps Pakistan's search for identity. The second issue arises from India's desire to be the paramount power in the subcontinent and the Indian Ocean and Pakistan's efforts to impede, if not stop, India from achieving this position.

Indians believe that Pakistan may have decided that neither conventional war nor nuclear war would benefit it, and that a more effective strategy is to encourage and aid the various divisive elements in India. India believes that Pakistan (ISI) is assisting the rebels in both Kashmir and the north-east. Pakistan reportedly has introduced members of the Afghan *mujahedeen* into Kashmir; these groups have not only been helping the insurgents, but also contributing to the level of violence by feuding among themselves. This Pakistani strategy is a relatively cheap one; it can be denied but it is a continuing financial drain on India and a distracting problem on an already heavily burdened Indian government. Pakistan appears to believe that its nuclear capability allows it to safely pursue its strategy of low-level conflict.

Pakistan has continued its nuclear development, and some of its top officials claim that it has the bomb: US Secretary of Defence Perry in January 1995 concurred. Pakistan believes that because it is so much smaller than India, it must have the bomb. It sees the bomb in a sense as an equaliser. In what circumstances Pakistan would use it, no one outside Pakistan knows. The United States has tried to persuade these two potential nuclear powers to cap their nuclear development, but neither has complied nor signed the NPT.

While the United States and a few other powers worry about

instability and possible nuclear war in South Asia, many Indians and Pakistanis believe that there is already a situation of nuclear deterrence in the area. One American scholar, George Perkovich, has called it 'non-weaponized deterrence'; Indians refer to it as 'recessed deterrence'. Nuclear weapons seem to cause more concern outside Pakistan and India than within either country. But although Pakistan's nuclear developments attract more attention, the known capability of China is seen by India as the real threat.

Indians have been dismayed by the US involvement in aggravating regional nuclear issues. In the late 1970s, Pakistan embarked upon a determined clandestine nuclear weapons programme that became the Pakistani factor in India's nuclear calculations. This was referred to for the first time in Parliament by Foreign Minister Atal Behari Vajpayee in April 1979. The Soviet invasion of Afghanistan in 1979 led to sizeable US aid to Pakistan which was seen as a 'front-line' state. Many Indians believe that Islamabad used this opportunity to mislead the United States about its nuclear intentions, and it soon attained a capability that was to add to the complexity of the nuclear proliferation issue. Indians have criticised the US administration's ambivalence in dealing with Pakistan's nuclear effort, including Washington's various attempts to bypass the Pressler Amendment passed by the US Congress in 1988. The non-proliferation law requires the cutoff of US military and economic support when an undeclared or aspiring nuclear weapons state carries its nuclear programme beyond a given point. The Pressler Amendment refers specifically to Pakistan.[11]

Indians continue to see Islam as a third threat. Having been invaded by different Muslim peoples for several centuries, then ruled by the Mughals for about 200 years, Indians are understandably sensitive to perceived Islamic threats. Today they are surrounded on their land borders by seven Muslim countries. Pakistan's destabilizing efforts in India, supported by other Muslim nations, is the clearest and nearest and most important Islamic threat. The recent formation of five independent republics in Central Asia, all with large Muslim populations, is seen as the latest manifestation of the Muslim presence. Iran is a nearby Muslim state seemingly with nuclear ambitions, but with which India has good relations.

Indians talk about this strategic Islamic threat, but when pressed, they confess that it is most unlikely that those countries could or would unite against India. However, the fact that other Muslim countries, such as Iran, Turkey and Saudi Arabia, are vying for influence and economic opportunity in Central Asia only increases India's concern about a possible Islamic bloc. The fact that the United States, other Western nations and China have also shown serious interest in the economic possibilities of this region and are concerned about Islamic fundamentalism has not allayed its concerns.

The second aspect of Islam, and probably the one that is taken most seriously, is the growth of militant or fundamentalist Islam. Small groups of Muslims are active both inside and outside the Muslim world, and India sees their activities as the nexus between Islamic countries and a possible source of unrest for India's Muslims. Many Indians believe that Islamic fundamentalists were responsible for the blasts in Bombay in January 1993.[12]

India has approximately 120 million Muslims, making it the nation with the second largest Muslim population after Indonesia. Indians note the challenge of the fundamentalists to the governments of Egypt and especially Algeria. They can read about Muslim terrorists who operate in much of the world, and who only a couple of years ago bombed the World Trade Centre in New York City. More important is their concern about the fundamentalists in Afghanistan and evidence that they are involved in Kashmir. Ideas know no political boundaries, a fact Indians are acutely aware of, and hence they fear the intrusion of militant ideas into India from any neighbouring country. If Islamic militancy were to spread to India, many Indians fear that it would trigger a Hindu fundamentalist backlash that would raise communal tensions and possibly result in the outbreak of communal violence.

The United States shares India's concerns about militant Islam. Washington seems to be developing a new policy of support for moderate Islamic governments, a policy with which some Indians sympathise. However, the two countries seem to disagree on which countries are moderate. For example, the United States is backing Pakistan, which it views as a moderate Islamic power; the Indians, needless to say, do not regard Pakistan in the same light.

Some Indians continue to see the Indian Ocean as an avenue of approach for unfriendly nations and thus a source of vulnerability; others see it as an area of increasingly important Indian interests;

still others see it as both. Those who see it as a threat recognise that the Europeans came by sea, but armies, not navies conquer nations. During the 1971 war, the United States sent the carrier *Enterprise* into the Bay of Bengal. Indians considered this an unfriendly act and still remember it with some bitterness, especially as it occurred when India was savouring its great military victory over Pakistan.

India has long opposed the presence of any foreign navies in the Indian Ocean, including those of the United States and the Soviet Union. Today it is mildly concerned about the presence of the French flotilla off the East African coast. The United States continues to maintain units of its 7th Fleet around the Persian Gulf, and to use its much expanded base at Diego Garcia. Improving Indo-US relations have made these deployments a little more acceptable to the Indians, and the end of the cold war has erased the threat of superpower confrontation and a hot war in this ocean.

Those who see the Indian Ocean as an area of Indian interests emphasise three concerns: the mid-ocean resources, some of which India has claimed; India's presence in Antarctica; and the need to keep the Indian Ocean and the Persian Gulf free and open for trade. Those who see the ocean as a threat and a challenge argue for a big navy. Those who are just interested in protecting India's interests there would perhaps settle for less.

It is difficult in 1995 to visualise a serious and immediate threat to India coming from the sea, though India worries about the Pakistan navy, which might be able to interfere with India's access to Persian Gulf oil. In the longer term, and this is very important as navies cannot be built in a day, Indians can visualise a threat from the Chinese navy which has already ventured into the Indian Ocean. To pose a threat to India, the Chinese navy would need a base in the Indian Ocean, and this may be in their minds as they build up Myanmar's road and port facilities. The Japanese already have large military forces, though defensively oriented, and could fairly rapidly develop power projection forces to protect Japan's lifelines to the Middle East and to Australia and Indonesia, should the need arise. Indian naval planners are concerned that people do not appreciate how much time and effort are needed to develop the navy that they believe India will need in the twenty-first century.

India has strategic aspirations that also play a role in its strategic considerations. First, it would like to be recognised as the pre-eminent power in the Indian Ocean. American approval of the Indian operations in the Maldives and in Sri Lanka suggest that the United States already views India as the regional power, a welcome development for New Delhi. Second, India wants to be recognised as a world power. Nehru wrote movingly of India's desire and, in his mind, its destiny to play a major role in world affairs. He hoped it would not be a military role, but one based on sound moral values. India still strives toward this goal, though some feel that only through its military strength can such a status be achieved. In today's world, however, economic strength may be the preferred route to world status. Prime Minister Rao's reform movement will likely contribute greatly to attaining this global status in a peaceful manner.

## SOME OBSERVATIONS AND CONCLUSIONS

One lesson to be drawn from the events of recent years is this: To effect major changes in its policies and government apparatus, India seems to require a great internal shock or powerful pressure from outside. Rapid changes may not be the Indian style, and India will likely follow its own more gradual approach to change. As it interacts with the global economy and with the world in other ways, however, it may have to adjust its behaviour somewhat if it is to succeed.

India's reaction to its severe economic and fiscal crises in the spring of 1991 illustrates this point. India was compelled to seek immediate aid from the International Monetary Fund (IMF) and the World Bank, both of which required greater fiscal responsibility and economic structural reform as a condition for India's obtaining the much-needed loans. India's subsequent budgets and economic reforms have reflected the influence of these internationally imposed conditions. In contrast, no such shock has occurred in the political arena, and political deterioration has progressively undermined the system. Political infighting, personal ambition and greed, wide-spread corruption at all levels, and a largely bloated, conservative, self-seeking bureaucracy raise serious questions about the governance of India. Problems are widely discussed, but one sees little action for reforms.

The present state of Indian politics, which focuses almost

exclusively on domestic issues, personal interests, and re-election, diverts politicians from considering security affairs. Traditionally politicians have shown little interest in foreign and security affairs. After independence, Pandit Nehru correctly focused domestic attention on building heavy industry, pursuing a policy of self-reliance and autarchy in economic affairs, and taking other actions, such as participating in the Non-Aligned Movement, to make India truly independent. He, his daughter Indira Gandhi, and his grandson, Rajiv Gandhi, aided by a small group of close confidants, tended to keep foreign and security policies in their own hands. This procedure was not conducive to the development of government institutions intended to address these matters in a more organised and coordinated manner.

Many Indians, mostly outside the government, have seen the need for government institutions or procedures for formulating and articulating a national strategy and implementing defence policies. The Cabinet Committee on Political Affairs (CCPA) has shown little interest, and in any case would require a supporting staff if it were to assume its rightful and much-needed role of formulating national goals and strategy. Today's politicians show little inclination to assume this responsibility, a reluctance that amounts almost to a dereliction of duty on their part. It cannot be expected that the ministries of External Affairs, Defence, Home Affairs, and other agencies can develop the correct and coordinated policies and actions if this guidance is not provided.

Foreign and security matters have not been ignored, however. In fact, a constant flow of prime ministers and other high-level official visitors to Delhi from the United States, Europe and other parts of Asia suggests a greater world-wide interest in India, a trend that has pleased India greatly. The Indian Prime Minister has visited Moscow, Washington and Beijing, as well as two Central Asian republics, Uzbekistan and Kazakhistan, several ASEAN states and Vietnam. There is already an increasing exchange of visits and interaction in spite of New Delhi's concentration on the domestic front, economic reforms, internal security and politics, especially the 1996 elections.

During the past five years, a large number of important international security developments and events have shown the need for a national strategy. Even a selective list suggests their importance to India. Some Pakistani officials claim that Pakistan has the nuclear bomb, and Islamabad seems to have adopted a low-intensity conflict strategy against India. The Chinese are modernising their armed forces and developing power projection capabilities. They continue to help Pakistan and are supplying weapons to India's neighbours. The situation in Afghanistan has deteriorated since the Soviet withdrawal, and civil war and inter-tribal struggles have dominated the country. This volatile situation could destabilise the entire region; it is already exacerbating the unrest in Kashmir, where there seems to be little hope for a peaceful resolution in the immediate future.

In 1991 the Soviet Union, India's friend and ally, collapsed and the cold war ended. The Gulf war highlighted the unipolar nature of the world, but even more the power of modern technology in warfare. Islamic fundamentalism seems to have spread to a large portion of Western Asia and North Africa. The United States, which to some extent has been the stabilising factor in Asia, has pulled back, notably from the Philippines, although it says it intends to stay in Asia. As China's strength grows and Japan and India become more important players, the situation has the potential to become even more complex.

India is increasingly involved in a dynamic and changing world. Economic problems, internal and external security and a host of new issues, including the environment, human rights, population control and peace-keeping demand practical, thoughtful and coordinated policies.[13]

There seems to have been more interest in having the government address national security areas in the 1989-91 period than is discernible today in a much more complex world. In 1990, the VP Singh government proposed the establishment of a National Security Council, but no such entity has been allowed to materialise. Also in 1990, the Ministry of Defence appointed a high-level Committee on Defence Expenditure (CDE), composed of civilian and military personnel and chaired by Mr Arun Singh, a former minister of state for defence. It prepared a far-ranging report with specific recommendations, but this report has never been released to the public. The government has, according to knowledgeable observers, acted on some of the report's recommendations but not all of the important ones.[14]

The following outline of an informal strategy formulation effort has been pieced together as a result of conversations with various

Indians who differ on parts of the account. The Army apparently developed a national strategy paper that was coordinated with the other services and endorsed by the Ministry of Defence (MOD), which sent it to the Ministry of External Affairs and other government agencies for comment. After considering all the comments, probably the Army prepared a final version, described as a 'national strategy paper.' It is not known, at least to the writer, what happened to the 'national strategy paper', or whether the process has ever been repeated.

A few have claimed that this *ad hoc* process has been somewhat formalised and that there now exists a means for developing, and modifying as necessary, both a national strategy and a defence policy. The exercise, if executed as claimed, demonstrates the desire and need of both the military and the ministries for a national strategy. While they essentially developed their own strategy, it is difficult to see how it can be considered an official national strategy unless the CCPA reviewed and endorsed it. However, unofficial documents such as this, since they are sometimes the only ones available, tend to become *de facto* national strategy. In any case, the exercise, if it took place, seems to show that strategies can be developed even if no central coordinating agency exists. In fact, this procedure seems to reflect an Indian way of developing policies and procedures whereby a small group may meet informally to discuss strategy and defence policy. The existence of such a procedure would indicate that India does have at least some strategic direction.

The Lok Sabha a few years ago created the Standing Committee on Defence, which has taken a more active interest in security matters. While it is new and still feeling its way, it has begun to question the government on defence matters. It recently recommended that the government make the CDE report available to the public, but this has not yet been done. The Nineteenth Report of the Estimate Committee (1992-3), also a creation of the Parliament, made public much information on defence policies and associated matters. The Committee concluded that there was no defence policy. It recommended that the government would be well advised to 'articulate a clear and comprehensive defence policy. This can only be based on a viable national security doctrine'.[15]

The Defence Planning Staff (DPS) was created in the MOD in

the mid-1980s to provide an integrated defence budget to the MOD. It also, according to observers, does some strategic planning. However, as of 1994, the DPS and other efforts do not seem to have provided for coordinated military planning. According to one leading defence expert, the services still plan separately and there is no national strategy to serve as an integrated defence policy. He urges India to 'examine her policy formulation mechanisms and bring them abreast of the times'.[16]

In 1995 it appears, at least to an outsider, that the public and the media are showing more interest in security matters than the government.[17] At least three English daily newspapers carry a full page weekly coverage of defence issues. At least two new defence journals, *Defence Today* and *Agni* have been established. In addition to the Centre for Policy Research (CPR), the Institute for Defence Studies and Analysis (IDSA) and the United Service Institution of India (USI), the latter two of which publish journals, several new research centers have recently been set up. The Forum for Strategic and Security Studies is just beginning and has started a new journal, *Agni* (April 1995); the Delhi Policy Group, composed of retired generals and foreign service officers, is also under way. The United Service Institute is establishing a new research cell in a new large building to house all its activities. Public interest in these issues is increasing and this may have some future impact on the government.

On the whole, India has adjusted its strategies and policies well despite some shortcomings in the strategy-making process. It has taken advantage of the end of the cold war to develop better relations with the United States while concurrently maintaining a good rapport with Russia. India is moving toward closer relations with Iran, partially as a check on Pakistan, but also as a gateway to Central Asia. The Look-east policy is developing slowly. Singapore and India have made the most progress so far, and India hopes that Singapore will promote closer relations with ASEAN and assist it in entering APEC. India would like to join the ASEAN Regional Forum created in Bangkok in June 1994, and it is also reaching out to Australia. It is participating in early talks about Indian Ocean Rim cooperation.

On the negative side, India has not developed a coherent strategy for domestic law and order, though it is coping with most of its separatist and insurgency problems. It has not developed an effective counter to Pakistan's policy of assisting these and other movements causing unrest in India, and no settlement is in sight in Kashmir.

A new tone is noticeable, particularly among the younger Indians when they talk about their country today. Many say that India is now a 'hard, tough, pragmatic' nation that will stand up for its rights and positions and make its own decision based on harsh realities and not on some vague ideology.[18] Something of this attitude has already been shown in India's policy switch on Myanmar from supporting the ideal of democracy to one of dealing with the very real problems India has with Myanmar. In April 1995, India's very warm welcome for Iran's President Rafsanjani and the signing of six agreements, one on arms, was a show of India's independence and a sharp rebuke to the United States for attempting to tell India what to do. India's toughening attitude also appears in New Delhi's differences with the United States on the deployment of Prithvi and the renewal of the NPT. Many of the young show increasing pride in their country and what it can do.

The budget problems continue to put all the military services on hold. They receive just enough funds to maintain themselves, and very little is allocated for new weapons and equipment though they received a modest increase in the 1995-6 budget, the first in several years. The situation will improve as the economic reforms succeed, but the services cannot expect much relief in the near future.[19] Military planners must take into account the somewhat reduced capabilities of the military. This situation, however, also provides an opportunity to develop realistic future requirements and plan for an enhanced military capacity. Modern technology would be an important consideration. Perhaps the politicians will see the need and the opportunity to develop a well-thought-out national strategy.

The greatest and longest term strategic challenge to India, however, is China. A huge China with a dynamically developing economy and a greatly improving military capability could early in the twenty-first century become the world's superpower.[20] China is already asserting its claims to the South China Sea region, and may well do so in other areas that it believes have been taken away from it in the past.[21] However, this giant, even without doing anything, casts a pall over East and South Asia because of its intensive dominance and sheer size. Whether China will be peaceful or assertive is much debated. Such discussion matters little as China could change its policy or intentions at any time, but its enormous economic and military capabilities will remain.

Few wish to face up to the problem of what could be done if China should begin to aggressively assert itself in the region. The US forces would not be able to play a stabilising role once China reaches its full power. Japan could play an important role, but alone it would be no match for China. Some in South-East Asia see India as a possible counter to China, and this could promote a closer security relationship between India and ASEAN, but any balancing lies in the future. China, because of its size and its increasing economic and military power, will pose a major problem for Indian and ASEAN strategists. These strategists might well try to devise means and policies to ensure that China remains a peaceful and constructive member of the region. At the same time, plans also need to be made for dealing with a more belligerent China.

India faces many strategic challenges in a world that is in a state of flux. How it handles them will help determine its future.

## NOTES

1 See Surjit Mansingh, *India's Search for Power*, pp. 358-60, for reasons for this view which she believes, however, was not justified.

2 Rajiv Gandhi had a major influence on the Congress platform for the 1991 elections, which called for more modernisation.

3 The policy of self-reliance requires a large research and development (R&D) effort, but the government spent only limited funds for defence R&D.

4 The rupee-rouble exchange rate was to cause problems later.

5 However, many feel it might have been better if the Soviet Union had stayed on, as it would have backed a secular government. Now Islamic fundamentalists seem to be on the verge of taking over Afghanistan.

6 The first deputy defence minister of Russia visited Delhi for a few days in March 1995. He said that India is more important to Russia as a strategic partner than it was to the Soviet Union.

7 India also sees other international agreements as discriminatory; it has strongly opposed the Nuclear Proliferation Treaty (NPT) and the Missile Technology Control Regime (MTCR).

8 Observers do not agree on the extent or nature of Chinese activities in Myanmar.

9 Some Indians argue that China may feel surrounded by unfriendly, or potentially unfriendly, countries.

10 The spring of 1995 confrontation between China and the

Philippines over disputed island claims shows how volatile the situation can be. However, ASEAN support for the Philippines and China's moderation has, at least, temporarily, reduced tension in the region.

11 The US administration has refused to allow Pakistan to take possession of 28 F-16s that it bought and paid for over $1 billion five years ago because Islamabad pushed its nuclear programme past the point where President Bush could certify that Pakistan did not have a nuclear capability, and the Pressler Amendment went into effect in 1990.

12 Others contend they came from political gang-fighting.

13 See VR Raghavan, *India's Security in the Emerging World Order,* Delhi Policy Group, 1995, pp. 32-6, for a discussion of current government inadequacies in this area. The author is a recently retired army general who should know the facts.

14 Shekhar Gupta has written, however, that the bureaucracy has blocked all efforts to implement the CDE's recommendations. See Shekhar Gupta, *India Redefines Its Role,* Paper 293, London, 1995, IISS, p. 47.

15 Lt Gen. KK Hazari, PVSM, AVSM, (Retd.) and Brig. Vijai Nair, VSM, PhD, 'Higher Defence Planning: the Need for Debate and Reform', *Indian Defence Review,* 1993, Vol. 8 (2), p. 34.

16 Lt Gen. KK Hazari, PVSM, AVSM (Retd.) 'National Interests: Formulation of National Policy and Strategic Concepts', *Indian Defence Review,* April 1994, Vol 9 (2), pp. 15-16.

17 However, in May, Prime Minister Rao said the NSC had not worked. Most observers thought it never came into existence. Rao said he was forming 'expert groups' to study certain aspects of strategy, and a group would oversee and coordinate these efforts. He was not very specific about these developments but they do suggest progress and that India may develop a strategy in its own fashion.

18 See Shekhar Gupta, op. cit., p. 56, for a brief discussion of this new spirit. However, Nehru's eloquent idealism masked a very pragmatic approach to India's problems, an approach India has continued to follow, though perhaps it has not been as vocal about what it is doing as are today's youth.

19 See George K Tanham and Marcy Agmon, *The Indian Air Force: Trends and Prospects,* Santa Monica, Calif., RAND, MR-424-AF, 1995.

20 It might split up after Deng's death in which case there would no longer be one China, but this does not seem likely.

21 The dispute between China and the Philippines in the spring of 1995 over some of the Spratley Islands is not a good omen. ASEAN sees the problem and is backing Manila. China may also be trying to ascertain the US reaction.

# STATE, SOCIETY, STRATEGY

KANTI P BAJPAI

Does India, a country with nearly one billion people, *have* strategy? With the fourth largest military and tenth biggest economy in the world, surely Indians have thought and organised strategically? The answer in George Tanham's first essay is that this potential Asian and global 'tiger' is, as in so much else, a laggard—not fierce and quick of foot but amiable and maundering, finding or getting its way, when it does, by instinct or by sheer preponderance.

Tanham's interpretation has been received with mixed feelings in India: gratification that an outsider should have bothered with Indian strategy; annoyance at his judgement that there does not seem to be much strategy to bother about; and self-reproach because he may be right. Three years later, Tanham has sought to review the situation. In his second intervention on Indian strategy, he finds that there is a greater awareness of the need for strategic thinking and that in a dramatically changed world India has made a number of strategic changes. I react to Tanham in three parts: the absence of a tradition of strategic thinking; the future of military strategic thinking in India; and India's grand strategy for a new century.

## THE ABSENCE OF STRATEGIC THINKING

First of all, then, what exactly is Tanham arguing when he claims India lacks strategic thinking? The word 'strategy' reflects two meanings—military strategy and grand strategy. Military strategy, strategy plain and simple, is 'the art of distributing and applying military means to fulfil the ends of policy'. On the other hand, 'grand strategy' is 'to coordinate and direct all the resources of a nation, or band of nations, towards the attainment of the political object of the war—the goal defined by fundamental policy'.[1]

Grand strategy is inclusive of but not coterminous with military strategy.

Strategic thinking, then, is systematic and sustained inquiry into the fundamental principles governing (i) the distribution of military means and (ii) the coordination of the nation's major resources—including the military—towards the aims of policy. When Tanham says that India lacks strategic thinking he refers to both meanings of strategy: the husbanding of force towards the ends of policy as also the overall husbanding of national resources to achieve the political objective.

It is important to underline the word 'thinking'. It is not Tanham's point that India lacks strategy and grand strategy *per se*: no political collectivity could survive without some actual distribution of the military means at its disposal and some coordination of its overall resources, physical and non-physical. Nor is Tanham's point absolutist: if India lacks a tradition of strategic thinking, it does so *relative* to Europe and its various offshoots. If this is Tanham's contention, it would seem he has the argument. India has had strategy and grand strategy, and one could distil these from Indian pronouncements and behaviour; but it cannot produce a canon of strategic thought of any great lineage, and certainly not comparable to Europe's.

Secondly, does Tanham get the causes of India's deficiency right? To answer that let me first pose and then answer another question: In terms of a 'strategic culture', is India exceptional or is Europe exceptional?[2] I would argue that Europe is the exception historically. If so, what conditions in Europe produced a tradition of strategic thinking unmatched anywhere in the world? It would be tempting to answer that the 'European Miracle', the whole course of European development from roughly the Late Middle Ages to the Industrial Revolution, was responsible.[3] But we can pick out two key elements or turning points: the Peace of Westphalia (1648) and the French Revolution (1789). The Peace of Westphalia signalled the end of empire in Europe and the legitimising of absolutist monarchical rule. Looking back, one can see that this was the beginning of a states system with no overarching authority: thus, 1648 was not the beginning of a perpetual peace but of a perpetual war-system, for, if there was no ultimate authority—Rome, the Holy Roman Empire—then, conceptually, war was the final arbiter of disputes. If war was the final arbiter of disputes, then systematic and rigorous inquiry into strategy *tout court*—the distribution of military means—became indispensable.

While the Peace of 1648 originated strategic thinking, the French Revolution was the origin of grand strategic thinking. The Revolution launched the idea that the state was accountable to the citizenry and responsible for its welfare. In return, the resources of civil society could be, and indeed should be, harnessed for the ends of state policy. The Revolution, and the rise of Napoleon, also changed the nature of war. Revolutionary and Napoleonic France brought an end to the sport of kings—limited wars for limited ends serviced by limited means. With state and civil society increasingly fused, and with war no longer limited but total, inquiry into grand strategy, i.e. the mobilisation and combination of a society's military and non-military resources, was essential.

It is these two changes that are the spur to a tradition of strategic thinking: exiting from an imperial system and entering a war-system, in which war is a constant shadow and is extensive rather than limited; and a growing integration of state and civil society. And it is these, much more than the factors Tanham identifies, that have caused Indian strategic thinking to be laggardly. Thus, it is not the absence of political unity but rather its opposite, namely, overwhelming unity under successive empires or near-empires, that obviated or retarded strategic thinking. So also, it is not so much Hindu culture—its conception of time, or its insistence that life is unknowable and largely uncontrollable—but a different path of political development, in which state and civil society stayed farther apart than in Europe, that is responsible for the leisurely pace of Indian strategic thought.

Things have of course changed, but not perhaps enough. India, after 1947, entered a state system which is a war-system, where war and the preparations for war are incessant; and its nationalist movement fused state and civil society as never before. Yet, as Tanham rightly contends, Indian strategic thinking—though not strategy—remains ephemeral. Why? Once again, it seems to me that there is nothing ineffably Indian at work, contrary to Tanham's view. First of all, India's entry into this kind of international and domestic society is recent: you need time for a tradition of thought to develop. Second, whereas India inhabits a war-system, its wars have been relatively limited, Pakistan being too modest an adversary and China too physically remote for total war. Thus, there has been no deep inquiry into military and grand strategy. Third, state and civil society, while more closely fused than before, lack the intimacy achieved by European states: the Indian state simply does not trust its civil society enough for total mobilisation and participation.

If Indian strategic thinking has been absent, is there any reason to think that things will change? The answer is not clear. Where strategy is understood as 'the art of distributing and applying military means to fulfill the ends of policy', i.e. military strategy, there is unlikely to be much progress towards a tradition of strategic thinking. This is in part because war with China and Pakistan will be limited, but also for a number of other reasons. On the other hand, where strategy means 'to coordinate and direct all the resources of a nation, or band of nations, towards the attainment of the political object of the war—the goal defined by fundamental policy', i.e. grand strategy, we should expect progress. State and civil society are more intimate, and therefore it is more and more imaginable that the nation's resources could be coordinated and directed towards the attainment of the political object. I shall not have much more to say on the prospects of grand strategic thinking in India, but I should like to elaborate on why military strategic thinking will remain impoverished.

## THE FUTURE OF MILITARY STRATEGIC THINKING

There are several reasons why military strategic thinking in India has been, and will remain, poor. First of all, assuming that Indian military objectives are defensive and regionally delimited, India does not have a military problem requiring great theoretical effort. China is the status quo power in relation to India, and has little or no interest in attacking and controlling a population of one billion fractious souls. Moreover, terrain and climate make it extremely difficult for China to do much more than it did in 1962. Distance, altitude, communications and climate make movement and supply for an army of several hundred thousand over many months, even years, a virtual impossibility. This does not mean that there cannot be fighting between India and China, but it will not amount to a war of survival, a full-scale invasion. Firefights along the border are the most likely prospect, but this is not a military problem that will attract and sustain the best and the brightest strategic minds.

Would an India-Pakistan war constitute a military problem which demands greater strategic attention and innovation? This too appears unlikely. The India-Pakistan strategic problem is not a terribly complex one. In the event of a Pakistani attack, in all likelihood in Kashmir, India has three options, none of which roils the strategic imagination. India can choose pure defence, a counter-offensive virtually all along the front, or a slicing counter-offensive in vulnerable or key sectors. Pure defence, that is, standing still and absorbing and destroying a Pakistani attack on its territory, is implausible: limiting the fight to Kashmir is politically unacceptable in India. On the other hand, a counter-offensive all along the front is logistically unviable.

After 1965, India's strategy therefore is to respond to a large-scale Pakistani attack on Kashmir by an immediate counter-offensive. One counter-offensive would be launched through Punjab to threaten Lahore, only fifty miles from the Indian border, and perhaps also Multan. This would involve heavy fighting because Pakistani forces will be thickly arrayed and backed by various obstacles—canals, land-mines, anti-tank ditches, and so on. A second counter-offensive, through Rajasthan, would threaten to cut Pakistan in half, separating Sind from Punjab. A key objective would be Hyderabad, which is only 125 miles from the border, and potentially Bahawalpur. The basic strategic choice is clear enough—a slicing offensive-defence rather than either pure defence or a general counter-offensive all along the front. There remain such operational level questions as what corridors would be used, what kinds of flanking moves, and so on, and the nature of tactics. However, this is not the stuff that stirs up the strategic imagination. India's responses and Pakistani counter-responses have been gamed to the point that there is little strategic excitement in gaming much further.

The space for strategic thinking is likely to be a modest space for various other reasons. For one, Indian forces must contend with rather severe logistical constraints. It is difficult to know exactly how long Indian forces can be supplied with subsistence, transportation, ammunition and spares, but present capabilities are likely to be sufficient for no longer than two weeks.[4] If so, there is not much room for strategic innovation. It is hard to plan great military plans when your fundamental posture is defensive and when, in addition, you can move only fourteen days supplies.

Another thing that cramps the Indian strategic imagination is a feeling of ineluctable preponderance. While the reports of Indian military superiority are exaggerated, Indian numbers, greater indigenisation of military supplies, strategic depth and economic strength encourage complacency. Why plan much if the Big Indian Machine can simply grind its opponent down?

Indian defence spending is yet another constraint on the strategic imagination. One might argue that for a poor country defence spending is already too high and that there are economies to be achieved. But, that said, from the point of view of strategising, one needs a looser purse. You can imagine all manner of strategic moves only if you have the men and material to deploy in the service of those moves.

If this was not enough, there are yet other factors which restrain the Indian strategic imagination. Military technology is one of these. The kinds of technology India possesses or is likely to possess relative to Pakistan, in the near future, does not allow it to dream great strategic dreams. Matters may be different in thirty years, but today there is no decisive system or capability at hand: nothing with the promise of the machine-gun in 1914, the tank in 1939, jet propulsion and missiles during the cold war, or present-day electronic warfare.

A final and perhaps decisive factor leading to the poverty of strategic thought is the presence of nuclear weapons capability in India and Pakistan. Everything said so far about the constraints on the strategic imagination is secondary to the effects of near-nuclearisation. India and Pakistan have come to believe that the other has nuclear weapons capability at short notice. If so, there is little to strategise about in the normal sense. A full-scale Pakistani attack in Kashmir or Punjab, an ambitious counter-offensive by India into West Punjab or Sind, both these appear fantastic. What rational ends of policy would be fulfilled by risking a nuclear war? Would any sane Pakistani leader risk an attack in Kashmir which could escalate to a nuclear exchange? In the shadow of nuclear weapons, would any reasonable Indian leader countenance a counter-offensive to take Lahore or to split Pakistan by a thrust into Sind?

The truth is that the Great Equaliser has left the region safe for only one form of warfare, which is sub-conventional. India and

Pakistan can fight each other by proxy and by no other means. New Delhi can subvert Sind in this way, as Pakistan can subvert Kashmir. Nuclear weapons are useless in dealing with subversives. They are also useless in punishing the hand behind the subversives. Neither side dares to respond with a large-scale conventional attack across the border: at best one might attempt hot pursuit, but even this is risky when nuclear weapons are about.

The great military problem facing India is therefore how to combat proxy wars in the shadow of nuclear weapons. It is also how to fight insurgency without destroying democracy. This is where Indian strategic thought could advance. Indeed, this is the one dimension of military strategy where India may have something to teach the world. As things stand, though, we know little about Indian counter-insurgency thought and practice. While one could infer something about practice from fifty years' experience in various theatres, Indian thinking—if it has been systematically articulated—remains veiled.[5] We need an Indian Tanham to part the veils.

## INDIAN GRAND STRATEGY FOR THE NEXT CENTURY

Tanham's new essay, 'Indian Strategy in Flux?', is an attempt to chart Indian policies in a new era. I agree with him that a series of occurences, internally and externally, in 1990-1 caused Indian policies to shift rather dramatically. I also agree broadly on the nature of those policies: economic reforms in the service of high growth rates; and a deepening engagement with the United States and subsidiarily with East and South-East Asia. What I shall do from here on is to focus on a clutch of grand strategic issues alluded to in Tanham's essays: economic reforms; China; Kashmir; and nuclear weapons. Specifically, I shall ask: What are the grand strategic implications of India's economic reforms? Is China truly a serious threat? Does India have a Kashmir policy and, if so, what are its prospects? Can India be secure without a nuclear weapons capability?

### *Reforming for Growth*

If the economic reforms work, what will be the strategic consequences? The economic reforms are intended to unleash a pattern of economic growth which will be sustained and rapid.

The Finance Ministry wants a long-term growth rate of at least 6 to 7 per cent. Given the pattern of growth in neighbouring South-East Asia over the past 10-15 years and the reportedly explosive rate in China (10-14 per cent), this is not unrealistic. India's present rate is around 5 per cent which means that a slight notching up is within reach.

At the rate of seven per cent per annum real growth, national income will double every ten years. If India's per capita GNP is roughly $400, this means that in thirty years the per capita GNP will stand at $3200. A conservative estimate of India's population in 2025 is roughly 1.3 billion.[6] This means a total GNP of $4.16 trillion, almost that of the US in 1986.[7] To see what this means, a further comparison with the US will help. Today, the US economy is some fifteen times the size of India's. If the US grows at an annual rate of 2.5 per cent for thirty years and if, at a conservative estimate, its total population is 300 million, its GNP in 2025 would be approximately $13-14 trillion, about three times the size of the Indian economy. Thus, in 2025, we can expect India to have perhaps the fourth or fifth largest economy in the world behind China, the US, Europe and Japan.

What are the implications of this? First, India will be a major technological and military power. With its scientific and technical manpower and an extensive industrial base built up since 1947, it will be an important force in global technology, both civilian and military. It would be a mistake to see India as perennially unable to break out of a low-level or intermediate-level technology trap. At a certain level of development, countries can perform scientific and technical leap-frogs, as the East Asians are showing. India in 20 years could suddenly be ready to enter the sunrise technology areas of the times. Further, it will want—and be able to afford — military power commensurate with its technological and economic power.

Second, India will be a cultural power. In 2025, with a fully literate population of 1.3 billion, it will be the biggest English-speaking country in the world. It will have a massive publishing, television, film and music industry, of which the English sector will be substantial. A new Indian popular culture, based on Indian regional languages, Hindustani and English, and leavened as before by non-Indian influences, will be a major source of 'soft power', globally.

Third, at a per capita income of $3200, India should have few, if any, people below the poverty line. Its citizens will live in much larger numbers in enormous towns and cities. This population will enjoy the basic amenities and will be educated and skilled, and will live its life in urban agglomerates as never before. It will therefore have a much greater propensity for social and political involvement and activity. The new India will be a bustling and participatory, but also often explosive, society and polity—with repercussions for neighbouring states and regions, to be sure, but also for the world at large.

Fourth, India will be a major consumer of key natural resources, especially oil. It will also be a major pollutant. Mahatma Gandhi once remarked that if India became an industrial power it would be a threat to civilisation. He meant that, like other advanced industrial powers, its need for resources and markets would make it an aggressive, militaristic society. Whether one subscribes altogether to this Gandhian judgment or not, it is not difficult to see that an India with a per capita income of $3200 and a population of 1.3 billion will put considerable added pressure on the global economic and ecological system, and therefore on the international political system. The international system will have to make room for India, and New Delhi will have to bear special responsibility for the stability of global economy and ecology. But this double adjustment will not necessarily be an easy process.

Fifth, if the pattern of high economic growth subsists, India will solve its problems with Pakistan and the US. With Pakistan this may take up to 30 years; with the US it should take much less time. An India with an economy of four trillion dollars will be an awfully large market to disdain, even for Pakistan. Already, there are signs that Pakistan's business community is urging its government to speed up trade links with India. Informal trade is growing fast, and the business community would prefer to conduct its transactions legitimately and more openly. Pakistani businessmen do not necessarily like India, but they do necessarily like profits.

The US, by contrast, is not an enemy, but there are numerous areas of disagreement and tension, especially in the strategic realm. New Delhi's policy increasingly is to 'do a China' on Washington. India has been identified as perhaps the biggest of the Big Emerging Markets, and it is doing its best to involve the US thoroughly in the Indian economy. An incidental benefit of this is that American businessmen will become a lobby for strategic restraint in the

White House and the Congress. If you do not have cultural affinity or strategic identity with the US, the best way to meliorate Washington's policies is *via* economic ties. India has finally—or almost finally—seen the light on this.

It is true of course that economic ties do not automatically lead to a more accommodative stance. It is also the case that they can cut both ways: the US may gain leverage too. But the question is: in terms of political influence, will the US or India gain more from increasing economic links? Since the US already has all manner of ways in which it can exert influence over Indian choices, India will gain more. India must therefore press on, and there is every sign that it will do so, periodic remissions notwithstanding.

### *The China Syndrome*

Tanham suggests that China is '[t]he greatest and longest term strategic challenge to India'. Since China is also a threat to East and South-East Asia, including Japan, India is a potential partner. Is China, though, the greatest and longest-term strategic challenge to India? Clearly, this is a view that has currency in India. It is used to justify India's nuclear option. Some use it to make India attractive to the West, especially the US, which is thought to fear China's rise to power. Others see it as a way of making India attractive to East and South-East Asians, who also worry about Chinese power. But is there a Chinese threat to India?

In a purely structural sense, one could admit China is a threat. Given its military and economic superiority and its contiguity with India, it is a threat by virtue of its power and placement. Threat assessment, though, is not just a matter of reckoning capabilities and opportunities. It does, and must, engage the issue of motives and intentions. Why should China threaten India?

Chinese intimidation might occur in various circumstances. First of all, there could be hostilities over the unresolved border dispute. Second, internal instabilities in China could encourage external adventurism. As the Chinese leadership struggles to assert or retain political control, it might be tempted to use external 'threats' to outmanoeuvre and discipline internal rivals. Third, the two countries are likely to be perennial rivals for influence in Asia, if not farther afield.[8]

Each of these propositions bears critical examination. First, while the border dispute is unresolved in a formal sense, Beijing has got most of what it wanted out of the issue. If its primary aim was to secure the route from Xinkiang to Tibet, it long ago accomplished its goal. China is the satisfied power on the border issue.

Second, there is considerable room for debate over the internal-external linkage. Is there any credible evidence that internal factors were responsible for Beijing's punitive wars against India and Vietnam? How vulnerable and unstable is China likely to be in the future? Can domestic political troubles be eased, in the new China, by external distractions? Most importantly, would war with India be credible, given that the only serious bilateral issue, viz., the border, favours China; and would it help or hurt an insecure regime or leadership to raise an *India* bogey in such circumstances?

Third, India is not a credible rival in South-East Asia; nor is it likely to be, any time in the near future. China has assets India does not and will not possess for a long time, if ever. It is contiguous to most of the South-East Asian states. There are powerful Chinese minorities throughout the region. And Chinese military and economic power leave India far behind. Militarily, China has nuclear weapons and conventional forces twice India's size, forces it is rapidly modernising with its growing economic strength. Economically, it has reputedly been growing two to three times as fast as the Indian economy. It is projected to become the largest economy in the world in the next decade or so, and it is a trading giant. In sum, China is a formidable presence in South-East Asia. India, by contrast, is a sideshow.

If these three counter-arguments are correct, it is unlikely that there is a Chinese threat to India. The *detente* with China will become a measured *entente*. India's greatest strategic problem is not China but various internal instabilities and rebellions, and if these are managed wisely the country will be secure internally as well as externally.

## *A Kashmir Policy*

Tanham suggests that India has not evolved a response to internal troubles, especially Pakistan-aided secessionism in Kashmir. Many in India would agree. But a closer look reveals that there is an Indian strategy.

At the heart of India's strategy is to evolve a political solution to the Kashmir problem.[9] This means that New Delhi is prepared to grant greater autonomy to Kashmir, if necessary beyond the limits of Article 370. While some oppose the devolutionist option—such as the BJP—it is clear that most Indians could live with this outcome. The question is: how can a political solution be found? The Indian method seems to consist of four inter-related elements.

First, the government will attempt to exhaust the militancy through counter-force methods. Counter-force has two components. The traditional component is to use large contingents of military, para-military and police forces to limit the inflow and outflow of militants, to carry out 'search and destroy' missions, and to maintain law and order in towns and cities. The new component, after Punjab, is to use so-called 'counter-insurgency groups' to combat the secessionists. These are the *tanzeem* (literally 'organisations') who are breakaway factions or are independent entities who have quarrelled with various secessionist outfits and are willing to cooperate with the government.[10] The Indian strategy seeks not only to tire out the militants through internal strife but also to tire out the populace through collateral damage. Already, six years of militancy have taken their toll, and there is growing fatigue with the privations and violence of the insurgency.

Second, India will continue to stand by its offer of bilateral talks with Pakistan. The offer is unconditional and has been rejected by the Benazir Bhutto government until India makes troop reductions in Kashmir. India's purpose is primarily tactical at this point, but the objective in the longer term is to move towards a partition of the state along the line of control (LOC). Since Islamabad has made it clear that the 'third option', i.e. an independent Kashmir, is not a viable strategic option for Pakistan, there is a convergence of interests here. India desperately needs a lever against Pakistan. Whether New Delhi likes it or not, there are only two levers in the short term: the US and China. A good bit of India's diplomacy must be to get either, or both, to pry Islamabad loose from its refusal to negotiate.

Third, the Indian government will attempt to build bridges to some organisation that is capable of negotiating a settlement. This is a delicate task. On the one hand, the government must step back and allow some entity to form and organise itself from a diverse and often mutually antagonistic ensemble of political activists and militants. It must give the incipient organisation the space to grow and to legitimise itself, even if this means giving it some political victories. On the other hand, it cannot give the organisation so much leeway that Kashmiri opinion comes to believe that the government is weak and that secession is plausible. The release of Kashmiri leaders over the past two years and the formation of the All Party Hurriyat Conference is part of the government's delicate balancing act.

Fourth, the government will hold elections in Kashmir, perhaps more than once. The goal will be to hand power back to an elected government and make it responsible for daily administration and law and order. Before elections, a number of confidence-building measures will be necessary: changing the present administration in Kashmir; a Prime Ministerial visit to Kashmir; the release of those detained for relatively minor offences; punishing the most serious human rights offenders; troop reductions or disengagement (i.e. confinement to barracks, except for election duty); and some form of special election supervision.

Will this four-stroke method work, at least to bring a tired, wary peace? Something like it 'worked' in Punjab. However, Kashmir is not quite Punjab. Counter-force in Punjab was helped by the fencing of the border with Pakistan and a hospitable terrain for police and military operations. The Pakistan factor was 'contained' by Islamabad's decision to draw down support in favour of the Kashmir militancy. While the Sikh militancy was fractionated, the Akalis and the Congress were mature and viable organisations. Finally, the level of popular support for the violence and for secession was limited, at least in part because roughly half the population was Hindu. Punjab had strengths that Kashmir does not. This suggests not that the basic strategy won't work, but that it will take longer.

As these lines are being written, the government's decision to hold elections has been rejected by the Election Commission. Reaction to the government's announcement had been negative—in Kashmir and amongst the major political parties outside Kashmir—and the Commission's countermanding seems rational. Clearly, the elections were called too early, for the Hurriyat has not yet established itself as an organisation that is capable of and willing to negotiate. The abruptness of the move was also a cause of failure. Various confidence-building measures were necessary as a prelude to the call for elections, yet virtually none were deployed.

The opening of the Hurriyat's 'Kashmir Awareness Bureau' in New Delhi is a step in the direction of increasing the group's visibility and credibility. If it begins a dialogue with the major political parties and with other elements of the policy community, its standing should grow. The government, for its part, should keep talking about elections—to be held at some later date but obviously not before the summer of 1996—while beginning to implement the kind of confidence-building measures listed earlier.

A Kashmir solution—a minimal peace—is not yet at hand, but a method is available, the broad outlines of which are familiar from the experience with Punjab and the North-eastern states. With some inflection, it will be the method of choice of any new government in New Delhi.

### *India's Nuclear Choices*

A key element of Indian strategy relates to nuclear weapons. Broadly speaking, India has three nuclear choices: ambiguity, weaponisation and abstinence. Ambiguity refers to a policy of opposition to nuclear weapons while keeping the weaponisation option open by maintaining a programme of research and development. This describes the present Indian policy. While there is a passionate lobby for weaponisation, it is not a widespread preference. Abstinence, on the other hand, has almost no support. I argue that weaponisation is unnecessary, ambiguity is dangerous, and abstinence is realistic.

Why is weaponisation unnecessary? India has two adversaries—China and Pakistan. China, as already argued, is not a military threat. Pakistan is. But India could deter a nuclear Pakistan without nuclear weapons—for two reasons.[11]

First of all, if India unconditionally and verifiably renounces nuclear weapons, Pakistan will be forced to reciprocate. International opinion and pressures will be exerted against Islamabad as never before. As a diplomatic weapon of last resort, Pakistan will claim that only nuclear weapons can counter India's superiority in conventional forces and strategic depth. But Pakistani deficiencies are correctable. First, Pakistani conventional forces can be strengthened sufficiently for deterrence and defence. Second, instead of 'levelling up' the quantum of conventional forces in South Asia, it is possible to 'level down'. With its dramatic nuclear gesture, India will have opened the door to negotiating a conventional forces balance consonant with Pakistani security needs. A South Asian balance will not be easy to construct, given that both sides have to maintain forces for other opponents and for internal security; but negotiated sufficiency and a non-provocative defence is not an impossibility either.[12]

Of the two correctives, levelling down is preferable. Even if India unilaterally abstained, Pakistan could object that it is cheaper to match India's conventional superiority with nuclear capability. Levelling down to a conventional balance which satisfies both sides and which avoids a costly arms race can overcome this objection. Negotiations would focus on reducing offensive weapons. All weapons can of course be used for offensive purposes, but the two countries could at least agree on which systems are *more* and which are *less* offensive and what should be the appropriate mix of these.[13]

Secondly, the threat of massive conventional retaliation could deter a nuclear-belligerent Pakistan. The threat of a nuclear attack could be matched by the threat of massive conventional retaliation. Specifically, India could threaten to retaliate with massive conventional bombing of Pakistani population, industrial, infrastructural, nuclear and symbolic targets. Indian bombers and missiles, armed with a variety of explosives and especially high incendiary weapons, could credibly threaten to carry out enormous punitive raids.

A conventional retaliatory strategy would encounter three limits or objections. First, if Pakistan's nuclear arsenal was sizeable enough, then India's most important air and missile installations would be vulnerable to a first strike, and massive conventional retaliation would become impossible. Secondly, massive conventional retaliation would be expensive. India would need to mount enormous raids capable of getting past Pakistani air defences. This would require considerable superiority in aircraft and missiles and enormous stocks of conventional explosives. The cost of these, plus the investments in skilled manpower, would add to India's defence bill. However, these added costs would need to be balanced against the costs of nuclear weapons which, if properly computed, are by no means modest. Moreover, since nuclear weapons are not necessarily substitutable for conventional weapons, a nuclear deterrent would entail large and expensive conventional forces as well.[14] Finally, massive conventional retaliation is open to the charge that if it mimics nuclear retaliation one might as well go nuclear. This is correct. But the obverse is also correct. Neither side needs to go nuclear to achieve mutual terror and mutual deterrence, if that is the objective.

If weaponisation is unnecessary, ambiguity is dangerous. First, with time, India will increasingly be seen as a nuclear power capable of striking well beyond the region. If so, the five declared nuclear powers will target India with nuclear weapons. Ambiguity may also expose India to non-nuclear threats. To persuade the Indian government to give up the ambiguity posture, the nuclear powers could exploit India's internal political problems, particularly its ethnic and religious divisions. Kashmir is a distinct vulnerability. Other punishments might include economic sanctions and technology denials. At a critical phase in India's economic reforms and development, these could be disastrous. The economic crisis of 1991, the recent plunge in the value of the rupee and the massive rise in the call money rates, all show that the Indian economy remains turbulent. It could be critically hurt by external manipulation if outsiders chose punitive action. Ten years from now India may be more or less invulnerable to such actions, but the present moment is fraught with dangers.

Second, if ambiguity deters, it is worth recalling what can be deterred and what cannot be deterred by a nuclear weapons capability—and with what strategic consequences. It bears repeating that nuclear weapons cannot deter perhaps the most important sources of violence in the region, namely, insurgency and terrorism. You cannot use a hammer to swat a fly. Worse, nuclear weapons capability in South Asia has made the region *positively hospitable to internal strife fuelled or instigated by one's neighbour*. With India and Pakistan at par in their nuclear postures, Islamabad has become free to export violence.[15]

It is a gloomy but nonetheless accurate thought that the seeds of Pakistan's present course in Kashmir were planted in the irradiated sands of Pokharan. The Indian nuclear test was a fillip to Pakistan's nuclear programme, and with nuclear equality Islamabad could fiddle while Kashmir burned. On the other hand, if both sides had abjured nuclear weapons capability, Pakistani intervention in Indian quarrels would have been exceedingly dangerous. Abstinent Pakistan would have had to reckon that abstinent India could retaliate by 'hot pursuit' strikes—with the promise of escalation to outright conventional war. One of the major benefits of abstinence would be to return the military advantage to India in the contest over Kashmir.

Thirdly, there is the argument that while ambiguity may be 'deterrence stable', it may not be 'crisis stable'. Whereas uncertainty of nuclear retaliation may deter in the general course of things, in a crisis, which is an environment marked by the dangerous lack of certitudes and by shortened decision-making horizons, what is likely to be stabilising is certainty of retaliation. Against this is the view of Kenneth Waltz and K Subrahmanyam who have argued the virtues of uncertainty in deterrence and even in crisis. They suggest that given the destructiveness of nuclear weapons what deters is not the certainty of response but the *mere possibility* that the other side could respond with nuclear firepower.

Notwithstanding the theoretic arguments for the virtues of uncertainty, the empirics are mixed. On the one hand, the nuclear powers, and India and Pakistan since the early 1980s, have run up a good list of crises, near-crises, or reputed crises without going to nuclear war. On the other hand, over the years, in a series of hints, half-truths, leaks and revelations, Pakistan has sought to reduce uncertainties about its nuclear capability. Most worryingly, since the mid 1980s, it has repeatedly used crises or crises-like situations to reveal its nuclear teeth—and to reveal more and more of them with each episode. The 1987 *Brasstacks* crisis and the 1990 Kashmir 'crisis' were the most serious instances.

Even more worryingly, India, for its part, has repeatedly denied seeing any teeth. The Indian strategic community does not apppear to believe there was a nuclear threat in either 1987 or 1990. Thus, Pakistan's escalating use of crisis as a means of signalling capability has run into India's bland refusal to acknowledge either the crisis or the capability: the harder Islamabad tries, the more stolid New Delhi becomes. In this situation, Islamabad may feel it has no option but to instigate more crises.

Two dangers exist. The first is that India is being lulled into complacency. The second is that someday, in the midst of a crisis, when India finally wakes up to Pakistani capabilities, it may well decide to go first. In a situation of nuclear asymmetry, where India has four or five times as many bombs as Pakistan, and where it confronts increasingly blatant nuclear exhibitionism and threat, the temptation to strike first may be difficult to control.

Theory suggests that uncertainty of capability is sufficient for deterrence and crisis stability. Yet, experience suggests otherwise. Over time, South Asians (as others?) seem to seek certainty of capability. In a situation of great asymmetry, this could be very dangerous. As Pakistan signals increasing certainty of capability, it may endanger itself by virtue of its signalling success. India, convinced at last of Pakistan's capability and conscious of its massive superiority, may decide it is better to fight now when Pakistani nuclear forces are minuscule than later when they are more mature. This would be a catastrophe for both countries.

In sum: if weaponisation is unnecessary and ambiguity is dangerous, nuclear abstinence is not utopian. Abstinence is a credible strategic choice; indeed, it is India's best choice.

## CONCLUSION

In reacting to Tanham's two lively essays I have argued that while India does indeed lack a tradition of strategic thinking, it is for somewhat different reasons than identified in *Indian Strategic Thought*. I have also argued that there is a poor future ahead for Indian military strategic thinking. Finally, I have suggested that India's change of grand strategic direction since 1991, with economics leading the way, is an opportunity to rethink old options and think through emerging options. I argue that economic reform will make India a great power, that there will be opportunities, dangers and special responsibilities as a result, and that relations with Pakistan and the US will be regulated by economics; that China is not a military threat to India; that there *is* a Kashmir policy and that it could well deliver a minimal but welcome peace; and that India can be safe without nuclear weapons. This is a vision of a more prosperous, mature, globalist and secure India than ever before. It is optimistic but not triumphalist.

George Tanham has written two engaging, informative and perspicacious essays on Indian strategy and strategic thinking. The first in particular was written for the eyes and ears of the US policy community, but together they have stirred the curiosity and imagination of Indians. His is not the final word on Indian strategic choices and thought, nor even the first, but it has been an important and much needed catalytic voice. *Indian Strategic Thought* and its companion will be an indispensable and inescapable reference point for the makers and thinkers of Indian strategy from here forward.

## NOTES

1 BH Liddell Hart, *Strategy*, New York, Signet, 1967, pp. 321-2.

2 This phrase is taken from George Tanham, 'Indian Strategic Culture', *The Washington Quarterly* 15 (Winter 1992), pp. 129-42.

3 For an account of European exceptionalism, see EL Jones, *The European Miracle: Environments, Economies and Geopolitics in the History of Europe and Asia*, 2nd edn., New York, Cambridge University Press, 1987.

4 The importance of logistics is neglected in strategic thinking, though not in strategic practice. On logistics in history, see Martin van Creveld, *Supplying War: Logistics from Wallenstein to Patton*, New York, Cambridge University Press, 1977.

5 On insurgency and counter-insurgency in India, see VK Anand, *Conflict in Nagaland: A Study of Insurgency and Counter-insurgency*, Delhi, Chanakya Publications, 1980, and B Varma, *Insurgency and Counter-insurgency*, New Delhi, Uppal Publishing House, 1988.

6 United Nations, *The Sex and Age Distribution of the World Populations*, New York, United Nations Publications, 1992, p. 441.

7 US GNP in 1986 is estimated to have been $4.2 trillion. For the US GNP figures, see Joseph S Nye, *Bound to Lead: The Changing Nature of American Power* (place of publication not mentioned), Basic Books, 1990, p. 163.

8 Some of these concerns are expressed by K Subrahmanyam, 'Implications of Nuclear Asymmetry', in K Subrahmanyam, ed., *Nuclear Myths and Realities*, New Delhi, ABC Publishing House, 1981, pp. 214-15.

9 On how India deals with separatist movements, see Shekhar Gupta, *India Redefines its Role*, Adelphi Paper 293, London, International Institute for Strategic Studies and Oxford University Press, 1995, and PS Datta, *Ethnic Peace Accords in India*, New Delhi, Vikas, 1995.

10 See Aditya Sinha, 'Militant Groups May Back Cong in J&K', *The Pioneer*, 28 October 1995, for an account of some of these groups and the government's use of them. Sinha points out that the strategy is not without risks. The behaviour of the counter-insurgent *tanzeem* may further alienate Kashmiri opinion from India and their rapid growth may make them more prone to Pakistani infiltration.

11 I draw here on my chapter, 'Abstaining: The Non-nuclear Option', in David Cortright and Amitabh Mattoo, eds., *India and the Bomb*, South Bend, Indiana, The Notre Dame University Press, forthcoming.

12 On defensive sufficiency, see Janne Nolan, ed., *Global Engagement: Cooperation and Security in the 21st Century,* Washington, DC, The Brookings Institution, 1994, Kanti Bajpai and Stephen P Cohen, 'Cooperative Security and South Asian Insecurity', in Nolan, ed., *Global Engagement,* pp. 447-80, Bjorn Moeller, *Common Security and Non-Offensive Defence: A Neorealist Perspective,* Boulder, Lynne Rienner,1992, and David Gates, *Non-Offensive Defence: An Alternative Strategy for NATO?*, London, St. Martin's Press, 1991.

13 For this argument, see Kanti Bajpai and Varun Sahni, *Secure and Solvent: Thinking About an Affordable Defence for India,* RGICS Paper No. 11, Rajiv Gandhi Institute for Contemporary Studies, New Delhi, May 1994, pp. 28-31.

14 On the broader costs of nuclear weapons, see the various essays in Kathleen Bailey, ed., *Weapons of Mass Destruction: Costs Versus Benefits,* New Delhi, Manohar Publishers, 1994.

15 This recalls Glenn Snyder's formulation of the 'stability-instability paradox': stability at the nuclear level would permit instability at lower levels. See his *Deterrence and Defense: Towards a Theory of National Security,* Princeton, Princeton University Press, 1961. See also PMS Blackett, *Fear, War, and the Bomb,* New York, Whittlesey House/McGraw Hill Book Company, 1948, p. 203: 'On the other hand the threat of use of weapons of mass destruction may prove far less a deterrent than an incitement of the rival power to strengthen its position by relatively unprovocative means. In fact, the obvious counter to the diplomatic use of the threat of atomic and similar weapons is the intensification of political warfare, or the actual waging of a guerilla type of war.'

# JUST ANOTHER BIG COUNTRY

VARUN SAHNI

*Indian Strategic Thought* could not have been written by an Indian. Even a cursory reading reveals the fingerprints of a non-Indian author. At a superficial level, this is evident in all sorts of errors: placing Bengalis in the *western* part of India, misspelling the names of Admiral Tahiliani and YB Chavan, getting the date of India's independence late by a day.[1] But this is merely sniping at the trivial. At a more substantial level, this essay is a serious attempt to understand and explain the Other. As the product of a research project commissioned by the Pentagon, this scholarly study obviously has a definite policy focus. In that sense, it is firmly within the state-sponsored area studies tradition: to deal with another people you have to figure out what makes them tick.

Nowhere is this tradition more in evidence than in the first section of the essay, which analyses the geographical, historical, cultural and British Raj influences on Indian strategic thought. George Tanham's analyses are sometimes tenuous, occasionally tendentious, but in the main unexceptionable. India as an alien culture is a particularly hard nut to crack, and one therefore has to admire the extent to which Tanham has been able to get to the kernel that is at its essence.

This commentary is an exercise in reflective thought. However, in trying to 'think Tanham through', I will neither tackle his central theme—that India lacks a culture or tradition of sustained and systematic thought on strategic issues—nor venture to suggest a grand strategy for India.[2] Instead, I will 'think through' the specific themes that came to the fore as I read and ruminated over Tanham's two essays.[3]

## GOING AROUND IN CIRCLES: THE MANDALA

Let me begin by commenting on a couple of Tanham's cultural conceptions. His analysis of how the world looks from New Delhi quite rightly emphasises that the strategic unity of the subcontinent is at the core of Indian notions and ideas about national security. However, this insight is tarnished by his allusion to Kautilya's *mandala* concept, which seems to suggest that there is something uniquely Indian about regarding one's immediate neighbours as potential adversaries over whom some sort of control is therefore desirable.

Far from being distinctly Indian, this strategic notion forms the bedrock of how most large countries view their place in the world. Egypt regards itself—in that ascending order—as a Nile valley, Arab/Islamic, African and developing country, and therefore views with understandable alarm the rise of militant Islam in Sudan, a neighbouring country with much the same geopolitical, historical-cultural and socio-economic attributes as itself. The attempt of Russia, as the dominant nationality in the erstwhile Soviet Union, to construct a *glacis* or *cordon sanitaire* on its western border after the Second World War is far too well known; witness Russia's deep unease over the demand of several of its former Warsaw Pact allies to be included in the North Atlantic Treaty Organisation (NATO). After unsuccessfully trying to remain 'of the West but not in it, in the East but not of it', Australia has come to terms with its geostrategic reality and is today actively engaged in influencing the evolving shape of the Asia-Pacific region. All nations, particularly big ones, are more concerned about what happens in their immediate geographical vicinity than in areas less proximate.

This rather pedestrian observation needs to be explicitly stated because our modes of thought on global power relations have been conditioned by the era of European imperialism when, for instance, the situation in Saigon mattered more to Paris than the situation in Lisbon. That exceptional period, which we may call the Columbian era or the 'Vasco da Gama epoch',[4] was undoubtedly the first phase of *world* history, but it is now over. Even the United States of America (USA), the only truly global power today, needs a North American Free Trade Area (NAFTA).

Thus, when India seeks to control the actions of its neighbours, or to restrict extra-regional influences on them, or to interfere in their domestic affairs, there is nothing specifically *Indian* about its behaviour. It is merely acting like a big power, or mimicking the way other big powers behave.

## CASTING AROUND FOR EXPLANATIONS: LIFE IN AN UNEQUAL WORLD

There is yet another example of Tanham seeking to explain Indian strategic notions through an exercise of cultural particularism. He argues that 'the caste system has given Indians a hierarchical view not only of India but of the world; they rank nations by size, culture and power.' This clearly will not do. The world *is* a hierarchical place, and *all* nations recognise this reality as they conduct their international relations. The Big Five in the UN Security Council, the nuclear 'haves' and 'have-nots' in the nuclear non-proliferation treaty (NPT), private investor excitement over the ten big emerging markets (BEMs), even Islamic revolutionary Iran's obsession with the Great Satanic USA, all testify to this being the case.

There is, therefore, nothing remarkable about the Indian strategic community regarding the world as hierarchical. On the contrary, what *is* remarkable is that India has been more vocal than most countries in its opposition to institutionalised discrimination in the international system, such as its criticism of the Big Five veto during the San Francisco Conference and its continued refusal to sign the NPT. To say this is not to assert that Indian strategic analysts or foreign police-makers do not think hierarchically. India seeks to be in the 'big league', however that may be defined, and opposes any international dispensation which places it among the 'have-nots'. Tanham recognises this as one of the 'complexities and paradoxes' of Indian strategic thinking: 'India argues for the legal and moral equality of all nations, yet it looks down on the smaller states and seeks a permanent seat on the UN Security Council.'

In other words, there is a distinct duality between principle and practice in Indian foreign policy; many observers, even friends of India, would call it hypocrisy. Hypocritical or not, this duality—an ideological opposition to hierarchy coupled with a pragmatic willingness to seek the best deal within a hierarchical system—is very real, and it is impossible to understand Indian foreign policy postures without understanding this.

Thus, India will continue to call for comprehensive global nuclear disarmament but will not sign the NPT because it is 'discriminatory'—it would prefer being left out in the cold as a 'nuclear holdout' to being included in the non-proliferation regime as a 'nuclear have-not'. India would rather see a UN General Assembly with real teeth, but will work towards the more modest goal of 'democratising' the Security Council—a codeword for Indian permanent membership with veto rights.

Incidently, this duality in foreign policy has its domestic cognate: although caste discrimination is constitutionally banned and has invited severe legislative and judicial sanctions, caste remains the basic category of Indian electoral politics.

### KNOWING ONESELF: THE IMPORTANCE OF NOT BEING PAKISTAN

Moving on from cultural issues to questions of strategy, we are faced with Pakistan, 'the regional destabiliser'. Tanham's analysis of the history of Indian-Pakistan hostility is well reasoned and rigorous. However, he does not quite explain why Pakistan remains the *bête noire* of not only the Indian strategic community but the Indian population at large. Unlike the Pakistani obsession with India, which is easily explained, the continual Indian obsession with Pakistan is quite remarkable and far less easy to comprehend. Tanham lists the various reasons why Indian strategists focus on Pakistan but does not critically examine them. Thus, he takes the centrality of Pakistan in Indian strategic thought as given without really explaining why that is the case.

Let us be clear about what the problem is. Let us compare the respective profiles of Pakistan and Bangladesh in Indian strategic thought. Tanham accurately reflects Indian strategic thought when he treats Bangladesh as merely one of 'India's smaller neighbours' which, unlike Pakistan, does *not* pose a serious military threat to India. Bangladesh may be economically poorer, geographically smaller and militarily weaker than Pakistan, but it is a *larger* country than the latter. Furthermore, Bangladesh and India have serious disagreements on a number of important issues ranging from river water management to unregulated population movement across the border. Bangladesh's national identity is based on Bengali-ness, a cultural attribute that is by no means exclusive to Bangladeshi citizens but which is shared by many Indian citizens as well. Bangladesh's geostrategic position south of the narrow 'chicken's neck' that connects north-eastern India to the Indo-Gangetic heartland poses a far greater threat to Indian territorial integrity than Pakistan's geostrategic location on the western front. And yet, while India and Pakistan are treated as strategic Siamese twins, no serious strategic analyst, either in India or abroad, has ever sought to strategically relate, let alone strategically equate, Bangladesh and India as potential military adversaries.

We really do need to figure out why this is so. Is it only because India and Bangladesh have not (yet?) fought a war, while India and Pakistan have fought at least three, and are even now engaged in undeclared hostilities on the Siachen glacier? I would argue that the answer lies in issues of ideology and identity rather than in military history. The central problem remains that Pakistan was founded on the 'two nation theory', an ideology that conferred distinct national identities on Hindus and Muslims. Tanham recognises that in the eyes of Indian strategists 'Pakistan's Islamic professions threaten Indian secularism', but places this last on his list of reasons for Indian antagonism toward Pakistan. The centrality of this factor in India-Pakistan hostility needs to be recognised if we are to have a proper perspective of the problem.

This also suggests that the passage of time is likely to be the best solution to the problem. For the post-Partition generation of the Indian elite, Pakistan has *always* been another country, coloured differently on the map in school. For them the equation '*Pakistan = homeland for Indian Muslims*' makes absolutely no sense; there are more Indian Muslims than the entire population of Pakistan! Thus, as the post-Partition generation reaches positions of power and influence in India, the centrality of Pakistan in India's *Weltanschauung* is likely to diminish considerably.

### GETTING TO KNOW THE SENAPATI: HIGHER DEFENCE ORGANISATION

Many observers of India's higher defence organisation have suggested that a country of India's size needs a Chief of Defence Staff (CDS) to coordinate the activities of the three service chiefs and their respective service headquarters. These observers usually suggest that successive governments have been reluctant to create this post because they fear that a single military commander-in-chief or *senapati* would increase the possibility of a military *coup*, or at the very least seriously subvert the principle of military subordination to civilian authority. Tanham too appears to see this issue largely in civil-military terms. In his own words, '[c]ivilians, bureaucrats, and politicians alike have consistently opposed creating the position of Chief of the Defence Staff and a joint staff, which most modern nations have and which India needs'. This view echoes a point made by Stephen P Cohen in his pioneering study of the Indian Army: 'The administrative and organizational changes introduced after independence indicate a fairly effective alliance between the civil service and the politicians, an alliance created for the purpose of reducing the role of the military in the decision-making process.'[5] I would like to suggest that the CDS issue actually has very little to do with civil-military relations *per se*. In my opinion, there are four separate points to be considered here.

The first point is that there is no unanimity, even within the Armed Forces, on the CDS issue. Going by the published views of senior military officers, several opinions would appear to prevail. Some officers, such as Lieutenant General SK Sinha, have strongly advocated a CDS system.[6] Others, such as General JN Chaudhuri, are considerably more ambivalent.[7] Finally, some senior officers, among whom Air Chief Marshal PC Lal's name would stand out, are totally opposed to the CDS system.[8]

Secondly, there is an inter-service dimension in the CDS debate. With a few significant exceptions, most Navy and Air Force officers are suspicious of the CDS system because of a deep-seated concern that this institutional change would lead to Army domination. To allay this concern, supporters of the CDS system suggest that the post could be rotated among the three services.[9] However, senior Army officers who have discussed the CDS system have not been coy in suggesting that only an Army general could fill boots CDS-sized.[10] What needs to be emphasised is that this institutional impulse will remain as long as the tripartite military institutional structure—Army, Navy and Air Force—persists. In the Indian context, the CDS system could work only if India were to adopt an integrated military institutional structure, *a la* Canada.

The third point we need to consider is the bureaucratic control of defence policy. As Air Marshal RD Sahni has pointed out, in India the formulation, sanction and execution of defence policy takes place at three levels: political, bureaucratic and service.[11] Although the Defence Minister is the political head of India's defence structure, it is the minister's civilian secretariat—the

Ministry of Defence (MOD)—which provides the interface between the political and the service levels, and 'processes' all formal communication between them. It is this sanctioning, processing and interfacing role of the civil service that has caused a high degree of dissatisfaction, resentment and irritation in the defence services. According to military officers, due to the daily interaction and symbiotic relationship between minister and bureaucrat, the latter is able to undermine or dilute the proposals of the service headquarters, invent inter-service complications where none exist, and otherwise influence policy in informal ways.

There is both a quantitative and a qualitative cause for the deep antipathy that many military officers have for the bureaucracy. The quantitative cause pertains directly to delays within MOD, which many military officers interpret as 'delaying tactics' but which in reality arise out of 'work overload'. Simply put, MOD is a 'bottleneck' in the defence policy process because it is far too small in size for the job assigned to it. This has been highlighted by Air Marshal Sahni:[12] a single joint secretary in MOD deals with the six principal staff officers, all air marshals, at Air Headquarters. The Defence Secretary interacts not only with his minister but with the three service chiefs, who though *senior* to him in protocol nevertheless have to consider his convenience and availability. This can obviously lead to bruised egos, and sometimes far worse. The answer is to triple or quadruple the number of higher civil servants in MOD. As Sahni remarks, 'it is unrealistic to expect just one person to head a secretariat which has to look after the needs of three services.'

There is, furthermore, a qualitative dimension to civil-military tension. In Sahni's words, 'It is not merely a question of size; the main issue is expertise. The main weakness in the present system is MOD's inability to make any positive contribution towards enhancing the effectiveness of the armed forces through its own knowledge of military matters.'[13]

In my opinion, if civil-military tension has spurred some senior military officers to advocate the CDS system, the root cause, the *causa causans*, is the hegemony that the elite Indian Administrative Service (IAS) exercises over the organs and activities of the Indian state. However, it is important to realise that the Armed Forces are by no means the only institutions of the Indian state that are at the receiving end of IAS domination. For instance, there is absolutely no reason why the Union Home Secretary, whose brief pertains essentially to internal law and order, should be an IAS officer rather than a member of the Indian Police Service (IPS). Only the Railway Board, the External Affairs Ministry, and lately the Finance Ministry, have managed to remain outside the jurisdictional hegemony of the IAS.

If this was simply a matter of India's elite government services playing power games with one another, the dominance of the IAS may not have been a significant issue. Unfortunately, embedded in the notion of IAS supremacy is the cult of the *generalists*. Most IAS officers are generalists *par excellence*. Administration and governance are seen by them as nothing more than the generalist supervising and controlling the activities of the specialist. Clemenceau may well have been right about war being too important a matter to be left to the generals. Civil-military relations in a democratic polity, as well as the 'total' character of modern warfare, undoubtedly require civilian involvement in national security and military matters. However, it is imperative to realise that national security, like almost everything else in the complex modern world, is the domain of the *specialist*. Civilians can, of course, be national and international security specialists; K Subrahmanyam, easily the most influential strategic thinker in India today, is a retired IAS officer.

The central question is therefore a simple one: Does civilian supremacy over the military in a democracy imply *civil service* supremacy? Or, to put it another way, in parliamentary democracy with a permanent civil service, can civilian control over military policy be operationalised in a manner to keep the generalists at bay? If this commentary is not an appropriate place to answer these questions, it is a good place to, at least, raise them. Perhaps the answer lies in creating a cadre of civil servants who spend their careers from the rank of Deputy Secretary onwards in MOD alone, thereby acquiring expertise in defence matters.

The fourth and final point is a straight-forward one. Although India does not have a CDS, it does have a perfectly adequate structure for inter-service coordination and planning since 1986, in the form of a Defence Planning Staff, headed by a three-star officer, which functions under the Chiefs of Staff Committee. For the advocates of the CDS system, this may not be the ideal situation. Nevertheless, it needs to be recognised that, since 1971, the three services actually function rather well in joint operations and exercises. The fact that a large number of military officers in India were cadets together at the National Defence Academy (NDA), well before they were commissioned in their respective services, makes for inter-service *camaraderie*. The impact of their first military experience at NDA probably lingers long after they have joined their regiment, ship or squadron. It is of such organic solidarity, rather than a new five-star post in the rarified realm of higher defence organisation, that effective inter-service coordination is truly made.

## FORGING OUR OWN SWORDS: SECURITY BEYOND SELF-RELIANCE

In his two essays, Tanham does not systematically analyse India's defence industry. In his second essay he makes a rather curious statement: 'India hopes to become self-sufficient by increasing exports to pay for imported military equipment.' Not being entirely certain what he means by this sentence, I will read my own meaning into it.

The lack of resources and a bureaucratic work culture apart, there are two other problems—both basic—faced by Indian defence industry. The first problem is *temporal* in nature, but it has a direct impact on the second problem, which is *structural* in nature. What do I mean by this rather opaque statement? For the last several years India has invested heavily in a number of projects, such as the Arjun main battle tank (MBT), the light combat aircraft (LCA) and the advanced light helicopter (ALH) projects, and the integrated missile development programme (IMDP). The level of success and rate of progress of these projects has been mixed, but one can safely say that most of these weapon systems will not be in regular service for at least another decade. In the meantime, India has no option but to buy costly and sophisticated foreign weapon systems in order to maintain a certain pace of military modernisation. This then is the temporal problem: India is *simultaneously* spending on overseas arms purchases to meet current security threats *and* on domestic arms production to meet future security threats. From this flows the structural problem: since domestic defence production capability has to be geared for *future* threats, the Indian defence industry not only has to keep in touch with current military technology but also has to anticipate future technological advances. But how does one leap-frog into the realm of frontier technologies of the future if one is barely able to keep abreast with the technological beakthroughs of today? This leads to an altogether harsher question: is Indian defence industry redundant?

There are, of course, excellent reasons for India to develop an indigenous military production capability. When India buys weapons from abroad, it is in effect financing someone else's research and development (R&D) programme. There are other liabilities: being forced to purchase obsolescent weapon systems, facing a perennial shortage of spare parts, living under the fear of being blackmailed by the weapon supplier in times of crisis, and the opportunity that arms imports provide for kickbacks and corruption in the political establishment. Supporters of defence production also argue that it is an important source for spreading technology in the economy. However, an excessive emphasis on establishing a military technology capability always runs the risk of creating high-tech islands amidst a low-tech ocean. The example of the former Soviet Union, with its supersonic high-performance combat aircraft and its primitive consumer durables on half-empty shop shelves, has a significance for India that should not be forgotten.

Defence production in India has been a state monopoly as a result of deliberate policy, exemplified by the Planning Memorandum of 1945 and the Industrial Policy Resolution of 1956. Apart from the 39 Ordnance Factories, eight public sector corporations—ranging from aviation to shipbuilding to electronics—are administered by the Department of Defence Production and Supplies in the Ministry of Defence. This state monopoly is further accentuated by the fact that the consumers of state-manufactured defence products are also state agencies, viz. the Armed Forces and other security forces. Some public sector defence undertakings, such as Bharat Earth Movers Limited (BEML), do sell their products in the civilian market, and some private companies do supply clothing and tents to the Forces, but these can hardly be regarded as military equipment or weapon systems. Although some public sector defence corporations, such as Hindustan Aeronautics Limited (HAL) and Mazagaon Docks Limited (MDL), have undertaken technical collaboration programmes with foreign companies, the defence industrial sector in India has, on the whole, remained closed to the private sector and foreign companies. Furthermore, military technology R&D is monopolised by the Defence Research and Development Organisation (DRDO).

The time has come to ask if the present state of affairs is desirable. Should India's defence industrial sector remain immune from the twin processes of liberalisation and globalisation that are now taking root in the economy? In policy terms, liberalisation of defence production would involve private sector participation in defence production, while globalisation would imply (i) seeking new markets for military products and (ii) building links, particularly in the form of collaborative programmes, with foreign firms.

Thus, if reducing the state monopoly in defence production by involving the private sector is one half of the equation, expansion of the market for defence products is the other half. In particular, the logic of globalisation would suggest that overseas markets need to be identified for Indian defence products and should be aggressively targeted. A successful arms export policy would reduce unit costs, help pay for military R&D and ensure that Indian defence products are up to international standards.

This is by no means an easy task. It is unclear what the next step should be. The experiences of other countries—China, Brazil, the United States, France, Israel—do not really provide India with beacons to mark the long road ahead.[14] As far as defence industry is concerned, for the temporal and structural reasons mentioned above, India's security dilemma is truly *sui generis*.

One thing is clear: this is a long-term problem. It takes 25 years to create a technologically competitive and commercially viable defence industry. Technological progress, in particular, is an evolutionary process with a few 'quantum leaps' along the way. Over the coming years, India will face some tough decisions. To give one example, there is the question of quality versus quantity—does one rely on advanced technology or on large numbers? Despite the experience of the Gulf war, the issue is far from settled in favour of advanced technology alone. Other wars have suggested other lessons: advanced technology did *not* win the Vietnam war. It is important to note that even in the US the high cost of advanced technology has forced it to prune the B-2 stealth bomber, the F-22 stealth fighter and the C-17A military transport programmes. Instead of a large number of F-22s, cheaper alternatives such as the CALF (Common Affordable Light Aircraft) programme are being vigorously pursued. For India's future needs—a large number of advanced weapon systems—the answer would appear to be an appropriate mix of quantity *with* quality. Thus, India's current emphasis on the MBT and the LCA is a first step in the right direction: it is these 'bread and butter' weapon systems—combat aircraft, tanks and submarines—that will continue to separate the strong from the weak.

## MAKING FRIENDS: ALLIES AND AXES IN AN UNCERTAIN WORLD

I would like to end this commentary with some strategic speculation of my own. Which countries will be India's friends—and India's enemies—in the years to come? Palmerstone's dictum about countries having permanent interests rather than permanent friends and enemies seems distinctly jaded today. As Paul Schroeder has shown in an elegant essay, alliances and associations between states in the international system have become ever more reliable and durable over the last four centuries.[15] Speculating about India's friends and enemies is therefore apposite.

In his essays Tanham talks about the importance of China and India's much-improved relations with the United States. Five future axes suggest themselves: (i) Washington-Jerusalem-New Delhi against international Islam: (ii) Teheran-New Delhi-Kuala Lumpur-Beijing, promoting 'Asian Values' against the West; (iii) New Delhi-Beijing-Tokyo, a future Asian 'Security Trinity'; (iv) Washington-New Delhi-Jakarta-Hanoi-Tokyo in a new game of containment, this time against China; and (v) Pretoria-New Delhi-Jakarta-Canberra in a new Indian Ocean Community of States. Unfortunately, the one axis that seems unlikely to emerge is Islamabad-New Delhi-Colombo-Kathmandu-Dhaka.

So much for allies and axes. What about the uncertain world? Three scholars have recently suggested powerful visions of the future, visions which suggest strongly etched but contrasting global fault lines. If Samuel Huntington is to be believed, future world politics will be a case of 'the West versus the Rest'.[16] In particular, Islam and Confucian civilisations will pose a threat to Western civilisation. Which side of this global fault line would India be on? India would seem to straddle the fault line: in civilisational terms it is emphatically not a part of the West, but as a state its major adversaries are Pakistan and China—in Huntingtonian terms, Islam and Confucianism.

A different vision is presented by Thomas Homer-Dixon.[17] In his version of the future, resource scarcity will make parts of the world extremely volatile and unstable. In contrast to Homer-Dixon, Francis Fukuyama presents a world in which liberal democracy has finally triumphed.[18] If we were to concatenate Homer-Dixon and Fukuyama, a terrifying new global fault line emerges: a post-historical world inhabited by Hegel's Last Man, and a pre-historical world inhabited by Hobbes's First Man, coexisting on the same planet at the same time. In this fractured world, India will unfortunately correspond to the Homer-Dixonian vision of the future.

### CONCLUDING WITH A BOW: CELEBRATING SPONSORED RESEARCH

There is, undoubtedly, a great deal else that could be said, both about Tanham's essays and about Indian strategic thought. The 1992 essay, in particular, deserves praise: it is a splendid piece which grows richer with every re-reading. This commentary, in its own way, salutes the author and his work. I would, however, like to conclude with a bow to the sponsor. We really must spare a thought for the US Department of Defence, which recognises scholars like Tanham as a valuable national resource and uses their intellectual abilities for *raison d'etat*. Is there any agency in India's security and foreign policy establishment which can claim to do likewise?

## NOTES

1 These errors were in George Tanham's original essay for the RAND Corporation, and have obviously been corrected in this book.

2 Kanti Bajpai and I have suggested a grand strategy for India in *Secure and Solvent: Thinking About an Affordable Defence for India*, RGICS Paper No. 11, Rajiv Gandhi Institute for Contemporary Studies, New Delhi, May 1994, pp. 40-5.

3 George K Tanham, *Indian Strategic Thought: An Interpretive Essay*, Santa Monica, California: RAND, 1992 and George K Tanham, 'Indian Strategy in Flux?', unpublished typescript, March 1995.

4 As KM Panikkar has described '[t]he 450 years which began with the arrival of Vasco da Gama in Calicut (in 1498), and ended with

the withdrawal of British forces from India in 1947 and European navies from China in 1949'. See KM Panikkar, *Asia and Western Dominance: A Survey of the Vasco Da Gama Epoch of Asian History 1498-1945*, Kuala Lumpur, The Other Press, 1993; first published 1953, p. 13.

5 Stephen P Cohen, *The Indian Army: Its Contribution to the Development of a Nation*, Berkeley, University of California Press, 1971, p. 171.

6 Lieutenant General SK Sinha, *Higher Defence Organisation*, New Delhi, United Service Institution of India, 1991, p. 40-6.

7 General JN Chaudhuri, *India's Problems of National Security in the Seventies*, New Delhi, United Service Institution of India, 1973, pp. 47-54.

8 Air Chief Marshal PC Lal, *Some Problems of Defence*, New Delhi, United Service Institution of India, 1977, pp. 38-45.

9 See Sinha, *Higher Defence Organisation*, op. cit., p. 45.

10 See Chaudhuri, *India's Problems of National Security*, op. cit., p. 51.

11 Air Marshal RD Sahni, 'New Defence Policy Structure Needed', *The Times of India* (New Delhi), 17 June 1987.

12 See RD Sahni, 'New Defence Policy Structure', op. cit.

13 See RD Sahni, 'New Defence Policy Structure', op. cit.

14 On this issue my views have shifted over the last year. In a paper I co-wrote with Kanti Bajpai in 1994, we had suggested that India could learn a lesson or two from the Brazilian experience in arms production and exports. See Bajpai and Sahni, *Secure and Solvent*, op. cit., pp. 16-21. I have now come to believe that India's fraught external security environment makes a comparison of Indian and Brazilian defence industries inappropriate: even at the height of its now-obsolete rivalry with Argentina, Brazil's external security environment was always far more secure than India's. Thus, Brazil has never faced the temporal problem—here and now versus tomorrow—that confronts India.

15 Paul W. Schroeder, 'The New World Order: A Historical Perspective', *ACDIS Occasional Paper*, University of Illinois at Urbana-Champaign, May 1994, pp. 4-5.

16 Samuel Huntington, 'The Clash of Civilizations', *Foreign Affairs*, vol. 72, no. 3, Summer 1993, pp. 22-49.

17 Thomas F Homer-Dixon, 'On the Threshold: Environmental Changes as Causes of Acute Conflict', *International Security*, vol. 16, no. 2, Fall 1991, pp. 76-116.

18 Francis Fukuyama, 'The End of History?', *The National Interest*, Summer 1989, pp. 3-18.

# OF ORAL TRADITIONS AND ETHNOCENTRIC JUDGEMENTS

WAHEGURU PAL SINGH SIDHU

The fact that India does not admit to broad generalisations and remains a complex and diverse society is an understatement. The myriad social, political, cultural and military strands that make up the fabric of India have defied simple explanation and are likely to keep scholars, trying to unravel the concept of Indianess, occupied for quite a while. Yet, it has not prevented some scholars from trying to draw general conclusions and provide some logical explanation, compatible with the accepted Western system of analysis, on the complexities and paradoxes of Indian strategic thinking. George Tanham's earnest essay (*Indian Strategic Thought: An Interpretive Essay*) belongs to this tradition, and consequently suffers the limitation of a painting with a broad canvas but not adequate number of strokes. It, however, provides a valuable starting point on the subject. In my appraisal of the essay, the endeavour is two-fold: First, to examine the general approach followed by the author in the essay; second, to evaluate some of the more specific conclusions made in the essay, especially those related to the role of the military and nuclear strategy.

Most Western scholars, coming from a well-honed tradition where the written word has more weight than the oral, tend to be uncomfortable with the concept of oral history, especially one that dates back several thousand years. The tendency is to look for documents and corroborate it with archaeological (or physical) evidence, and ignore or treat with great suspicion any oral input.[1] And when there does not appear to be any document or physical evidence, the inclination is to assume that history was not 'discovered' or that a strategy or doctrine 'does not exist'. In fact, one could argue that the Indians not only knew their history well, but lived it every day. The only difference is that the world discovered Indian history after the middle of the eighteenth century.

This is not to say that the study of oral history is not without its own problems. There is the obvious one about its credibility and reliability, and therefore the precedent of oral history would have to be examined before it is used. However, in the Indian context, oral history has a respectable lineage and substantial credibility, and for several centuries the traditions, norms, military strategies and law books were passed on by word of mouth. As noted Indian historian Romila Thapar observes: 'During the early Vedic Period, instruction remained entirely oral. There is a delightful description of frogs gathering and croaking during the rainy season, echoing each other's voices, a description which is compared with that of pupils repeating lessons after a teacher. However, the method of memorising was highly systematic. In the later Vedic period, the institution of the *brahmacharin* had become regularised—the student lived with a teacher for a number of years away from urban life'.[2] Similarly, there is evidence in the Indian epic *Mahabharata* of a military strategy to break into and out of an encirclement (*chakravyu*) being imparted orally. Hence, given a strong oral tradition, this particular method is still favoured to impart basic military tactics, at least at the level of the foot soldier. In fact, even today it is a common sight in cantonments to see infantry soldiers being imparted instructions while sitting under trees in the open air, not unlike the *brahmacharin* institution of the Vedic times. The oral tradition is still practised in several cultural spheres too. The most obvious one is Indian classical music. Although the basic *raag* (composition) structure has been written down, it is primarily imparted orally. There are no musical notation sheets and Indian classical musicians can play for hours purely from memory.

Another obvious strand of Indian strategic thought, which has remained constant since the time of Chandragupta Maurya, through even Gandhi's non-violence era and right till the present day (but has been mentioned only in passing in the essay under review), is the concept of realism.[3] Clearly, it was not described as 'realism' by Kautilya, the official strategist for the Mauryan empire, or for that matter by Gandhi or Nehru. Yet it was more than evident in their writings and in their actions. The mistake that most analysts make in interpreting the relevance of the *Arthasastra* is to study modern Indian policy in the specific context of the *mandala* concept, which propounded that neighbouring states should be treated as enemies or potential enemies and that states beyond the neighbouring states should be treated as friends, since these, according to the *mandala* theory, would be the enemies of neighbouring states.[4] This, however, does not conform to the modern reality of India and its neighbours and shows the dangers of interpreting the *Arthasastra* narrowly.

The relevance of the *Arthasastra* is to be found in its broader and strategic philosophy. For instance, according to Kautilya, there are six forms of foreign policy: Peace (agreement with pledges); War (offensive operations); Neutrality (indifference); Marching (making preparations); Alliance (seeking the protection of another); and Double Policy (making peace with one and waging war with another). All of these are relevant as a basis of foreign policy even today. While a king 'desirous of expanding his own power shall make use of the six fold policy', Kautilya prefers the Double Policy over even Alliance 'for whoever adopts the double policy enriches himself, being ever attentive to his own works, whereas an allied king has to help his ally at his own expense'.[5]

The same realism (which is often overlooked in the face of the forceful moral argument) could also be attributed to Gandhi's philosophy, which several authors have cited as an influence in the idealist policies of Nehru. For instance, Raju GC Thomas asserts that Gandhi's 'philosophy is implicit in Nehru's idealistic vision that security was better achieved through profession of peaceful coexistence and diplomacy rather than through arms build up—an approach to security that was manifest in the 1950s at least in India's policy towards China, if not Pakistan'.[6] This, however, does not explain why the policy of peaceful coexistence was applicable only to China. Here, Ashok Kapur should be credited for sifting out the realism in the Gandhian inspired policy. He has rightly evaluated peaceful coexistence as a 'transitional phase in Indian foreign relations, that is until India's economic and military strength was sufficient to defend India's interests'.[7]

That this is an accurate interpretation is evident from Gandhi's own writings and reveals that his decision to opt for the non-violent method was as much a realist choice as it was an idealist motivation. He notes: 'I contend that the revolutionary method cannot succeed in India. If an open warfare were a possibility, I may concede that we may tread the path of violence that the other countries have and at least evolve the qualities that bravery on the battlefield brings forth. But the attainment of Swaraj through warfare I hold an impossibility for any time that we can foresee.'[8] Underlying this idealism is the harsh reality of the futility of trying to carry out an armed insurrection against a well-equipped and organised British force. Besides, the use of force by the freedom fighters would automatically legitimise any retaliatory violence on the part of the British, whereas by using force against unarmed revolutionaries the British not only lost the high moral ground, but had no way to legitimise their use of force.

However, Gandhi was not averse to the use of force to ensure the nation's territorial integrity. Speaking in the specific context of Pakistan, Gandhi said: 'I do believe that, where there is only a choice between cowardice and violence, I would advise violence. I would rather have India resort to arms in order to defend her honour than that she should, in a cowardly manner, become or remain helpless witness to her own dishonour.'[9]

And this brand of realism was also evident in the actions and policies of Nehru. While it is true that he advocated Panchsheel and Non-Alignment, it was a diplomatic attempt to counter the dangers posed by China and the cold war, respectively. Hence, even Tanham admits: 'Nehru's primary foreign policy doctrine of non-alignment was intended to steer an independent course between the two superpowers. Rather than neutralism, it represented India's right to take positions in India's interest.'[10] With regard to China, Nehru realised that the Indian army, which was undergoing a process of reorganisation and Indianisation, was in no position to take on the Chinese, who had the advantage of sheer numbers on their side. Thus, '...though by the late 1950s he had come to realize that the PRC was a "hostile" state, still he did not change his mind about the military'.[11] Interestingly, however reluctant Nehru may have been to use force in other situations, it was under his orders that the Army was used in Goa and in Kashmir, because even Nehru did not envisage a peaceful solution to these problems.

In his section on the four principal factors that help to explain India's strategic actions, Tanham has been more than generous to the contribution made by the British Raj, especially to the elusive concept of the nation-state and Indian unity. In doing so, the essay ignores the fact that in India, the evolution of a nation-state and the creation of nationhood was interrupted by British colonisation. And hence, the nationalist movement, which under normal circumstances could have focused exclusively on nation building (as it did in other nascent states in Europe), had to contend with throwing off the burdensome yoke of colonisation. In the bargain, the process of nation-building was put off to after independence and continues. In fact, the legacy of the Raj (especially the British policy of 'divide and rule') created several other complications in the cumbersome process of nation-building, the repercussions of which are being felt even today. However, it is a measure of the resilience of the Indian nation-state that the often violent movements against the state have been managed and controlled, unlike the United States which had to undergo a bloody and traumatic civil war.

Interestingly, while the essay argues that the strategic policies of independent India are a legacy of the British Raj, it also admits that some of the military policies of the British in India were a continuation of the policies of the Mughals, thus identifying the cohesion in India's strategic concepts and interests, which have remained remarkably consistent despite a variety of rulers and empires. For instance: 'The British, as the Mughals had before them, gained the tribesmen's support with subsidies.' And later: 'The British empire at the end of the nineteenth century and the first half of the twentieth century had become a status quo power. Its main purpose was to protect what it had. Consequently, British strategy was defensive in general, and particularly so for India. By World War I, the British had recognized Chinese suzerainty over Tibet but still advocated its independence.'

Similarly, in his section on Geography, the essay argues the 'Indians have long regarded the mountains and seas as a protective barrier against outside interference and invasion', which, while essentially correct, needs to be examined more realistically and substantially. The Indian attitude towards the natural 'protective barrier' has evolved to a more 'forward posture' over the centuries and reveals remarkable realism. In ancient times, when the ability of the invader was limited, in terms of logistics, it made sense to use the natural barrier as a buffer, rather than challenge the intruder at the passes. There are two explanations for this policy. First, by the time the invader managed to cross the natural barrier and came down to the plains, his supply lines and troops were bound to be on the verge of exhaustion. And any army based on the plains could take advantage of this situation. An interesting example is that of Alexander, who, while he defeated Porus on the banks of the Indus, hesitated from going further east and subsequently retreated from Punjab. Second, till the time of the Delhi Sultanate, the invasions were few and far between and it made no military sense to maintain forces on these passes for an intermittent eventuality. However, when the frequency of raids increased (from about AD 1000 till about 1300), especially during the Sultanate period, the Sultans recruited the help of the local tribesman to act as the first layer of defence. Subsequently, the Mughals and British, who feared the Russians, extended their first line of defence to Afghanistan and Iran.[12]

In the section titled 'The Absence of Strategic Thinking', Tanham's essay argues that there are very few military or government leaders directly involved with strategic planning and laments the absence of 'serious strategic planning institutions', all of which clearly are to be readily found in the Western system of policy planning. But if one examines the Western system of strategic planning, it is evident that while there is a surfeit of think-tanks, very seldom is there a direct correlation between their policies and official policies. Whereas in the Indian case, because all the strategic planning is done in official circles, it is more akin to the policy of the government. Again, while the assertion that Indian policy planning remains informal and personality-oriented is fundamentally correct, there is evidence of long-term planning in crucial sectors, including defence. For example, the plan that most naval planners will quote today dates back to the 1950s. Similarly, the path that India's atomic programme would follow was clearly delineated by Homi Bhabha way back in the late 1940s and early 1950s and this plan of development has been more or less adhered to till now. Again, while there is no doubt that Bhabha was the central individual in the formulation of this plan, it was also dictated by technical and monetary considerations (for instance, one reason that Indian scientists cite for following the plutonium reprocessing path is that it is cheaper than the uranium enrichment path). In a similar vein, the long-term policy of non-alignment dictated India's foreign policy behaviour virtually till the end of the cold war. It is important to realise that this policy was vocally supported not only by the several Congress governments, but also by the opposition in Parliament.[13]

Tanham's essay argues that modern military technology is beginning to shape India's strategic policy. While this is substantially true in the case of imported hardware, it certainly does not hold true for the indigenous weapon systems.[14] Most of the weapon systems being developed by DRDO are against very specific Staff Requirements. And in most cases, they are being built around very specific strategic requirements. For example, the LCA is regarded as a successor to the MiG-21 and is merely an updated version of that multi-role aircraft. All it intends to do is incorporate contemporary technology (such as fly-by-wire), which has become standard for fighter aircraft the world over.

In the case of missiles, the essay is factually incorrect when it asserts that the IGMDP 'has developed a family of missiles that could cover the entire region and, of course, carry nuclear warheads'. In fact, the 'family' of five missiles ranges from Nag (an anti-tank missile with a maximum range of four kilometres—hardly adequate to cover 'the entire region' and it would be a miraculous technological breakthrough if it could be fitted with a nuclear warhead!)—to Agni (the IRBM). And of the five missiles—the others being Trishul (a quick reaction SAM); Akash (essentially an anti-aircraft missile); and Prithvi (a SSM with a maximum range of 250 km)—only the Prithvi and Agni can be considered to be capable of covering the 'region'. And while both Prithvi and Agni are considered to be nuclear capable, Indian officials assert that Prithvi is designed only for conventional warheads. Moreover, the contention that the missile programme has popular support is also debatable. While it does have some popular support now, that was certainly not the case when the programme began in 1983.[15]

While examining the complexities and paradoxes of Indian strategic thinking, Tanham's essay argues that 'Indians see poverty as a condition of life and maintain that it has nothing to do with military might'. In fact, during the 1980s, an argument was propounded by several economists and strategists to the effect that there is a direct correlation between military spending and economic growth. For instance, Jasjit Singh of the IDSA argues that it was the adequate level of spending on defence since 1971and right through the 1980s that contributed to the long period of peace (the longest since independence) and, hence, to the development of the economy.[16]

In his section on the Role of the Military, Tanham has erroneously stated that Nehru had a strong anti-military attitude because 'the army did not take part in the nationalist movement'. This is certainly not borne out by the facts. Indeed, the Indian National Army (INA) led by Subhash Bose consisted of officers and men of the Indian Army who had been left behind after the British withdrew from Malaya and Burma and others who had been taken prisoner—there were 60,000 of them in Malaya alone.[17] And when this army was defeated by the British, several of its officers, who were still in the British Indian Army, were tried for treason. In fact, in a celebrated public trial of three INA Officers in Delhi's Red Fort, Nehru himself appeared for the defence of these three (putting on his barrister's gown after 25 years).[18] So, Nehru could hardly claim ignorance of the involvement of the Indian Army in the nationalist movement.

In addition to the INA trials, there was also the Royal Indian Navy (RIN) revolt, where ratings in Bombay went on hunger-strike in February 1946 and this action was supported by the Communist Party of India which called for a general strike. While Sardar Patel opposed the strike, arguing that 'discipline in the Army cannot be tampered with', Nehru's first reaction too was to be 'impressed' by the necessity for curbing the wild outburst of violence'. However, later he hailed the strike for breaking down the 'iron wall' between the army and the people.[19]

In his Note on Nuclear Strategy, Tanham claims that the Department of Atomic Energy categorically maintains that it works only for peaceful purposes. This, however, is not the position that the Department has held. While it has never highlighted or boasted about its weapon manufacturing capability, it has never denied this ability either. In fact, several nuclear scientists, from Bhabha to Raja Rammana, have insisted that they do have the capability to make weapons, if asked to do so. Similarly, the missile programme, especially the Agni and Prithvi programme, has never been described as having a 'peaceful purpose'. In fact, one of the reasons to launch the IGMDP was to separate the military missiles from the peaceful, civilian rocket programme of ISRO. Besides, the description of the Agni as a 'technology demonstrator' does not mean that it is being manufactured for peaceful purposes (several early American military missiles were also labelled as 'technology demonstrations'). Indeed, in the case of Agni, senior scientists have categorically stated its nuclear capability.[20]

Although Tanham is correct in his assessment that the nuclear debate is not as public here as it is in the West, especially in the United States, there is adequate unclassified material to provide more than a glimpse of the various strands of nuclear strategic thinking within India. Briefly, there are several contending schools of thought ranging from doves who want to give up the option, at one extreme, to the overt weaponisers who also speak in terms of a war fighting capability, at the other extreme. The armed forces, for instance, have consistently asked for nuclear weapons at the level of the Joint Chiefs of Staff since 1964. The Indian Army has persisted in its demand for tactical nuclear weapons since the mid-1960s.[21] In fact, some analysts have argued that were the Army to be more involved in shaping strategy, the nuclear stance would harden.[22] There is also evidence that some Army officers have thought through the various possible methods of 'using' nuclear weapons, albeit using the models of deterrence developed in the Western context.[23] Similar studies have also been carried out by the Indian Navy. The only service which has shied away from this type of an academic study is the Air Force. One possible explanation is that in the event of the country going nuclear, the Air Force is the most obvious choice as the service which is likely to deliver the weapons. Hence, they do not feel the need to make a case, whereas the Army, which is an unlikely contender, feels that it has to be vocal to stake its claim.

The fact that the country has still not tilted to either side but retains the 'option policy' clearly shows where the consensus lies. This is possible because the 'option policy' offers more alternatives to Indian strategists than the straitjacket acceptance or rejection of the option. It provides diplomatically the ability to withdraw if global nuclear disarmament is commensurate with India's own security interests. On the other hand, it provides the ability to weaponise if deterrence is necessary for its security. Interestingly, some strategists, especially Jasjit Singh of the IDSA, have propounded the concept of 'recessed deterrence' which, while adhering to the overall policy of keeping the weapon option open, enables both sides to behave like nuclear weapon states, albeit without nuclear weapons. That this concept is now gaining acceptability is apparent in the series of articles that have appeared in the Western literature, examining the stability of non-weaponised deterrence.[24]

In the sphere of nuclear strategy, the primary contention of the earlier essay is that Indians may not address the problem of nuclear strategy seriously unless a real crisis arises and that there is an inherent tendency not to plan ahead. This is reiterated in 'Indian Strategy in Flux?', which avers that India seems to need a great internal shock or powerful pressure from outside to change policies. However, this is not borne out by developments in the sphere of long range missiles and nuclear weapons capability. In both these areas there is ample evidence that the organisations concerned did plan well in advance and, in fact, anticipated the possible hurdles along the way.

For instance, after the 1974 test, both the United States and Canada imposed severe restrictions on India, and Canada broke off all nuclear cooperation. The Canadians were particularly upset that the plutonium for the 1974 test had come from CIRUS, the 40 MW reactor supplied by them which used heavy water supplied by the United States. India justified this use by saying that the explosion was for peaceful purposes, but the Canadians were far from convinced. This, according to one nuclear scientist, caused a setback to the Indian nuclear programme. The atomic establishment was, according to Rammana, 'still basking in the problems created by this [the test]—total embargo, RAPP reactors were stopped and we were treated as rogues.... So, this anti-business was going on, and we had to lie low'.[25]

However, even while lying low, a couple of important decisions were taken to ensure the future availability of unsafeguarded fissile material. The first was the decision to build a reactor that would provide unsafeguarded fissile material and would reduce the dependency on CIRUS. Consequently, construction started on 30 October 1975 on Dhruva, a 100 MW indigenous high flux nuclear reactor.[26] On 8 August 1985, Dhruva, the 100 MW research reactor, achieved criticality. This reactor, like CIRUS, is located on the BARC premises. Significantly, the fuel for the reactor is fabricated at BARC itself and not the Nuclear Fuel Complex at Hyderabad. The official role for Dhruva was described as 'production of isotopes and development of power reactor technology'.[27] However, nuclear experts noted that Dhruva's true capability lay in the fact that it could produce unsafeguarded weapon-grade plutonium. It was 'basically a scaled-up version of CIRUS. This reactor can annually produce about 20 to 25 kgs of weapon-grade plutonium, which is separated in the enlarged Trombay facility'.[28]

Although, theoretically, India could use the plutonium generated in most of its six power reactors, there are technical reasons (apart from the safeguard agreements) which lend credence to the fact that India's weapon grade plutonium is derived from Dhruva. Basically, plutonium derived from power reactors contains the Pu-240 isotope in addition to Pu-239 (which is the ideal isotope for explosives). This means that larger quantities of plutonium would have to be used and even then the yield would be uncertain. Moreover, to get weapon grade-plutonium, the power reactors would have to be run uneconomically at a low burn rate, which is contrary to the basic principles of a dominantly civilian nuclear programme. Thus, for a weapon programme a dedicated production/research reactor is perfect. This makes Dhruva ideal for military purposes.[29]

Similarly, the missile programme was also the result of a long term perspective plan, rather than a reaction to a real crisis. This is obvious from the fact that the IGMDP (which includes the nuclear capable Prithvi and Agni missiles) was launched in 1983, at a time when there was an attempt at rapprochement on the part of India and Pakistan and India and China. With the former, it was the negotiations for the no-war pact, while with the latter it was the decision to talk about the disputed border. Hence, if one were to accept Tanham's theory to the effect that nuclear capable missiles were an *ad hoc* response to a real crisis, then the programme should have actually started around the late 1980s when the first reports of Chinese deployment of tactical nuclear missiles in Tibet surfaced and information about the Chinese supply of nuclear capable missiles to Pakistan was leaked. And yet, it is a well known fact that the IGMDP was taken up in 1983 and was provided adequate support, both in terms of technical and financial inputs, at least five to seven years before a real crisis arose.

The IGMDP planners also anticipated the obstructions that might be placed once the Agni was launched and took steps right from the inception of the Programme to ensure that the missiles, which were seen as imperative for the development of the nation's nuclear strategy, remained unaffected by any subsequent embargo. That this was one of the crucial components of the IGMDP is admitted by Dr APJ Abdul Kalam, who headed the IGMDP in 1983. It is worth quoting him at length here. He observed:

> In 1983, when the IGMDP was launched, one decision was taken. Once Agni is launched, there will be many countries which will stop some critical components. We identified certain critical areas—and what we did was to make a consortium, of industries, of laboratories and academic institutions, and we worked two to two and half years, and today many of the components are under production. One was the C-band phase shifters. Like that, there are many elements—carbon-carbon perform—[which] only two or three countries make and they will not give it to us. Four institutions joined together and in 18 months we got the product. Like that, critical areas were identified and funded, and today nobody can do anything. We are self sufficient. We anticipated the areas where they were going to throttle us and prepared to acquire the technology. In 1986, MTCR was formed. They cannot do anything to us.[30]

The five critical technologies identified were: phase shifters for radars; impact diodes that act as high frequency power sources; carbon composites to withstand the heat of re-entry; key sensors for guidance systems; and computerised fluid dynamic models.[31] Thus, at least in the case of the missile programme, it is obvious that it was not an *ad hoc* reaction to powerful pressure from outside, but in anticipation of it.

Of course, one could argue that both the nuclear weapon capability and the missile programme were dictated by the fear of external embargos and to that extent were a response to powerful pressure from outside. But it is important to recognise that unlike the case of conventional weaponry, where the country's arms acquisition policy did flounder following the dramatic and sudden collapse of the Soviet Union, there was no significant disruption in missile capability following the imposition of the MTCR. This can only be the result of some amount of forward, long term planning.

One could also argue that the nuclear and missile policy was technology driven and to that extent has a direct bearing on the formulation of strategy. And some weapons encourage offensive thinking. But technology also has its limitations, which could adversely affect strategy and operations. This is particularly true in the case of the Prithvi missile which uses a highly toxic liquid fuel, and that has created a number of operational problems for the potential users—the Army—who worry about handling such toxic material so close to the front line.

However, it is also important to appreciate the policy that led to the technology being unleashed in the first place. And, hence, it is crucial to understand the process of policy formulation. For instance, why was the decision to launch the IGMDP taken in 1983? Why were two nuclear capable missiles approved? Why not one or three? And what of the technical capabilities of the missiles? Why, for example, is it important for both Prithvi and Agni to have a throw-weight of one ton? Here, the technical capabilities provide the answers. The capabilities of the Prithvi make it a Pakistan-specific weapon. Its range and altitude make it unsuitable in the northern sector (against China). Even if it was deployed at the furthest point on the Indo-Chinese border, and even at its extended range of 250 km, it could not cover any worthwhile military targets. Whereas, in the Western sector (against Pakistan), the missile not only covers the tactical battlefield, but, at its extended range, also covers strategic targets.

Similarly, while the official assertion holds that the Agni is a 'technology demonstrator' yet, upon scrutiny, it is possible to discern the hint of a future role. For instance, it is deliberately pointed out that Agni can 'carry payloads of 1000 kg and less as far as 2500 km and heavier payloads up to 1500 km'.[32] These assertions reveal a tacit debate regarding its mission. For instance, why was the weight of 1000 kg selected? Why not 2000 kg? Also, why 2500 km range? Considering that the maximum range of the Prithvi is 250 km, why was the Agni designed to cover ten times that distance? Why not five times or fifteen times? Was there any specific mission that the creators had in mind? In attempting to answer some of these questions, we learn that the technological capabilities of the Agni missile make its possible mission requirement obvious. Given its range and throw-weight, the missile is a logical vehicle for delivering nuclear weapons against China. And that may explain why the targeted range of the missile is slated to be between 1500 to 2500 km. At its maximum range, Agni would be able to target Beijing while at 1500 km it could hit cities in southern China. This may explain why in March 1992 the then Foreign Secretary, JN Dixit, could calmly state that China has tactical nuclear weapons in Tibet.

As to the articulation of nuclear strategy, the general trend among nuclear weapon states has been that strategies have come in the wake of weaponisation and not the other way around. This probably holds true in the case of India also. However, there has been some serious thinking on the issue since the 1980s, particularly in the wake of the Pakistani nuclear programme and the revelations of China's tactical nuclear weapons in Tibet. This led to the first wave of a semi-public debate on the issue of how to fight without nuclear weapons.[33]

However, in the wake of the possible nuclearisation of the Indian forces, especially the advent of the missile programme, which gives India the delivery capability, there has been a spurt in this debate.[34] And more recently, officials of the MEA have gone as far as to propose a no-first-strike clause to Pakistan, which clearly reveals the Indian option of a second strike capability, at least against Pakistan. However, a similar proposal has not been forwarded to China, against which India tacitly holds a first strike capability.

The indications are that as the country moves closer to conventional nuclearisation, the nuclear debate will also emerge from the dusty files of the bureaucracy out into the open. It has already become an election issue, with the BJP making it a part of its manifesto. Thus, it would be correct to say that Indian nuclear doctrine is finally coming of age.

In conclusion, it is obvious that while Tanham's essay is an earnest and diligent exercise in attempting to unravel the strategic thought process of India, it is far from perfect in its contentions and, occasionally, even in its facts. Yet, the singular service of the treatise is to offer a platform to continue the debate and attempt to understand the evolution of India's dynamic, if somewhat enigmatic, strategic thought.

## NOTES

1 In more recent times, however, some scholars have turned to the oral tradition to recreate contemporary history. But here the oral history has been used to supplement documents and physical evidence. One such exercise was conducted to re-enact the Cuban Missile Crisis. See, for instance, *Cuba on the Brink* by James Blight, Bruce Alcyn and David Welch, New York 1993. Another was the reconstruction of the Brasstacks crisis between India and Pakistan.

See *Brasstacks and Beyond: Perception and Management of Crisis in South Asia* by Kanti Bajpai, PR Chari, PI Cheema, SP Cohen and Sumit Ganguly. Indeed, Tanham's own essay could well fall into this category, but for the author's confession that it was perhaps not as rigorous and was dependent on 'informal conversations'.

2 Romila Thapar, *A History of India, Volume 1,* Penguin, Harmondsworth, 1979 edition, p. 42.

3 In the section titled 'The Complexities and Paradoxes of Indian Strategic Thinking', Tanham notes 'Indians can be expedient and pragmatic in their foreign policies and strategies, but they like to emphasize the moral and spiritual aspect of India', p. 68 in the original essay.

4 See Raju GC Thomas, *Indian Security Policy*, Princeton University Press, NJ, 1986 and George Modelski 'Kautilya: Foreign Policy and International System in the Third World', *American Political Science Review* 58, No. 3, September 1964.

5 Kautilya, *Arthasastra*, Book VII, translated by R Shamasastry, 2nd edn, Mysore, 1923.

6 Raju GC Thomas, *Indian Security Policy*, Princeton, NJ, 1986.

7 Ashok Kapur, *India's Nuclear Options: Atomic Diplomacy and Decision Making*, New York, 1976.

8 NK Bose (ed.). *Selections from Gandhi*, Ahmedabad, 1948, pp. 122-3.

9 Ibid., p. 155.

10 George Tanham, *Indian Strategic Thought*, p. 57 in the original essay.

11 Ibid. Although it must be noted that, by the late 1950s, Nehru had hoped to revamp the Indian Army and create an armaments infrastructure, a process which was taken up in earnest with the appointment of Krishna Menon in 1957. While the modernisation did not prepare the Army for the 1962 Chinese war, it was well equipped to take on the Pakistanis in 1965, a mere three years later.

12 Interestingly, the 1992-3 Annual Report of the Ministry of Defence also cites the possible threat from Iran. 'The modernization and expansion of the Iranian Armed Forces presents the possibility of Iranian assistance to Pakistan in a future conflict situation' (p. 3). While this may partly be a reaction to the "defence in depth" concept propounded by the former Pakistani army chief, MA Beg, it could also be regarded as a logical evolution to the 'forward posture' concept on the part of the Indians.

13 By the late 1980s, Indian officials were already starting to pave the way for a quiet burial of the non-aligned policy. The first clear indication of this reversal, however, came in 1990-1 when the

United States was allowed refuelling rights in India in the build up to the Gulf war.

14 For instance, the IL-76, which was essentially a replacement for the An-12, provided the Indian Air Force with a strategic airlift capability.

15 See, for instance, Steven Flank, *Reconstructing Rockets: The Politics of Developing Military Technology in Brazil, India and Israel,* PhD thesis submitted at the Massachusetts Institute of Technology, June 1993.

16 The elaborate economic argument for this phenomenon can be found in BB Bhattacharya, *Defence and Development Strategy in India*, unpublished paper, 1991.

17 Bipin Chandra, Amles Tripathi and Barun De (eds), *Freedom Struggle,* New Delhi, 1972, p. 224

18 Sumit Sarkar, *Modern India* 1885-1947, Delhi, 1983, p. 418.

19 Ibid. pp. 423-5.

20 In an interview in *India Today*, 15 June 1989, soon after the first Agni launch, Dr AJP Abdul Kalam, then the head of the IGMDP, in reply to a question on its nuclear capability stated: 'It can also carry nuclear warheads. In India we are not making nuclear warheads. We provide the carrier and the policy makers decide how to use it'.

21 Major General Som Dutt, *India and the Bomb*, Adelphi Paper 30, London: IISS, 1966.

22 Shekhar Gupta, *India Redefines its Role*, Adelphi Paper 293, London: IISS, 1995.

23 See, for instance, Brigadier VK Nair (Retired), *Nuclear India*, New Delhi, Lancers, 1992, which estimates that India needs a total of 132 nuclear bombs to provide an effective deterrence against both China and Pakistan. A total of 60 bombs would give India a second strike capability against Pakistan. Another interesting version of this school of study is General K Sundarji (Retired), *The Blind Men of Hindoostan*, New Delhi, UBSPD, 1993, which attempts to work out an indigenous Indian nuclear doctrine through the medium of war games.

24 See Susan Burns, *Non-weaponized Deterrence: Symbolic or Verifiable?* ACDIS, University of Illinois, unpublished paper, August 1994.

25 Interview with Dr Raja Rammana at Bangalore on 17 March 1995.

26 'CIRUS had been working for a long time. But we took an immediate decision. We knew that the CIRUS plutonium had been used for Pokhran and we took a decision to build Dhruva. It is the best reactor and it is designed entirely by the locals.' Interview with Rammana, at Bangalore, on 17 March 1995.

27 Department of Atomic Energy publication 'Atomic Energy in

India', Section 10, Research and Development.

28 David Albright and Mark Hibbs, 'India's Silent Bomb', *The Bulletin of Atomic Scientists*, September 1992, p. 28.

29 See PR Chari, *Indo-Pak Nuclear Standoff: The Role of the United States*, Manohar, 1995, p. 39.

30 Interview with Dr APJ Abdul Kalam, at Hyderabad, October 1990.

31 Raj Chengappa, 'The Missile Man', *India Today*, 15 April 1994, p. 44.

32 See Kalam interview, 'We Can Design Any Missile', *India Today*, 15 June 1989, p. 31.

33 The best example of this debate is in Lt Gen. K Sundarji (ed), 'Effects of Nuclear Asymmetry on Conventional Deterrence', *Combat Paper*, No.1, May 1981.

34 Again, for an unclassified version of military thinking on nuclear weapons see Lt Gen. K Sundarji (ed), 'Nuclear Weapons in a Third World Context', *Combat Paper*, No. 2, August 1981.

# THE LIMITS TO NAVAL EXPANSION

RAHUL ROY-CHAUDHURY

It is heartening that George Tanham devotes special attention to naval and maritime affairs in his monograph on the wide-ranging subject of Indian strategic thought. These aspects of Indian security are examined in relation to factors such as geography, history and the British Raj, as well as the Indian Ocean region. While separate sections of the monograph deal with the roles and objectives of the Indian Navy, the aims of Indian naval strategy are also discussed. In addition, two of the three maps provided tend to emphasise India's geographical position in the Indian Ocean and the adjacent seas.

This attention to naval and maritime affairs is due probably to two main reasons. First, the appreciation of the Indian Ocean as a vital frontier of the country (along with the north-west and the north-east land boundaries), which presents both opportunities and threats. As a consequence, the entire Indian Ocean region is perceived to form the fourth circle or ring in India's *ad hoc* and pragmatic defence strategy.

The second reason is the much-publicised, and often exaggerated, expansion of Indian naval forces at the time the monograph was written. This was essentially symbolised by the Navy's acquisition of its second aircraft-carrier from Britain and the three-year lease of a nuclear-powered submarine from the erstwhile Soviet Union, both vessels being commissioned during the tenure of Rajiv Gandhi as Prime Minister.

While this focus on the maritime aspects of Indian security is wholly justified, it could have been stressed even further. This would have primarily involved an analysis of the crucial relationship between India and the seas surrounding it on three sides. While some of its constituent elements have been discussed in the monograph, it does not tackle the fundamental basis of this relationship—the growing dependence of India on the Indian Ocean. The continuing increase in the population of the country and the consequential dwindling of resources on land make this fact even more critical in the future.

The nature and extent of India's dependence on the sea includes the following dimensions:

- Sea-borne trade accounts for virtually all of India's external trade; this constitutes a staggering 97 per cent of the country's total external trade. The value of total sea-borne trade for 1992-3 is estimated at over Rs 100,000 crore. This is confidently expected to grow much more by the turn of the century, in view of the expansion of the economy and increased trade links.
- Sea-borne trade involves the import of nearly 20 million tonnes of petroleum annually, primarily from the oil-rich states of the Persian Gulf. This satisfies some 36 per cent of the total demand for petroleum in the country.
- Petroleum extracted from offshore areas in the Arabian Sea and the Bay of Bengal meets 41 per cent of the total demand in the country. This constitutes 64 per cent of the total production.
- Offshore supplies of natural gas presently constitute 77 per cent of the total domestic production.
- The proposed construction of submarine pipelines in the Arabian Sea will facilitate the transportation of much-needed natural gas from countries of the Persian Gulf, primarily Oman and Iran.
- The formalisation of the 1982 UN Convention of the Law of the sea as part of international law in November 1994 enhances the importance of the Exclusive Economic Zone (EEZ) as a critical source of economic wealth.
- In November 1995 India is expected to be granted control over an additional area of 150,000 sq km in the central Indian Ocean for the exploitation of the sea-bed.
- The mining of polymetallic nodules from the Indian continental margin as well as the site in the central Indian Ocean is expected to satisfy, to a large extent, the demand for mineral resources in the near future.

Meanwhile, the pace of Indian naval expansion has clearly

decreased since the late 1980s. The Indian Navy has not acquired a single principal surface combatant, the mainstay of any naval force, since the commissioning of a destroyer in early 1988. The first such warship to be commissioned into the fleet in the future is expected to be the Delhi-class destroyer in 1996. This situation has largely been the result of the severe national economic crisis in mid-1991 and the disintegration of the Soviet Union later that year. While the former limited additional funding for major naval projects, the latter forced the Navy to contend with disruptions in the supply of crucial spare parts and services for a majority of its warships. For the next few years, therefore, the Navy will continue to be forced to simply consolidate its forces and strive to maintain the country's ship-building capacity. None the less, the Indian Navy will continue to constitute a medium-sized blue water fleet as well as remain the largest indigenous naval force in the Indian Ocean for some time to come.

The central thesis of the monograph, even in relation to maritime and naval affairs, is sound. That there is a relative lack of strategic thinking in naval development cannot be disputed. Although the expansion plans of Naval Headquarters over the years have emphasised the shape and size of the fleet India is desirous of possessing in the future, they have not been prepared in tandem with the other two armed services nor based on a realistic assessment of the availability of financial resources. Moreover, these naval plans have not been prepared on the basis of a comprehensive policy directive provided by the political leadership of the country, which would have set out the major priorities to be kept in mind. This is not surprising in view of the complete absence of a security doctrine for the country. In essence, defence policy, and consequently naval policy, cannot be made in any sort of vacuum but needs to flow from a national security doctrine. This would have to take various geographical, historical, political, economic and technological perspectives into account. Unfortunately, such a national security doctrine does not exist in the country today. As a result, as the monograph makes only too clear, 'no authoritative government statement exists on Indian naval strategy'.

In this respect, it is important to note that Tanham gallantly ascribes two aims of Indian naval strategy which appear to represent an ideal, rather than the realistic, state of affairs. The monograph states that India's defence strategy in relation to the Indian Ocean, though informal and *ad hoc*, aims to 'develop naval capabilities that (1) could deny any extra-regional power from achieving a meaningful naval presence in the Indian Ocean and (2) would give India superiority over any combination of local navies, thereby seeking legitimacy for Indian predominance in the Indian Ocean'. These aims of naval policy suggest a 'sea denial' strategy (against superpower or extra-regional naval forces) along with a 'sea control' strategy (against naval forces from within the region).

Although the Indian Navy would gladly emphasise both these missions simultaneously, its role in ensuring the security of the country over the years, and the lack of sufficient funding, have forced it to stress a 'sea control' strategy at the cost of an effective 'sea denial' one. The nature of the Navy's force of aircraft carriers, destroyers and frigates, and the construction of additional principal combatants, should all be seen in terms of an attempt to primarily acquire a regional 'sea control', rather than a super or great power 'sea denial', capacity. The Navy aims to assert control over the use of the sea during a war against regional adversaries not super or great power naval forces. If the 'sea denial' of naval forces was the primary objective of Indian naval strategy, an alternative force structure comprising missile-launching submarines and mainland and island-based strike and Airborne Early Warning (AEW) aircraft could have evolved. Although 'sea control' is directed only against regional navies, it is expected that the development of such a capability could provide an element of 'sea denial' against super or great power naval forces. This could be achieved by increasing the perceived costs of such an intervention (thereby complicating hostile naval missions against Indian maritime assets) and possibly even deterring a coercive application of force in the first place.

Furthermore, even though the Indian Navy's stress on the defence of 'growing maritime interests' since the 1980s undoubtedly took account of foreign naval forces in the Indian Ocean, it primarily indicated a perceptible reduction in the perception of threats from super or great power (read primarily the United States) naval forces. Despite a massive increase in American military capacity in the Indian Ocean in the 1980s, and consequently a perceived increase in the vulnerability of India's maritime assets, the Indian Navy stressed the nature and extent of its interests in an extended maritime zone. In effect, the Indian Navy was emphasising that the expansion of its forces was not necessarily dependent upon the presence of superpower or other naval forces in the Indian Ocean. A 'sea control' strategy also has the inherent advantage of being able to execute a wider array of naval missions (including power projection), as befits a medium-sized naval power such as India.

In the monograph, Tanham also suggests that the development of a blue water navy ought primarily to be seen in terms of India's attempt at recognition as a great world nation. While it may be correct to assume that a blue water navy could provide a country a status such as this, it should be appreciated that India has considerable interests in the Indian Ocean—political, economic and military. Therefore, the development of a blue water navy is primarily in order to maintain the defence and security of these 'growing maritime interests' rather than simply an attempt at achieving the status of a global power.

In essence, the flexibility and mobility of naval forces, and the unique nature of the medium upon which they traverse, necessitate a perspective on maritime affairs broader than simply one of threat-perception from neighbouring countries alone. The varied dimensions of India's maritime security include the growing dependence of the country on the sea and the increasing importance of marine resources to its prosperity (discussed above), the defence of vast and extended maritime assets (including island territories) and the long lead-time required for naval development. The possibility of threats arising from beyond the Indian Ocean, and the Navy's role in the support of foreign policy objectives (including peace-keeping operations and confidence-building measures) are also apparent. Since these considerations differ in a marked manner from the development of both the Army and the Air Force, they are often ignored.

Finally, there are four inaccuracies, in Tanham's study relating to the pre-1971 period of naval development, which I note because there are so many misperceptions and misapprehensions about the Indian Navy.

First, the formation of a predominantly Indian-staffed Indian Navy was not encouraged in order to ensure the maintenance of sea communications with Britain, upon which colonial rule rested. Therefore, although an 'Indian Navy' has existed under various nomenclature since 1612, its ratings and officers have been predominantly non-Indian until Independence in 1947. In this respect, the possibility of the small Indian naval force serving with the Royal Navy during the Second World War ranking as an independent navy does not arise. In a similar manner, the creation of a very small 'Indian navy' in 1924 is of no consequence.

Second, the Indian Navy did not have to start almost from scratch in the 1960s. As a result of the First and Second Plan papers soon after Independence, and the implementation of various expansion plans, the Indian Navy comprised a fairly effective fighting force by the early 1960s. In terms of principal combatants alone, its fleet consisted of an aircraft carrier, two cruisers, three destroyers and fourteen frigates.

Third, the Navy received more funding after 1963 only in relation to the 1961-3 period, not the earlier 1958-61 period, in terms of both total expenditure as well as its share of defence expenditure amongst the armed forces. From 1958 the Navy received over Rs 30 crores annually till 1961-2, when its financial allocation was reduced by a sixth. In 1959-60, such a sum of money accounted for nearly 13 per cent of the defence budget. From 1965-6, the Navy was given more than Rs 30 crores annually once again, which accounted for less than 4 per cent of the total defence budget, in view of the vast increase in funding for both the Army and the Air Force in the period immediately after the 1962 war with China. In essence, the Navy suffered considerably in financial terms from 1961-5. It was only after the 1965 Indo-Pakistan war that the Navy began, once again, to receive some attention from the government.

Fourth, till the 1960s the Royal Navy did not defend India from the sea. Although the British Admiralty influenced the shape and size of the Indian Navy in order to make it conform to a desired role in the defence of the Commonwealth against the Soviet Union and China, India's non-aligned foreign policy specifically precluded the determination of such an option prior to a situation of global war. Moreover, in view of the retirement of the last of the three British Admirals in charge of the Indian Navy in the late 1950s, and the expansion of the Pakistan Navy, increased attention began to be paid to a local war against Pakistan, during which the Royal Navy would have no active role.

Notwithstanding some differences in perception presented above, Tanham's monograph remains a crucial document that Indian policy-makers ought to read, and more important, from which some very pertinent lessons must be learnt. Its central thesis, particularly in relation to naval and maritime affairs, is of great importance for the future of the country. In this respect, it is frustrating that in the past three years since the monograph was first published, there has been little, if any, attempt to formulate a coherent and systematic formal defence strategy.

The nature of international relations in the future will present a large number of challenges and opportunities to India in the Indian Ocean region. In order to deal effectively with, and take advantage of, these increasingly complex situations, the country needs to formulate a coherent and integrated naval strategy based upon a viable defence policy and a national security doctrine. If India continues to fail to carry out these tasks, it will have only itself to blame.

George Tanham's new monograph, 'Strategy in Flux', essentially examines four critical events of 1991 which continue to have a major impact on India's foreign and domestic policies. These comprise the economic crisis in the country in the spring, the sudden collapse of the erstwhile Soviet Union in the late summer of that year, along with the Gulf crisis and war of 1990-1, and the rapid growth of China's economic and military power. In this respect, the nature of India's defence relationship with the United States, and China's increasing influence in Myanmar, represent the more important maritime and naval concerns of India in the 1990s.

Tanham points out that India's major strategic change as a result of the end of the cold war has been the growing defence relationship with the United States. Indo-American naval relations had begun to improve even before the end of the cold war. The formal proposal for the conduct of Indo-American joint naval exercises, for example, preceded by two years the often quoted Kickleighter proposals of the autumn of 1991 (not 1992, as the typographical error in the monograph indicates).

In September 1989, the then Commander-in-Chief of the US Pacific Fleet, Admiral David Jeremiah, presented a set of proposals to the then Indian Chief of Naval Staff, Admiral JG Nadkarni. These included the conduct of joint exercises between the two navies. These proposals were followed in late 1991 by a 14-point programme from the American side for the improvement of naval relations between the two countries. As a result, the first meeting of the Indo-US naval steering committee took place in March 1992 at which the first set of joint naval exercises (Malabar 92) was approved for late May that year.

The second round of Indo-American joint naval exercises (Malabar 95), which finally took place in May 1995, were the largest and most important set of naval exercises carried out so far by the Indian Navy since 1991. It involved the most important dimension of naval warfare in the present day, that of Anti-Submarine Warfare (ASW). This included ASW tactics and communication as well as the detection and mock destruction of submarines, and encompassed the participation of all three dimensions of naval power—air, surface and sub-surface.

In addition to the participation of destroyers and frigates—two on each side—the four-day exercise involved, on the American side, two P-3C Orion Maritime Reconnaissance planes and two nuclear-powered submarines, and on the Indian side, two ex-Soviet Kilo-class submarines. The selection of the strike aircraft and the submarines for the exercise indicated a subtle trade-off between the navies of the two countries.

For the Indian Navy, the presence of the Orions was crucial to gain tactical knowledge of their capabilities and deficiencies. This is particularly relevant as Pakistan has already paid $ 170 million to the United States for three of these aircraft and associated Harpoon anti-ship missiles. These weapon systems are expected to be transferred to the Pakistani Navy by the end of the year. For the US Navy, the presence of two Kilo-class submarines provided critical knowledge of their operational capabilities in the waters of the Arabian Sea. This was particularly important in view of Iran's acquisition of two such boats in the past three years, and the order for a third submarine of this type.

Notwithstanding the importance of this exercise, the nature and pace of Indo-US naval relations in the future will be determined by the manner in which some of the challenges and concerns of the Indian Navy are met. These include the potential transfer of American defence technology to the Indian military and the final size and pattern of fleet deployment of the American Fifth Fleet (revived in May 1995) for the Persian Gulf.

Furthermore, to make Indo-American defence relations meaningful in the future, both countries must take into account each other's limitations. For India, this means accepting the position that an improvement in defence ties will not mean the erosion of America's relationship with Pakistan, or the supply of American weaponry in the future. For the United States, this means the acceptance of India's security considerations in both the nuclear and missile spheres. Once these factors are understood, defence relations between the two countries could advance effectively.

Tanham is quite correct to point out that China represents the greatest and longest term strategic challenge to India. This can be seen from the continuing growth of its military forces and power projection capabilities as well as its dynamically developing economy. During the Ninth Five Year Plan, to begin in 1996, China is scheduled to embark upon a massive military modernisation programme. China's growing influence in Myanmar, along with the establishment of a signal intelligence station on the Cocos Island, and the construction of naval facilities on Hianggyi island are quite obviously of grave concern to the Indian Navy.

The establishment of naval facilities in Myanmar could enable Chinese warships to resupply and carry out routine maintenance tasks in the area, thereby augmenting to a great extent China's ability to operate in the Indian Ocean. Although preliminary intelligence estimates indicate that the expansion of Hianggyi naval base, located at the mouth of the Bassein river, may continue to be too small to host Chinese principal surface combatants of the size required for operations in the Indian Ocean, it would suffice for the batch of new Kilo-class diesel/electric submarines ordered from Russia. In this respect, a Chinese naval presence in the Indian Ocean could well come into effect in the early part of the next decade.

An early indication of the dilemmas involved in this regard were brought out by India's policy of maritime cooperation as a confidence-building measure between states. While the Indian Navy carried out exercises with warships of several countries, including those of extra-regional powers, it stopped short of similar interactions with the Chinese Navy. Although it realises that this may be a good way to moderate its influence in the area, it is not keen to encourage a Chinese naval presence in the Indian Ocean through joint exercises. In view of this paradox, the Indian government has hesitated from suggesting anything beyond visits by Indian and Chinese warships to each other's ports.

Tanham's central thesis, that there is a relative lack of strategic thinking in India, is sound indeed. However, he perceives this lacuna as an integral part of India's history and culture, and thereby appears to condemn India to eternal *ad hocism* in national strategy and higher defence planning. Such a perception is unnecessarily gloomy and pessimistic, and not wholly correct. This ought not to be seen as a prescription for prospective events. Modern-day India does not have to live by its history. Increasing urbanisation and the establishment of modern institutions also serve to break the shackles of cultural rigidity and hierarchy. The lessons of the past and the increasing pressures on various economic, political, and ecological fronts in the future, encourage these developments.

It is heartening to note, therefore, that in the new monograph, Tanham acknowledges that India does at least have some strategic direction. He reaches this conclusion on the basis of informal strategy formulation by the armed forces and the government as well as the conduct of several informal exercises regarding organisational arrangements for national security management. These appear to indicate that strategies can be developed, even if no central coordinating agency exists.

None the less, far more work needs to be done in this area. A major priority for the Indian government is to formalise these *ad hoc* arrangements as soon as possible. The formal enunciation of an official national strategy as well as a defence policy for the country is critical in order to effectively meet the challenges and take advantage of the opportunities provided by a complex and uncertain international security environment.

# *RAISON D'ETAT* OR ADHOCISM?

AMITABH MATTOO

George Tanham's essay on Indian strategic thought deserves special attention for at least three reasons. First, the essay was specially 'prepared' for the Under Secretary of Defence for Policy in the Bush administration. Published in 1992, Tanham's work needs to be read, therefore, as part of a larger review of American policy towards India in the post-cold war period. This renewed American interest in understanding 'India's Future Strategic Role and Power Potential' is clearly a recognition of the country's potential (economic and military) to be an important player in the international system in the years to come.

Tanham's mandate was straightforward. He was asked to provide answers to at least the following questions: How does India's elite view the world? What factors have shaped their views? What are the goals that India is aspiring towards? What strategies are being designed in the pursuit of these goals? And what impact will these ideas, strategies and goals have on the US-Indian relationship? These questions and Tanham's answers are of interest not just to the policy-makers located in Foggy Bottom and the Pentagon, but must engage every concerned Indian. That is the second reason to read and debate Tanham.

The third reason to give Tanham a wider audience is because of the unusual sensitivity with which he has grappled with the subject matter. Rarely has an American scholar attempted to systematically disinter Indian thinking on strategic issues for a Western audience. And few analysts, South Asians included, have made an effort to explore the strategic mindset of the Indian elite with an almost anthropological keenness. Tanham's contribution is even more remarkable given that this is his first intellectual engagement with India. Admittedly, Tanham's essay is rooted in the controversial genre of writings on strategic culture[1], but it does bravely attempt to correct the American ethnocentric bias that Joseph Nye and

Sean Lynn-Jones believe has characterised most of strategic studies.[2] Such an exercise is important because, in the words of one recent study,

> the possibility that strategic choice is in large measure determined by values or assumptions with roots deep in a state's ideational history is an intriguing one both theoretically and in policy terms. Theoretically, it fundamentally challenges structural explanations of choice that rely on ahistorical calculations of interests and capabilities . . . In policy terms, the notion of strategic culture leaves open the possibility that strategic preferences are somewhat more amenable to purposive change than structural realists might assume. . .[3]

Indeed, Tanham's essay, while hardly flawless, displays a rich understanding of India's complexity and its uniqueness, even while the main arguments are refreshingly fresh—untainted by the long-standing 'love-hate' relationship that many established American 'South Asianists' seem to have with India.

Not only is Tanham's in many ways a pioneering study, but the principal conclusion of his work is both perceptive and provocative. Even Prime Minister Narasimha Rao read the essay and referred to it in at least one speech. A serious attempt, therefore, at analysing Tanham's essay must begin by examining his central thesis: 'Indian elites show little evidence of having thought coherently and systematically about national strategy.' It is this sweeping generalisation about a country, which Tanham concedes does not 'admit easily to broad generalizations', that has generated most discussion and controversy. And in this debate Tanham has found a powerful ally in one of India's best known contemporary strategic thinkers, K Subrahmanyam, who—in his review of the study—argued that 'the absence of strategic tradition has resulted in *ad-hocism* all around'.[4]

At least three questions are provoked by Tanham's thesis. First, is there really such an absence of systematic strategic thinking in India? Second, are the factors that Tanham identifies as being responsible for this deficiency the right ones? Finally, how has this lack of strategic planning (if it is assumed that Tanham's thesis is correct) affected India's pursuit of its national interest?

The term 'strategy', as the war historian Michael Howard put it, needs continual definition.[5] Unfortunately, Tanham does not provide a definition in his essay. Hence, this review will have to test his thesis both against the narrower view of strategy—the art of distributing military means to fulfill the ends of policy—and the grander view of the term—the mating of domestic and international resources to achieve national security.

As far as military strategy is concerned, Tanham is quite right. There has been and remains a singular lack of coordinated military planning in independent India. There is no evidence to suggest that careful thought has gone into devising a plan of action on the basis of which specific policies, related to the armed forces, are being executed. This is not to suggest that some of the individual 'tactical' dimensions of military strategy have not been developed. Surely some thinking seems to have gone into the organisational, operational, and the technological dimensions—as Tanham is no doubt aware.

Peacetime exercises routinely carried out by the armed forces, as well as the insightful articles that regularly appear in the 'in-house' journals of the armed forces, for instance, clearly reveal that as far as conventional weapons are concerned there is an operational strategy in existence. Moreover, India has fought four wars since 1947, and in at least two of them the armed forces put forward a remarkably sophisticated operation in the pursuit of clear political objectives. In the sphere of military technology, India has made significant advances; the Defence Research and Development Organisation is known to be one of the most competent wings of the government of India and its scientists, led most ably by Dr APJ Abdul Kalam (the chief designer of the Agni intermediate range ballistic missile), have demonstrated great innovativeness in the face of a severe resource crunch.

It has to be admitted, however, that India has paid little attention to fusing the operational, the technological, the logistical and the social dimensions into a coherent security policy. There is no institution or process at the highest level by which such a policy could have been formulated, and those that exist are pre-occupied with mostly routine administrative matters. As K Subrahmanyam, an insider, puts it,

> The chiefs of staff committee, the committee on defence planning, the defence ministry and the secretaries committee are all shuffling papers and taking ad hoc decisions on routine administrative issues in the absence of dedicated staff for national security planning.[6]

This reviewer, therefore, has no problem with Tanham's thesis if his argument about the absence of strategic thinking relates only to the narrower definition of strategy.

If it is, however, also Tanham's contention that India has not developed a grand strategy, then he is quite off the mark. India's first prime minister, Jawaharlal Nehru, may have seemed like a woolly-headed idealist, but he was arguably one of the most sophisticated grand strategists of this century. Nehru had a clear vision for India and its place in the world, and had devised prudent domestic and international strategies that could enable the country to realise these goals. The two pillars of Nehru's grand strategy were Non-Alignment and Self-Reliance, both sharing a close symbiotic relationship. Nehru's grand strategy enabled India to do two things: first, to carve out a niche for itself in the international system during the early years of the US-Soviet cold war; second, to create conditions of relative internal autonomy and stability which enabled the country to build an enviable scientific and technological infrastructure

If *realpolitik* in foreign policy means attempting to get the best deal for one's country, then Nehru's policies did just that. Take, for instance, the concept of non-alignment which, in the first decade at least, helped India not just to avoid 'entrapment in great power rivalries', but enabled New Delhi to gain considerable leverage *vis-à-vis* the great powers. In fact, it could be convincingly argued that in the Nehru years, non-alignment helped India to gain greater international influence and authority than it would have had had it aligned itself with either of the super-powers or devoted its efforts only towards maximising its military strength. Nehru's grand strategy was certainly not flawless, and it did not accurately gauge, for instance, Chinese intentions, but a strategy it was, and a carefully thought out one at that.

It is, however, true that while today the Nehruvian vision has faded, no clear *Weltanschauung* has replaced it. This crisis of identity has been accentuated by the disintegration of the Soviet Union and the erosion of what one might call the post-colonial agenda. In this sense, the real challenge for India lies not merely in articulating a new grand strategy, but in defining aims, objectives and goals on the basis of which such a strategy can be developed and new partnerships forged.

Is the absence of strategic thinking rooted in Indian geography, culture and history as Tanham seems to suggest? It is difficult for this commentator to agree with Tanham on this score. For every cultural trait or historical factor that Tanham believes has inhibited the development of strategic thought, one can easily identify an opposing trait or factor which should have promoted such thinking. However, the real problem with accepting Tanham's view of Indian history is that not only is it far too selective, but it focuses only on—what can be loosely termed—Hindu India. Were the later Mughals, the descendants of Tamerlane, Genghis Khan and Babar, and some of the greatest warriors and military expansionists in the annals of human civilisation, any less Indian than the Hindu kings whom they fought? Perhaps Tanham relied far too much on the Brahminical views of the 'Delhi nationalist elite'. Alastair Iain Johnston's critique of the 'first generation' of writers on strategic culture holds good for Tanham as well:

> . . . the alleged homogeneity of a society's strategic culture across time is problematic. It seems somewhat muddled to argue that a single strategic culture emerges from its multiple inputs when each of these inputs could produce alternative, even contradictory strategic cultures . . . it would be more logical to conclude that the diversity of a particular society's geographical, political, cultural and strategic experience will produce multiple strategic cultures, but this possibility is excluded by the narrow determinism . . .[7]

In any case, for all those engaged in attempting to generate a wider debate on national security issues, Tanham's deterministic view is not very helpful. It suggests that Indians are inherently incapable of thinking systematically about issues of power and security. Instead, it may have been more useful if Tanham had focussed on institutions and processes which have prevented clear thinking. He may then have discovered that bureaucratic inertia, political ineptitude and the state of civil-military relations—during the last 48 years—may have more to do with the absence of strategic thinking than India's ancient past.

The second question that Tanham's thesis provokes is no less important. Has the absence of strategic thinking affected India adversely? Yes and no. A narrow strait-jacketed strategy could have prevented flexibility and innovativeness, crucial in international politics and a hallmark of Indian diplomacy during the Nehru era. And yet it must be conceded that the lack of clear thinking on strategic issues has often prevented India from anticipating events or acting quickly enough. For instance, the fiasco of the Indian Peace-Keeping Force (IPKF) in Sri Lanka may have been avoided had there been a more comprehensive strategic assessment of the situation on the ground. The lack of strategic planning during the IPKF operation is starkly borne out by the fact that the Indian Army landed in Jaffna without contour maps of the region!

Having dealt with Tanham's central thesis, this review will focus on two issues that were raised in the essay on Indian strategic thought and updated in the later essay, 'Indian Strategy in Flux?' The first issue that will be discussed is the nuclear one. It is here that the absence of clear strategic thinking is most glaring. 'Strategic ambiguity' may, at one stage, have seemed like a carefully thought-out policy, but today it is synonymous only with confusion. Indeed, political indecision, bureaucratic incompetence and dangerous secrecy seem to have forced India's policy into a time warp; neither is the country's nuclear policy serving a *realpolitik* interest nor is it promoting a principled message. In other words, India is neither being able to claim the benefits (small as they may be in the present international climate) of being a non-nuclear state, nor is it gaining the prestige or influence that are traditionally associated with being a nuclear power. The deterrent value of such an ambiguous posture is also debatable.

A large part of the confusion has less to do with India's history or culture than with the regime of secrecy that is in operation. As in many other countries, the decisions about India's nuclear programme are usually taken in secret by a few individuals.[8] India's vast nuclear establishment continues to function even today without any real public accountability. The chairman of India's Atomic Energy Commission, for instance, has the absolute power to 'initiate, formulate, plan and execute India's nuclear programme in total secrecy'[9] and is responsible only to the Prime Minister. Informed observers have referred to India's nuclear decision-making process as 'scientific and political czarism'[10] or as virtual 'nuclear sub-government'[11]. Reasoned public discussion of nuclear policy options is almost entirely lacking in the country which otherwise has a rich and vibrant democratic tradition of dialogue and debate. Not much emphasis is laid on nuclear policy in the media, in public fora, or in the two houses of Parliament—all of which seem otherwise preoccupied with domestic problems. India's nuclear policy has never been an issue in general elections, and even among non-governmental organisations discussion of national security and nuclear issues is scarce. As K Subrahmanyam puts it:

As a consistent advocate of the nuclear option for India for the last quarter of a century and as a person very familiar with the general thinking at the top levels of military and bureaucratic leadership, though not privy to their secrets, I despair whether the Indian establishment can be persuaded to apply their mind at all to a nuclear strategic policy . . . [India's] approach to security issue is purely reactive and *ad hocist* . . .[12]

There is, admittedly, a steady stream of articles on the subject in quasi-official journals and a few newspapers. But this discourse has been almost totally appropriated by a handful of scholars and former military and government officials, who usually present no more than a justification of official policy. On sensitive subjects such as national security, the government can, and often does, restrict the availability of information, and even those given access to nuclear secrets are prevented from disseminating them through the special Atomic Energy Act of 1962 or the more pervasive Official Secrets Act. Even then there are few, if any, civil servants, political leaders (outside the Prime Minister) or military officers who can claim to know the exact state of India's nuclear programme. Under Section 18 (i) of the Atomic Energy Act, the government has the power to restrict the disclosure of information in any form which relates to an existing or proposed plant used for the purpose of producing, developing or using atomic energy. Through state patronage of research institutes and universities and the release of selected information to sympathetic investigators, the government is able to control much of the discussion that takes places on nuclear policy options. Informed policy formulation in these circumstances is very difficult.

There are indications, however, that this situation may be changing. Regional tension and international pressure may now be forcing India to review its policy. There are three pointers in this direction.

First, in early 1990, at the peak of the insurgency in Kashmir, the Government of India is believed to have set up a study group to 'look into' the possibility of a Pakistani nuclear strike against India and devise appropriate responses. This was done during a particularly tense period in India-Pakistan relations and after the government received information from US intelligence and other sources that Pakistan had deployed nuclear warheads on its American-made F-16 fighter planes. The study group had representatives from India's nuclear establishment, the armed forces, the political leadership and the civil service.

Second, in March 1993, the government set up an eminent persons' group to examine 'various policy options available to India in the nuclear field so as to help the government to choose the one most suited in the present-day security and political environment'. The group included serving and retired officials of the Atomic Energy Commission and other official and non-official experts. The group was also asked to recommend measures that India should take to respond to growing non-proliferation pressures from the Clinton administration.

Finally, the recommendations made at a seminar on 'External Pressures on India's Nuclear Options' (which included a virtual 'who's who' of India's strategic thinkers, including serving officials) held in September 1995 reveal the new directions towards which India's nuclear policy is most certainly moving. Some of the recommendations are reproduced here:

> . . . in this changed new situation following the permanent extension of the nuclear Non-Proliferation Treaty (NPT) both the comprehensive test ban treaty (CTBT) and the fissile material cut-off treaty (FMCT) have also become untenable and India should oppose both these treaties unless explicitly, in a time-bound framework, they are made part of total and comprehensive disarmament . . .
>
> . . . in this changed situation the present policy position of 'keeping the nuclear option open' has become meaningless. There is need now to examine how best to translate this into effective deterrence . . .
>
> . . . India's current capabilities can take care of Pakistan but not the other larger challenges. And, therefore, even in case India decides not to resume nuclear testing, we must continue developing longer range delivery systems and, towards that end, expedite research and development, and testing of the systems required.
>
> . . . India should proceed ahead with the serial production and induction into service of the Prithvi, and with the further development of the Agni for induction into service.
>
> . . . India should first start by presenting its case in clear-cut national security policy and start working towards developing its capabilities.

The other issue of concern is China. Tanham says, 'the greatest and longest term strategic challenge' to India comes from China, and yet on no other issue is there greater elite, especially government, complacency. While the lack of uneasiness in the government about Chinese intentions is frightening, the all-pervasive 'revisionist' thinking about Beijing is almost seditious.

At a recent seminar held near Delhi, which included top defence journalists, almost all the Indian participants blamed India for the Sino-Indian war of 1962. In the late-1960s when Neville Maxwell claimed that it was Nehru's forward policy which caused the war, his book was banned. Today Maxwell's thesis seems to be becoming the accepted wisdom of India's intelligentsia. The Indian elite's swing from one extreme to another is symptomatic of the government's short-sighted thinking about China. Ironically, the threat from China has been undermined, almost marginalised, while Pakistan's capabilities have been always overestimated.

There are several reasons why a political and military threat from China needs to be taken seriously. First, and most frightening, is the growing evidence of nuclear cooperation between Beijing and Islamabad. Beijing, recent reports have suggested, may even have provided Islamabad with the design of a nuclear weapon. Second, there is great uncertainty about China's future in the post-Deng era. Sinologists are divided about the expected outcome. Many believe that China could be breaking into its provinces. As evidence they point to the devolution of power and economic activity that has already taken place. But the final disintegration of China may not be peaceful, and the whole country could be thrown into a civil war. From India's point of view, this outcome, unfortunate as it might be, is the most preferred option. A smaller China would be more manageable, and it is highly improbable that domestic Chinese conflicts would spill over to South Asia.

But the more likely scenario is that China will emerge as a military and economic superpower in the next ten years. In 2004, if China maintains the rate of growth it has had in the last decade (9.2 per cent), its GNP—after correcting for price differences—would be higher than Japan's and only second to that of the United States. In this scenario, the Chinese army and the Communist party will continue to be in control and Beijing's economic expansionism would be buttressed by its military strength. Could Beijing, under these circumstances, be willing to stand competition from India which would be seeking similar greener economic pastures in the Asia-Pacific region? Economic rivalry would inevitably lead to a political conflict, and India could once again be overwhelmed by China.

Third, China has begun to display imperial ambitions. All those who felt that Tibet and Vietnam were aberrations and that Beijing has not demonstrated expansionist tendencies should observe the inroads that China has made into Myanmar, or its aggressiveness over the Spratley islands dispute. The relationship with Myanmar, for instance, which began on a commercial basis (arms sales to the generals in Yangon) is now translating into a close political and military bond. Reports have even suggested that China is being allowed to set up a naval base near Yangon. This base could be used to monitor Indian space and missile launches. Although India has been attempting to create its own area of influence in Myanmar, there is no doubt that it is in no position to compete with China. In other words, Myanmar may only be the first move in China's grand design.

Fourth, the nuclear threat from China is alive and real. It is well known, and most ably documented by Tibetan refugees, that China has deployed nuclear missiles in Tibet. While not much is known about Chinese targeting doctrines, nor is the precise location in Tibet known, it is clear that these missiles can have only one target: India. True, Chinese inter-continental ballistic missiles elsewhere could also target India, but the potential psychological and political impact of these missiles—literally a few hundred miles from India's border—cannot be underestimated.

Fifth, the presence of thousands of Tibetan refugees is a continuing irritant which is likely to get even worse as the scale of Chinese atrocities in the region gets worse. The Tibetans led by the Dalai Lama have been model refugees, but as the younger generation of radical and militant Tibetans takes over, they would not be averse to confronting the Chinese more directly. If the Government of India crushes the Tibetan uprising, it could face domestic and international opprobrium.

Finally, the truth is that India faced a humiliating and traumatic defeat at the hands of the Chinese in 1962. That defeat has deeply embedded itself on the national psyche. The defeat of 1962 was the biggest rupture in Nehru's worldview and in India's thinking about foreign policy. It changed the way India thought about the world and it was in many ways the basis of the Indian nuclear programme. Indians may not want to avenge that defeat, but an increasing number of 'ordinary' Indians believe that so-called Sino-Indian *detente* has been built principally on a history of Indian concessions. The line of tranquility was made possibly because of Indian appeasement of Beijing and was not an agreement between equal partners.

To conclude, George Tanham's essays, insightful as they are, are not (nor perhaps were they intended to be) a definitive study of India's strategic thought. Rather, Tanham's essays are a most useful beginning, and will certainly provoke a wider debate on the subject. Hopefully, they will also persuade the Indian elite to think a little more systematically on issues relating to India's security in a world of ever-increasing turbulence.

## NOTES

1 See Alastair Iain Johnston's excellent survey of writings on strategic culture: 'Thinking about Strategic Culture', *International Security*, vol.19, no. 4, pp. 32-64.

2 See Joseph S Nye, Jr, and Sean M Lynn-Jones, 'International Security Studies: A Report on a Conference on the State of the Field', *International Security*, vol. 12, no. 4 (Spring 1988), pp. 14-15; and Ken Booth, *Strategy and Ethnocentrism*, New York, Holmes & Meier, 1979.

3 Johnston, op.cit., p. 63.

4 See K Subrahmanyam, 'Strategic Thinking in India', *Economic Times*, 9 March 1994.

5 Michael Howard, 'The Forgotten Dimensions of War' in his *The Causes of War*, London, Temple Smith, 1983, p. 101.

6 Subrahmanyam, op.cit.

7 Johnston, op. cit., p. 38.

8 For an insightful study of India's nuclear decision-making, see Ashok Kapur, *India's Nuclear Option: Atomic Diplomacy and Decision Making*, New York, Praeger, 1976. Also see Onkar Marwah, 'India's Nuclear and Space Programs: Intent and Policy', *International Security*, No. 2, Fall 1977, pp. 96-121, and Ziba Moshaver, *Nuclear Weapons Proliferation in the Indian Subcontinent*, New York, St Martin's Press, 1991.

9 Dhirendra Sharma, *India's Nuclear Estate*, New Delhi, Lancers, 1976, p. 149.

10 Kapur, *India's Nuclear Option*, op. cit.

11 Sharma, *India's Nuclear Estate*, op. cit., p. 2. Also see Achin Vanaik and Praful Bidwai, 'India and Pakistan' in *Security Without Nuclear Weapons?*, Regina Cowen Carp, ed., Oxford, SIPRI/OUP, 1991. Vanaik and Bidwai are two other prominent dissenters.

12 K Subrahmanyam, 'Nuclear Policy, Arms Control and Military Cooperation', paper presented at a conference on 'India and the United States After the Cold War' sponsored by the India International Centre and Carnegie Endowment for International Peace, New Delhi, 7-9 March 1993.

# SELECT BIBLIOGRAPHY


Agarwal, Rajesh K, *Defence Production and Development*, Arnold-Heinemann Publishers, New Delhi, 1970.

Aiyanger, Rangaswami, KV, *Some Aspects of Ancient Indian Polity*, Eastern Book House, Patna, 1988.

Akbar, MJ, *India: The Siege Within: Challenges to a Nation's Unity*, Penguin, Harmondsworth, 1985.

———, *Nehru: The Making of India*, Penguin, London, 1988.

———, *Riot after Riot: Report on Caste and Communal Violence in India*, Penguin, London, 1988.

———, *Kashmir: Behind the Vale*, Viking Press, New Delhi, 1991.

Ali, Akhtar, *South Asia: Nuclear Stalemate or Conflagration?*, Research on Armament and Poverty, Karachi, 1987.

Ali, Tariq, *Can Pakistan Survive?*, Penguin, Harmondsworth, 1983.

Altekar, AS, *State and Government in Ancient India*, Motilal Banarsidass, New Delhi, 1984.

Alvares, Claude Alphonse, *Homo Faber: Technology and Culture in India, China and the West From 1500 to the Present Day*, Martinus Nijhoff Publishers, The Hague, 1980.

Anand, VK, *Conflict in Nagaland: A Study of Insurgency and Counter-Insurgency*, Chanakya Publications, Delhi, 1980.

Another India, *Daedalus*, vol. 118, no. 4, Fall 1989.

Appadorai, A, *Domestic Roots of Indian Foreign Policy*, Oxford University Press, New Delhi, 1971.

———, *Indian Political Thinking in the Twentieth Century: From Naoroji to Nehru, An Introductory Survey*, Oxford University Press, Calcutta, 1971.

Appadorai, A and MS Rajan, *India's Foreign Policy and Relations*, South Asian Publishers, New Delhi, 1985.

Aram, M, *Peace in Nagaland: Eight Year Story (1964-72)*, Arnold-Heinemann Publishers, New Delhi, 1979.

Arora, Satish Kumar, *American Foreign Policy Towards India*, Suneja Book Centre, New Delhi, 1954.

Ayoob, Mohammed, and Subrahmanyam K, *The Liberation War*, S Chand, New Delhi, 1972.

Ayoob, Mohammed, *India, Pakistan, and Bangladesh: Search for Relationship*, Indian Council of World Affairs, New Delhi, 1975.

———, *India and South East Asia: Indian Perception and Policies*, Routledge, London, 1990.

Azad, Maulana Abul Kalam, *India Wins Freedom*, Sangam Books, London, 1988.

Babbage, Ross, and Sandy Gordon (eds), *India's Strategic Future: Regional State or Global Power?* St. Martin's Press, New York, 1992.

Bains, JS, *India's International Disputes: A Legal Study*, Asia Publishing House, Bombay, 1962.

Bajpai, Kanti P and Stephen P Cohen, (eds), *South Asian Security After the Cold War: International Perspectives*, Westview Press, Boulder, Colorado, 1993.

Bajpai, Kanti P and Varun Sahni, *Secure and Solvent: Thinking About an Affordable Defence for India*, RGICS Paper No.11, Rajiv Gandhi Institute for Contemporary Studies, New Delhi, 1994.

Bajpai, Kanti P, PR Chari, Pervaiz Iqbal Cheema, Stephen P Cohen, Sumit Gauguly, *Brasstacks and Beyond: Perception and Management of Crisis in South Asia*, Manohar Publishers, New Delhi, 1995.

Bajpai, US, (ed), *India's Security: The Politico-Strategic Environment*, Lancers Publishers, New Delhi, 1983.

————, *India and Its Neighbours*, Lancer International, New Delhi, 1986.

Bakshi, PM (ed), *The Constitution of India: With Comments*, Universal Book Traders, New Delhi, 1995.

Bandyopadhyaya J, *The Making of India's Foreign Policy*, 2nd edn, Allied Publishers, New Delhi, 1987.

Barnds, William J, *India, Pakistan and The Great Powers*, Praeger Publishers, New Delhi, 1972.

Basham, AL, *The Wonder That was India*, Sidgwick & Jackson, London, 1967.

Basu, Tapan, Pradip Datta, Sumit Sarkar, Tanika Sarkar, S Sen, *Khaki Shorts and Saffron Flags: A Critique of the Hindu Right*, Tracts For The Times/1, Orient Longman, New Delhi, 1983.

Baxter, Craig, *Jana Sangh*, Oxford University Press, London, 1971.

Baxter, Craig, Yogendra K Malik, Charles H Kennedy, and Robert C Oberst, *Government and Politics in South Asia*, Westview Press, Boulder, Colorado, 1987.

Bayly, CA, *The New Cambridge History of India: Indian Society and the Making of the British Empire*, Cambridge University Press, Cambridge, 1987.

Begum, Khurshida, *Tension Over the Farakka Barrage: A Techno-Political Tangle in South Asia*, KP Bagchi, Calcutta, 1988.

Berkes, Ross N, and Mohinder S Bedi, *The Diplomacy of India: Indian Foreign Policy in the United Nations*, Stanford University Press, Stanford, 1958.

Bhaduri, Major Shankar, and Major General Afsir Khan, *The Sri Lankan Crisis*, Lancers Paper 1, Lancer International, New Delhi, 1990.

Bhagwati, Jagdish, *India in Transition: Freeing the Economy*, Clarendon Press, Oxford, 1993.

Bhagwati, Jagdish and TN Srinivasan, *Foreign Trade Regimes and Economic Development: India*, Columbia University Press, New York, 1975.

Bhagwati, Jagdish and TN Srinivasan, *India's Economic Reforms*, Ministry of Finance, Government of India, New Delhi, July 1993.

Bhandarkar, DR, *Some Aspects of Ancient Hindu Polity*, Eastern Book House, Patna, 1988.

Bhargava, GS, *The Battle of NEFA: The Undeclared War*, Allied Publishers, Bombay, 1964.

Bhargava, ML, *Indian Ocean Strategies: Through the Ages (with Rare and Antique Maps)*, Reliance Publishing, New Delhi, 1990.

Bhat, Sudhakar, *The Challenges of the North East*, Popular Prakashan, Bombay, 1975.

Bhatia, BM, *Food Security in South Asia*, Oxford & IBH, New Delhi, 1985.

Bhatia, Shyam, *India's Nuclear Bomb*, Vikas Publishing House, New Delhi, 1979.

Bidwai, Praful, Anuradha Chenoy, Arun Ghosh, Muchkund Dubey, Seema Mustafa, SP Shukla, V Sudershan and Achin Vanaik, *India Under Siege: Challenges Within and Without*, Wiley Eastern, New Age International, New Delhi, 1995.

Bindra, SS, *India and Her Neighbours: A Study of Political, Economic and Cultural Relations and Interactions*, Deep & Deep Publications, New Delhi, 1984.

———, *Indo-Bangladesh Relations*, Deep & Deep Publications, New Delhi, 1982.

Birla, KK, *Indira Gandhi: Reminiscences*, Vikas Publishing House, New Delhi, 1987.

Birla Institute of Scientific Research, Economic Research Division, *India and the Atom*, Allied Publishers, New Delhi, 1982.

Blinkenberg, Lars, *India-Pakistan: The History of Unresolved Conflicts*, Dansk Udenrigspolitisk Institute, Munkgaard, 1972.

Bouton, Marshal M, and Philip Oldenburg, *India Briefing, 1989*, Westview Press, Boulder, Colorado, 1989.

Bowman, Leslie W and Ian Clark (eds), *Indian Ocean in Global Politics*, Young Asia, New Delhi, 1983.

Bradnock, Robert, *India's Foreign Policy Since 1971*, Chatham House Council on Foreign Relation Press, New York, for the Royal Institute of International Affairs, London, 1990.

Brands, HW, *India and United States: The Cold Peace*, Twayne Publishers, Boston, 1990.

Brar, Lt General KS, *Operation Blue Star: The True Story*, UBSPD, New Delhi, 1993.

Brass, Paul R, *The New Cambridge History of India: The Politics of India Since Independence*, Cambridge University Press, Cambridge, 1990.

Brata, Sasthi, *India: Labyrinths in the Lotous Land*, William Morrow & Co. Inc., New York, 1985.

———, *India: The Perpetual Paradox*, Rupa, Calcutta, 1986.

Braun, Dieter, *Indian Ocean: Region of Conflict or Peace Zone*, Oxford University Press, New Delhi, 1983.

Brecher, Michael, *The Struggle For Kashmir*, Oxford University Press, New York, 1953.

———, *India and World Politics: Krishna Menon's View of the World*, Oxford University Press, London, 1968.

Brines, Russell, *The Indo-Pakistani Conflict*, Pall Mall Press, London, 1968.

Brown, Judith M, *Gandhi: Prisoner of Hope*, Yale University Press, London, 1985.

Brown, Judith M, *Modern India: The Origins of an Asian Democracy*, Oxford University Press, New Delhi, 1988.

Brown, W Norman, *The United States and India, Pakistan, Bangladesh*, Harvard University Press, Cambridge, Mass. 1972.

Bruce, Robert H (ed), *The Modern Indian Navy and the Indian Ocean*, Centre for Indian Ocean Regional Studies, Curtin University of Technology Perth, Australia, 1989.

Buarik, Erik and Jon Sigardson, *India-China: Comparative Research Technology and Science for Development*, Scandivanian Institute of Asian Studies, 1981.

Burke, SM, *Mainsprings of Indian and Pakistani Foreign Policies*, University of Minnesota Press, Minneapolis 1979.

Buzan, Barry, and Gowher, Rizvi, *South Asian Insecurity and the Great Powers*, Macmillan Press, London, 1986.

Byres, TJ (ed), *The State and Development Planning in India*, Oxford University Press, New Delhi, 1993.

Calman, Leslie J, *Protest in Democratic India: Authority's Response to Challenge*, Westview Special Studies on South and South-East Asia, Westview Press, Boulder and London, 1985.

Carnegie Task Force on Non-Proliferation and South Asian Security, *Nuclear Weapons and South Asian Security*, Carnegie Endowment for International Peace, Washington, DC, 1986.

Chakravarti, PC, *India's China Policy*, University of Indiana Press, Bloomington, 1962.

Chakravarty, BN, *India Speaks to America*, Orient Longman, Bombay, 1966.

Chakravarty, Sukhamoy, *Development Planning: The Indian Experience*, Oxford University Press, New Delhi, 1987.

Chandra, Satish (ed), *Indian Ocean: Exploration in History, Commerce and Politics*, Sage Publications, New Delhi, 1987.

Chari, PR, *Indo-Pak Nuclear Standoff: The Role of the United States*, Manohar, New Delhi, 1995.

Chaudhuri, General JN, *Arms, Aims and Aspects*, Manaktalas, Bombay, 1966.

———, *India's Problems of National Security in the Seventies*, USI National Security Lectures, USI, New Delhi, 1973.

Chellaney, Brahma, *Nuclear Proliteration: The US-Indian Conflict*, Orient Longman, New Delhi, 1993.

Chibber, Aditya, *National Security Doctrine: An Indian Imperative*, Lancer International, New Delhi, 1990.

Chibber, Lt General ML, *Military Leadership to Prevent a Military Coup*, Lancer International, New Delhi, 1986.

———, *Solider's Role in National Integration*, Lancer International, New Delhi, 1986.

Chisti, Lt General Faiz Ali, *Betrayals of Another Kind: Islam, Democracy and the Army in Pakistan*, Asia Publishing House, London, 1989.

Chopra, Maharaj K, *India: The Search for Power*, Lalvani Publishers, Bombay, 1969.

Chopra, Pran, *Before and After the Indo-Soviet Treaty*, S Chand, New Delhi, 1971.

Chopra, Pran, (ed), *The Challange of Bangladesh: A Special Debate*, Humanities Press, New York, 1971.

Chopra, Pran, *et al.*, *Future of South Asia*, Macmillan, New Delhi, 1986.

———, *India, Pakistan and the Kashmir Tangle*, Harper Collins, New Delhi, 1994.

Chopra, Surendra, *UN Mediation in Kashmir: A Study in Power Politics*, Vishal Publishers, Kurukshetra, 1971.

Choudhury, GW, *India, Pakistan Bangladesh and The Major Powers: Politics of A Divided Subcontinent*, Frec Press, New York, 1975.

Chufrin, G, *Economic Cooperation and Collective Security in Asia*, Vikas Publishers, New Delhi, 1976.

Coelho, Vincent, *Across the Palk Straits: India-Sri Lanka Relations*, Palit and Palit, Dehradun, 1976.

Cohen, Stephen P, (ed), *The Security of South Asia: American and Asian Perspectives*, Vistaar Publications, New Delhi, 1987.

———, *The Indian Army: Its Contribution to the Development of a Nation*, rev edn, Oxford University Press, New Delhi, 1990.

———, (ed), *Nuclear Proliferation in South Asia: The Prospects for Arms Control*, Westview Press, Boulder, Colorado, 1991.

Cohen, Stephen P, and Richard L Park, *India: Emergent Power?* Crane Russak, New York, 1978.

Campbell-Johnson, Alex, *Mission with Mountbatten,* Athaneum, New York, 1985.

Cordesman, Anthony H, *US Strategic Interests in the India- Pakistan Military Balance,* The English Bookstore, New Delhi, 1988.

Cottrell, Alvin J, and RM Burrell (eds.), *The Indian Ocean: Its Political, Economic and Military Importance*, Published for the Centre for Strategic and International Studies by Praeger Publishers, New York, 1972.

Cottrell, Alvin J, (ed), *Sea Power and Strategy in The Indian Ocean*, Sage Publications, London, 1981.

Crunden, Robert M, *et al.* (eds), *New Perspectives on America and South Asia*, Chanakya Publications, New Delhi, 1984.

Dalvi, Brig, JP (Ret.), *Himalayan Blunder: The Curtain-Raiser to the Sino-Indian War of 1962,* Thacker and Company, Bombay, 1969.

Damodaran, AK and US Bajpai (eds), *Indian Foreign Policy: The Indira Gandhi Years,* Radiant Publishers, New Delhi, 1990.

Das, Suranjan and Sekhar Bandopadhyay, *Caste and Communal Politics in South Asia*, KP Bagchi, New Delhi, 1993.

Das, Tapan, *Sino-Pak Collusion and US Policy*, Asia Publishing House, New Delhi, 1972.

Das Gupta, Ashin and MN Pearson (eds), *India and the Indian Ocean, 1500-1800,* Oxford University Press, Calcutta, 1987.

Dhar, PN, *India and the Changing World: An Indian Perspective.* RGICS Paper No.1, Rajiv Gandhi Institute for Contemporary Studies, New Delhi, 1993.

Dikshitar, VR Ramchandra, *War in Ancient India,* Motilal Banarsidass, New Delhi, 1987.

Dowdy, William L and Russell B Trood (eds), *Indian Ocean: Perspectives on a Strategic Area*, Himalayan Books, New Delhi, 1981.

Drekmeir, Charles, *Kingship and Community in Early India*, Stanford University Press, Stanford, 1966.

Dubey, Ravi Kant, *Indo-Sri Lankan Relations: With Special Reference to the Tamil Problem,* Deep and Deep Publications, New Delhi, 1990.

Dutt, Srikant, *India and the Third World: Altruism or Hegemony?,* Zed Books, London, 1984.

Dutt, VP, *India and the World,* Sanchar Publishing House, New Delhi, 1990.

Eldridge, PJ, *The Politics of Foreign Aid in India*, Shocken, New York, 1970.

Embree, Ainslie T, (ed), *The Hindu Tradition: Readings in Oriental Thought*, Vintage, New York, 1972.

———, *India's Search for National Identity*, rev. edn, Chanakya Publications, New Delhi, 1987.

———, *Imagining India: Essays in Indian History*, Oxford University Press, New York, 1989.

———, *Utopias in Conflict: Religion and Nationalism in Modern India*, University of California Press, Berkeley, California, 1990.

Engineer, AA, *Secular Crown on Fire: The Kashmir Problem*, Ajanta Publication, Delhi, 1991.

Farmer, BH, *An Introduction to South Asia*, Methuen, London, 1983.

Fischer, Louis, *The Life of Mahatma Gandhi*, Grafton Books, Collins Publications Group, London, 1982.

Fisher, Margaret W, Leo E Rose, and Robert A Huttenback, *Himalayan Battleground: Sino-Indian Rivalry in Ladakh*, Praeger Publishers, New York, 1963.

Fishlock, Trevor, *India File: Inside the Subcontinent*, John Murray, London, 1983.

Frankel, Francine, *India's Political Economy 1947-77: The Gradual Revolution*, Princeton University, Princeton, 1978.

Galbraith, Peter, *United States Security Interests in South Asia*, Government Printing Office, Washington, DC, 1984.

Gananathan, VS, *Geopolitics and India*, Puna Municipal Gazette, Pune, 1962.

Ganguly, Shivaji, *US Policy Towards South Asia*, Westview Press, Boulder, Colorado, 1990.

Ganguly, Sumit, *Origins of War in South Asia: Indo-Pakistani Conflict since 1947*, 2nd edn, Westview Press, Boulder, Colorado, 1994.

Gascoigne, Bamber, *The Great Moghals*, Dorset Press, New York, 1971.

Ghosh, Partha S, *Cooperation and Conflict in South Asia*, Manohar Publishers, New Delhi, 1989.

Ghosh, SK, *Unquiet Borders*, Ashish Publishing House, New Delhi, 1993.

Glazer, Sulochana and Nathan Glazer (eds), *Conflicting Images: India and the United States*, Riverdale, Maryland, 1990.

Gopal, Madan, *India As A World Power: Aspects of Foreign Policy*, Rajkamal Publication, Delhi, 1948.

Gould, Harold S and Sumit Ganguly (eds), *The Hope and the Reality: From Roosevelt to Reagan*, Westview Press, Boulder, 1992.

Government of India, *Economic Reforms: Two Years After and The Task Ahead*, Discussion Paper, Ministry of Finance, Government of India, New Delhi. n.d.

Goyal, Narendra, *Prelude to India: A Study of India's Relations With Himalayan States*, Cambridge Book and Stationary Store, New Delhi, 1964.

Gulati, Niranjan D, *Indus Water Treaty: An Exercise in International Mediation*, Allied Publishers, Bombay, 1973.

Gundevia, VD, *War and Peace in Nagaland*, Palit and Palit, New Delhi, 1975.

Gupta, Karunakaran, *India in World Politics: A Period of Transition, Fall 1956 to Spring 1960*, Scientific Book Agency, Calcutta, 1969.

Gupta, Rajnikant, *Military Traits of Tantya Tope*, S Chand, New Delhi, 1987.

Gupta, Shekhar, *India Redefines its Role: An Analysis of India's Changing Internal Dynamics and Their Impact on Foreign Relations*, Adelphi Paper, No.293. IISS, Oxford University Press, 1995.

Gupta, Sisir, *India and Regional Integration in South Asia*, National Publication House, Bombay, 1964.

————, *Kashmir: A Study in India-Pakistan Relations*, Asia Publishing House, Bombay, 1966.

Gupta, SP, *Modern India and Progress in Science and Technology*, Vikas Publishing House, New Delhi, 1979.

Gururaj Rao, HS, *Legal Aspects of the Kashmir Problem*, Asia Publishing House, Bombay, 1967.

Haass, Richard N, *Conflicts Unending: The United States and Regional Disputes*, Yale University Press, New Haven, 1990.

Habibullah, Major General E and Col BK Narayan, *Compulsions of Indian Security: A Plea for Geographic and Demographic Defence*, ABC Publishing House, New Delhi, 1984.

Haksar, PN, (ed), *Nehru's Vision of Peace and Security in the Nuclear Age*, Patriot Publishers, New Delhi, 1987.

————, *India's Foreign Policy and Its Problems*, Patriot Publishers, New Delhi, 1989.

Handa, Rohit, *Policy For India's Defence*, Chetana Publications, New Delhi, 1976.

Hansen, Waldemar, *The Peacock Throne: The Drama of Moghul India*, Holt Rinehart, New York, 1972.

Hardgrave, Robert L, *India: Government and Politics in a Developing Nation*, 5th edn, Harcourt Brace Jovanovich, New York, 1994.

Harrison, Selig S, *India: The Most Dangerous Decades*, Princeton University Press, Princeton, NJ, 1960.

————, (ed), *India and the United States*, Macmillan Press, New York, 1961.

Harrison, Selig S and Geoffrey Kemp, *India and America After the Cold War*, Carnegie Foundation Endowment for International Peace, Washington, DC, 1993.

Harrison, Selig S and K Subrahmanyam (eds), *Superpower Rivalry in the Indian Ocean: Indian and American Perspective*, Oxford University Press, New York, 1989.

Hart, D, *Nuclear Power in India*, Allen and Unwin, London, 1983.

Heimsath, CH and Surjit Mansigh, *A Diplomatic History of Modern India,* Allied Publishers, Bombay, 1971.

Heptulla, Najmah, *India's Progress in Science and Technology,* Oxford and IBH Publishing, New Delhi, 1986

Hoffman, Steven A, *India and the China Crisis,* Oxford University Press, Delhi, 1990.

Horn, RC, *Soviet-Indian Relations: Issues and Influences,* Praeger Publishers, New York, 1982.

Inden Ronald, *Imagining India,* Basil Blackwell, Oxford, 1990.

Isaacs, Harold, *Scratches on Our Mind,* Massachusetts Institute of Technology Press, Cambridge, 1958.

Israel, Milton (ed), *National Unity: The South Asian Experience,* Promilla, New Delhi, 1983.

Iyer, Nandhini, *India and the Indian Ocean,* ABC Publishing House, New Delhi, 1985.

Jackson, Richard L, *The Non-Aligned, the UN and the Super Powers,* Praeger Publishers, New York, 1983.

Jackson, Robert, *South Asian Crisis: India-Pakistan and Bangla-desh,* Chatto and Windus Publishers, London, 1975.

Jain, BM, *South Asian Security: Problems and Prospects,* Radiant Publishers, New Delhi, 1985.

Jain, BM, *Nuclear Politics in South Asia,* Rawat Publications, New, Delhi, 1995.

Jain, Girilal, *India Meets China in Nepal,* Asia Publishing House, Bombay, 1959.

————, *Panchseela and After: A Reappraisal of Sino-Indian Relations in the Context of the Tibetan Insurrection,* Asia Publishing House, New York, 1960.

Jain, JP, *Nuclear India,* 2 volumes, Radiant Publishers, New Delhi, 1975.

Jaipal, Rikhi, *Non-Alignment: Origin, Growth and Potential for World Peace,* 2nd edn, Allied Publishers, New Delhi, 1987.

Jaisingh, Hari, *India After Indira: The Turbulent Years, 1984-1989,* Allied Publishers, New Delhi, 1989.

Jalan, Bimal (ed), *The Indian Economy: Problems and Prospects,* Viking Press, New Delhi, 1992.

Januzzi, F Thomasson, *India in Transition,* Westview Press, Boulder, Colorado, 1989.

Jayaramu, PS, *India's National Security and Foreign Policy,* ABC Publishing House, New Delhi, 1987.

Wilson, Jayaratnam, and Dannis Dalton (eds), *The States of South Asia: Problems of National Integration,* Vikas Publishing House, New Delhi, 1982.

Jeffrey, Robin, *What's Happening to India? Punjab, Ethnic Conflict, Mrs*

*Gandhi's Death and the Test for Federalism.* Macmillan Press, Basingtoke, 1986.

Jha, Shree Krishna, *Uneasy Partners: India and Nepal in the Post-Colonial Era,* Manas Publishers, New Delhi, 1975.

Joeck, N (ed), *Strategic Consequences of Nuclear Proliferation in South Asia,* Frank Cass, London, 1986.

Johnson, BLC, *South Asia: Selective Studies of the Essential Geography of India, Pakistan and Ceylon,* Heineman Educational Books, London, 1989.

Jones, Kenneth W, *The New Cambridge History of India: Socio- Religious Reform Movements in British India,* Cambridge University Press, Cambridge, 1989.

Kadian, Rajesh, *India and Its Army,* Vision Books, New Delhi, 1990.

———, *India's Sri Lanka Fiasco: Peacekeepers at War,* Vision Books, New Delhi, 1990.

Kapur, Ashok, *India's Arms Control and Nuclear Policy: A Quest For An Altered World Order,* Carleton University, Ottawa, 1974.

———, *India's Nuclear Option: Atomic Diplomacy and Decision Making,* Praeger Publishers, New York, 1976.

———, *Indian Ocean: Regional and International Power Politics,* Praeger Publishers, New York, 1983.

Kapur, BD, *Building a Defence Technology Base,* Lancer International, New Delhi, 1990.

Kapur, H, *The Embattled Triangle: Moscow-Peking-New Delhi.* Humanities, New Delhi, 1973.

———, *India's Foreign Policy 1947-1992: Shadows and Substance,* Sage Publications, New Delhi, 1994.

Kapur, Rajiv, *Sikh Separatism: The Politics of Faith,* Allen and Unwin, London, 1986.

Kar, Lt Col HC, *Military History of India,* Firma KLM, Calcutta, 1980.

Karim, Maj General Afsir, *Counter Terrorism: The Pakistan Factor,* Lancers Paper 2, Lancer International, New Delhi, 1991.

———, *Kashmir: The Troubled Frontier,* Indian Defence Review Team, Lancers Publishers, New Delhi, 1995.

Karnad, Bharat (ed), *Future Imperilled: India's Security in the 1990s and Beyond,* Viking, New Delhi, 1994.

Karunakaran, KP, *Alignment and Non-alignment in Asia: An Examination of the Inter-relation Between the Domestic and Foreign Policies of the Continent,* People's Publishing House, New Delhi, 1961.

Kathpalia, Lt General PN, *National Security Perspectives,* Lancer International, New Delhi, 1986.

Kaul, BM, *The Untold Story,* Allied Publishers, Bombay, 1967.

———, *Confrontation with Pakistan,* Barnes and Noble, New York, 1972.

Kaul, Ravi, *India's Strategic Spectrum,* Chanakya Publications, Allahabad, 1969.

———, *India's Nuclear Spin-Off,* Chanakya Publications, Allahabad, 1974.

Kaur, Amarjit, *et al., The Punjab Story,* Roli Books International, New Delhi, 1984.

Kavic, Lorne J, *India's Quest for Security,* University of California Press, California, 1967.

Keay, John, *India Discovered,* Rupa, Calcutta, 1989.

Kennedy, DE, *Security of Southern Asia,* Chatto and Windus, London, 1968.

Khanna, DD (ed), *Strategic Environment in South Asia During the 1980s,* Naya Prakash, Calcutta, 1979.

Khanna, DD and PN Mehrotra, *Defence Versus Development: A Case Study of India,* Indus Publishing, New Delhi, 1993.

Khera, SS, *India's Defence Problems,* Orient Longman, New Delhi, 1968.

Kochanek, Stanley, *Business and Politics in India,* University of California Press, Berkeley, 1974.

Kodikara, Shelton U, *Strategic Factors in Interstate Relations in South Asia,* Heritage Publishers, New Delhi, 1984.

———, *South Asian Strategic Issues: Sri Lankan Perspectives,* Sage Publications, New Delhi, 1990.

Kohli, Atul, *Democracy And Discontent: India's Growing Crisis of Governability,* Cambridge University Press, Cambridge, New York, 1991.

Kohli, Atul, (ed), *India's Democracy: An Analysis of Changing State-Society Relations,* Orient Longman, New Delhi, 1991.

Kohli, SN, *The Indian Ocean and India's Maritime Security,* United Services Institute, New Delhi, 1981.

Kothari, Shanti, *Applied Politics,* Indian Institute of Public Administration, New Delhi, 1989.

Kulkarni, VB, *Is India A Big Power?,* Orient Publishers, New Delhi, 1972.

Kumar, DP, *Challenges To India's Unity. Assam Students Agitation and Government,* BR Publishing, New Delhi, 1990.

Kunju, N, *Indian Army: A Grassroots Review,* Reliance Publishing House, New Delhi, 1991.

Kux, Dennis, *Estranged Democracies: India and the United States 1941-1991,* Sage Publications, New Delhi, 1993.

Labh, Kapileshwar, *India And Bhutan,* Sindu Publications, New Delhi, 1974.

Lamb, Alastair, *The China-Indian Border: The Origin of the Disputed Boundaries,* Chatham House Essay, Oxford University Press, London, 1964.

———, *The Kashmir Problem: A Historical Survey*, Praeger, New Delhi, 1967.

———, *Tibet, China and India 1914-1950: A History of Imperial Diplomacy*, Roxford Books, Hertfordshire, 1989.

———, *Kashmir: A Disputed Legacy*, Roxford Books, Hertfordshire, 1991.

Levi, W, *Free India in Asia*, University of Minnesota Press, Minneapolis, 1953.

Limaye, DH, *Some Aspects of India's Military Defence*, New York, Bombay.

Longer V, *The Defence and Foreign Policies of India*, Oriental University Press, London, 1988.

Low, CR, *History of The Indian Navy*, 2 Vols, Manas Publications, Delhi, 1985.

Madhok, Balraj, *Indianisation: What, Why and How?*, S Chand, New Delhi, 1970.

Madhok, Balraj, *Rationale of Hindu State*, Indian Book Gallery, Delhi, 1982.

Mahmud, SF, *A Concise History of Indo-Pakistan?*, Oxford University Press, Karachi, 1988.

Malhotra, Inder, *Indira Gandhi: A Personal and Political Biography*, Hodder and Stoughton, London, 1989.

Malik, Hafeez, *Dilemmas of National Security and Cooperation in India and Pakistan*, St. Martin's Press, New York, 1993.

Mansingh, Surjit, *India's Search For Power*, Sage Publications, New Delhi, 1983.

Marshall, PJ, *The New Cambridge History of India. Bengal: The British Bridgehead in Eastern India, 1740-1828*, Cambridge University Press, Cambridge, 1987.

Marwah, Onkar and Jonathan D Pollack, *Military Power and Policy in Asian States: China, India, Japan*, Westview Press, Boulder, Colorado, 1980.

Mascaro, Juan (translator), *The Bhagavad Gita*, Penguin, London, 1982.

Mason, Philip, *The Men Who Ruled India*, Norton, New York, 1985.

———, *A Matter of Honour. An Account of the Indian Army, Its Officers and Men*, Macmillan, New York, 1986.

Mathews, Ron, *Defence Production in India*, ABC Publishing House, New Delhi, 1989.

Mattoo, Amitabh and David Cortright (eds.), *India and the Bomb*, Notre Dame University Press, South Bend, Indiana, 1996.

Maxwell, N, *India's China War*, Jonathan Cape, London, 1971.

Mellor, John W, (ed), *India: A Rising Middle Power*, Select Book Service, New Delhi, 1981.

Menon, VP, *The Transfer of Power in India*, Princeton University Press, Princeton, 1957.

———, *The Story of the Integration of the Indian States*, Orient Longman, New Delhi, 1958.

Mirchandani, GG, *India's Nuclear Dilemma*, Popular Book Services, New Delhi, 1968.

Mishra, BB, *The Unification and Division of India*, Oxford University Press, New Delhi, 1990.

Mishra, KP, *Quest For an International Order in the Indian Ocean*, Allied Publishers, Bombay, 1977.

Moorehouse, Geoffrey, *India Britannica*, Harper, New Delhi, 1983.

Moshaver, Ziba, *Nuclear Weapon's Proliferation in the Indian Subcontinent*, St. Martin's Press, New York, 1991.

Mullick, BN, *My Years With Nehru: The Chinese Betrayal*, Allied Publishers, Bombay, 1971.

Muni, SD and Anuradha Muni, *Regional Cooperation in South Asia*, National Publishing House, New Delhi, 1984.

Muni, SD, *Pangs of Proximity*, Sage Publications, New Delhi, 1993.

Murty, K Satchidananda, *The Quest for Peace*, Ajanta Publishers, New Delhi, 1985.

Murty, TS, *India-China Boundary: India's Options*, ABC Publishing House, New Delhi, 1987.

Nagar, KS and Lt Colonel Gautam Sharma (eds), *India's Security and Superpower Threat*, Reliance Publishing House, New Delhi, 1979.

Naipaul, VS, *India: A Million Mutinies Now*, Viking, New York, 1990.

Nair, Brig VK, *Nuclear India*, Lancer International, New Delhi, 1991.

———, *War in the Gulf: Lessons for the Third World*, Lancer International, New Delhi, 1991.

Nambiar, K, *Our Seafaring in the Indian Ocean*, Jeevan Publications, Bangalore, 1975.

Namboodiri, PKS, *et al.*, *Intervention in the Indian Ocean*, ABC Publishing House, New Delhi, 1982.

Namboodiri, PKS and GG Mirchandani, *Nuclear India. A Technological Assessment*, Vision Books, New Delhi, 1981.

Nanda, BR, (ed), *Indian Foreign Policy: The Nehru Years*, University Press of Hawaii, Honolulu, 1976.

Nanda, Col Ravi, *Evolution of National Strategy of India*, Lancers Books, New Delhi, 1987.

Narayanan, MK, *National Security: The Internal Dimension*, RGICS Paper No.16, Rajiv Gandhi Institute for Contemporary Studies, New Delhi, September 1994.

Nath, Maj General Rajendra, *Military Leadership in India, Vedic Period to Indo-Pak Wars*, Lancers Books, New Delhi, 1990.

Nath, Maj General Rajendra, Shayan Kosia and Ashok Malik (eds), *Indian Security: Threats and Strategies*, Panchanand Research Institute, Chandigarh, 1990.

Naval Foundation, *Proceedings of the Seminar on the Indian Ocean: Challenges and Opportunities*, New Delhi, 1992.

Nawaz, Hamsa, *Indian Nuclear Weapons Programme*, Progressive Publishers, Lahore, 1985.

Nayar, Baldev Raj, *Violence and Crime in India: A Quantitative Study*, Macmillan, New Delhi, 1975.

———, *American Geo-Politics and India*, Vikas Publishing House, New Delhi, 1976.

———, *Indian Quest for Technological Independence*, 2 Vols, Lancers Publishers, New Delhi, 1983.

Nayar, Kuldip, *Distant Neighbours: A Tale of the Subcontinent*, Vikas Publishing House, New Delhi, 1972.

Nayar, Kuldip and Khuswant Singh, *Tragedy of Punjab: Operation Bluestar and After*, Vision Books, New Delhi, 1984.

Nayar, Lt General VK, *Threat from Within: India's Internal Security Environment*, Lancers Publishers, New Delhi, 1992.

Nehru, Jawaharlal, *India's Foreign Policy*, Publication Division, Government of India, New Delhi, 1983.

———, *The Discovery of India*, 4th ed, rev., Meridian Books, London 1960.

———, *The Discovery of India*, Oxford University Press, New Delhi, 1982.

Noorani, AG, *India, South-East Asia And Vietnam*, Democratic Research Service, Bombay, n.d.

Norman, Dorothy (ed), *Nehru: The First Sixty Years*, John Day, New York, 1965.

Omissi, David, *The Sepoy and the Raj: The Indian Army, 1860-1940*, Macmillan, Madras, 1995.

Paarlberg, Robert L, *Food Trade and Foreign Policy: India, the Soviet Union and the United States*, Cornell University Press, Ithaca, 1985.

Palit, DK, *War in the High Himalaya: The Indian Army in Crisis*, Lancer International, New Delhi, 1991.

Palmer, Norman D, *South Asia and United States Policy*, Houghton Mifflin, Boston, 1966.

———, *The United States and India: The Dimensions of Influence*, Praeger Publishers, New York, 1984.

Pandey, BN, *South and South East Asia 1945-1979: Problems and Policies*, Macmillan Press, London, 1980.

Panikkar, KM, *The Strategic Problems of the Indian Ocean*, Kitabistan, Allahabad, 1944.

———, *A Survey of Indian History*, Asia Publishing House, Bombay, 1947.

———, *In Two Chinas*, George Allen & Unwin, London, 1951.

———, *Geographical Factors in Indian History*, Bhartiya Vidya Bhawan, Bombay, 1955.

———, *Problems of Indian Defence,* Asia Publishing House, London, 1960.

———, *The Foundation of New India,* George Allen & Unwin, London, 1963.

Pathak, KK, *Nuclear Policy of India: A Third World Perspective*, Gitanjali Prakashan, New Delhi, 1980.

Patil, RLM, *India: Nuclear Weapons and International Politics,* National Publishing House, New Delhi, 1969.

Paul, TV, *Reaching For The Bomb: The Indo-Pak Nuclear Scenario*, Dialogue Publications, New Delhi, 1984.

Pearson, MN, *The New Cambridge History of India: The Portuguese in India*, Cambridge University Press, Cambridge, 1987.

Phadnis, Urmila, SD Muni, and Kalim Bahadur, (eds.), *Domestic Conflicts in South Asia,* 2 Vols., South Asian Publishers, New Delhi, 1986.

Phadnis, Urmila, *Ethnicity and Nation-building in South Asia,* Sage Publications, New Delhi, 1990.

Poulose, TT (ed), *Indian Ocean Power Rivalry*, Young Asia, New Delhi, 1974.

———, (ed), *Perspectives on India's Nuclear Policy*, Young Asia, New Delhi, 1978.

Power, Paul F (ed), *India's Non Alignment Policy,* DC Heath, Boston, 1967.

Paranjpe, Shrikant, *India and South Asia Since 1971,* Radiant Publishers, New Delhi, 1981.

Prasad, Beni, *Theory of Government in Ancient India,* 2nd edn., Central Book Depot, Allahabad, 1968.

Prasad, Bimal, *Indo-Soviet Relations, 1947-1972: A Documentary Study,* Allied Publishers, Bombay, 1973.

———, (ed), *India's Foreign Policy: Studies in Continuity and Change*, Vikas Publishing House, New Delhi, 1979.

Praval, Major KC, *The Indian Army After Independence*, Lancer International, New Delhi, 1990.

Press Council of India, *Crisis and Credibility*, Lancer Paper 4, Lancer International, New Delhi, 1991.

Puri, Balraj, *Kashmir: Towards Insurgency*, Tracts For The Times/4, Orient Longman, New Delhi, 1993.

Radhakrishanan, S, *Eastern Religions and Western Thought,* Oxford University Press, New Delhi, 1989.

Rahul, Ram, *The Himalayan Borderland,* Vikas Publishing House, Delhi, 1969.

Rajan, MS and Shivaji Ganguly (eds), *Great Power Relations, World Order and the Third World,* Vikas Publishing House, New Delhi, 1981.

Ramakant, *Nepal-China and India,* Abhinav Publishers, New Delhi, 1976.

Ramaswamy, TN, *Essentials of Indian Statecraft: Kautilya's Arthasastra For Contemporary Readers,* Asia Publishing House, New Delhi,1962.

Rana, AP, *Imperatives of Non-alignment: A Conceptual Study of India's Foreign Policy Strategy in the Nehru Period*, Macmillan, New Delhi, 1976.

Rana, AP, (ed), *Four Decades of Indo-US Relations: A Commemorative Retrospective,* Har-Anand and USEFI, New Delhi, 1994.

Rao, General KV Krishna, *Prepare Or Perish: A Study of National Security,* Lancers Publishers, New Delhi, 1991.

Rao, K Krishna, *The Sino-Indian Boundary Question and International Law,* The Indian Society of International Law, New Delhi, 1963.

Rao, PR, *Indian Heritage and Culture*, Oriental University Press, London, 1988.

Rao, PVR, *Defence Without Drift*, Popular Prakashan, Bombay, 1970.

Rao, Ramakrishan, and RC Sharma (eds), *India's Borders: Ecology and Security Perspectives,* Scholar's Publishing Forum, New Delhi, 1991.

Rasgotra, M, VD Chopra and KP Misra (eds), *India's Foreign Policy in the 1990s,* Patriot Publishers, New Delhi, 1990

Ray, Hemen, *Sino-Soviet Conflict Over India: An Analysis of the Causes of Conflict Between Moscow and Beijing Over India Since 1949,* Abhinav Publishers, New Delhi, 1990.

Rikhye, Ravi, *The Fourth Round: Indo-Pak War 1984,* ABC Publishing House, New Delhi, 1982.

————, *The War That Never Was: The Story of India's Strategic Failures,* Chanakya Publishers, New Delhi, 1988.

————, *The Militarization of Mother India,* Chanakya Publishers, New Delhi, 1990

Robert P Goldman, (tr.), *The Ramayana of Valmiki, Vol.1, Balkanda,* Princeton University Press, New Jersey, 1984.

Rowland, John, *A History of Sino-Indian Relations: Hostile Coexistence,* Van Nostrand, Princeton, 1967.

Roy, Vice Admiral Mihir K, *War in the Indian Ocean,* Lancers Publishers, New Delhi, 1995.

Roy-Chaudhury, Rahul, *Sea Power and Indian Security,* Brassey's, London, 1995.

Rudolph, LI, and SH Rudolph, *In Pursuit of Lakshmi: The Political Economy of the Indian State,* University of Chicago Press, Chicago, 1987.

Rustomji, Nari, *Imperilled Frontiers: India's North-Eastern Borderlands,* Oxford University Press, New Delhi, 1983.

Saksena, KP, *Cooperation In Development: Problems And Prospects for India And ASEAN,* Sage Publications, New Delhi. 1986.

Sardesai, DR, *Indian Foreign Policy in Cambodia, Laos and Vietnam,* University of California Press, Berkeley, 1968.

Sardeshpande, Lt General SC, *Assignment Jaffna,* Lancers Publishers, New Delhi, 1992.

Sarhadi, Ajit Singh, *Indian Security in Resurgent Asia,* Heritage Publishers, New Delhi, 1979.

Sarkar, JN, *The Art of War in Medieval India,* Munshiram Manoharlal Publishers, New Delhi, 1984.

Sarkar, Bidyut (ed), *PN Haksar: Our Times and the Man,* Allied Publishers, Ahmedabad, 1989.

Sen, Gautam (ed), *India's Security Considerations in the Nuclear Age,* Atlantic Publishers, New Delhi, 1986.

Sen, LP, *Slender Was the Thread,* Sangam, New Delhi, 1973.

Sengupta, Bhabani, *Nuclear Weapons? Policy Options for India,* Sage Publications, New Delhi, 1983.

Sengupta, Bhabani (ed), *Regional Cooperation and Development in South Asia,* 2 Vols, South Asian Publishers, New Delhi, 1986.

————, *Fulcrum of Asia: Relations among China, India, Pakistan and the USSR,* Konark Publishers, New Delhi, 1988.

————, *South Asian Perspectives: Seven Nations in Conflict and Cooperation,* BR Publishers, New Delhi, 1988.

Seshagiri, N, *The Bomb Fallout of India's Nuclear Explosion,* Killas Publishing House, Delhi, 1975.

Shamasastry, R (tr.), *Kautilya's Arthashastra,* Mysore Printing and Publishing House, Mysore, 1967.

Sharan, Vyupakesh, *India's Role in South Asian Regional Cooperation,* Commonwealth Publishers, New Delhi, 1991.

Sharma , Dhirendra, *India's Nuclear Estate,* Lancers Publishers, New Delhi, 1983.

Sharma, Lt Colonel Gautam and RS Nagar (eds), *India's Northern Security,* Reliance Publishing, New Delhi, 1987.

Sharma, Ram Sharan, *Aspects of Political Ideas and Institutions in Ancient India,* 3rd rev. edn, Motilal Banarsidass Publishers, New Delhi, 1991.

Sharma, RC and PC Sinha, *India's Ocean Policy,* Khama Publishers, New Delhi, 1994.

Sheppard, Eric William, *A Short History of the British Army to 1914,* Constable, London, 1926.

Shoemaker, Michael M, *The Ancient Empires of Southern India and South East Asia,* Mittal Publishers, Delhi, 1987.

Sidhu, KS, *The Role of Navy in India's Defence,* Harnam Publishers, New Delhi, 1983.

Singh, Lt Colonel Bawa Sunder, *Tradition Never Dies: The Genesis and Growth of the Indian Army*, Lalvani Publishing House, Bombay, 1972.

Singh, Lt General Depinder, *IPKF in Sri Lanka,* Trishul Publications, Noida, n.d.

Singh, Lt General Harbakhsh, *War Dispatches: Indo-Pakistani Conflict 1965,* Lancer International, New Delhi, 1991.

Singh, Air Commodore Jasjit, *Air Power in Modern Warfare,* Lancer International, New Delhi, 1990.

Singh, Air Commodore Jasjit (ed), *India and Pakistan: Crisis of Relationship,* Lancers Publishers, New Delhi, 1990.

———, *Indo-US Relations in a Changing World: Proceedings of the Indo-US Strategic Symposium,* Lancers Publishers, New Delhi, 1992.

———, *Maritime Security,* Institute for Defence and Strategic Analysis, New Delhi, 1993.

Singh, Air Commodore Jasjit, and Vatroslav Vekaric (eds), *Non-Provocative Defence: The Search for Equal Security,* Lancer International, New Delhi, 1984.

Singh, KR, *Indian Ocean: Big Power Presence and Local Response,* Manohar Publishers, New Delhi, 1972.

Singh, Mahesh Kumar, *India's Defence Strategy and Tactics: A Geographical Analysis,* Shree Publishing House, Delhi, 1984.

Singh, Sarva Daman, *Ancient Indian Warfare,* Motilal Banarsidass, New Delhi, 1987.

Singh, Major General Sukhwant, *India's Wars Since Independence,* 3 volumes, Vikas Publishing House, New Delhi, 1982.

Singh, Tavleen, *Kashmir: A Tragedy of Errors,* Viking, New Delhi, 1995.

Singham, AW and Shirley Hume, *Non-Alignment in an Age of Alignments,* Zed Books, London, 1973.

Sinha, Lt General SK, *Of Matters Military,* Vision Books, New Delhi, 1987.

Sinha, NK and Nitish R Ray, *A History of India,* Orient Longman, Hyderabad, 1987.

Sinha, PB and RR Subramanian, *Nuclear Pakistan: Atomic Threat to South Asia,* Vision Books, New Delhi, 1980.

Sinha, Sureshwar D, *Sailing and Soldering in Defence of India,* Chanakya Publication, New Delhi, 1990.

Sinha, SK, *Operation Rescue: Military Operations in Jammu and Kashmir 1947-49,* Vision Books, New Delhi, 1977.

Sisson, Richard, and Leo E Rose, *War and Secession: Pakistan, India and the Creation of Bangladesh,* University of California Press, Berkeley, 1990.

Spear, Percival, *A History of India,* Vol. 2, Penguin, London, 1965.

Sreenivasan, MA, *Of the Raj, Maharajas and Me*, Ravi Dayal, New Delhi, 1991.

Stein, Arthur, *India and the Soviet Union: The Nehru Era*, University of Chicago Press, Chicago, 1969.

Subramaniam, KS, *Political Violence, Social Movements and the State in India*, Discussion Paper 308, Institute of Development Studies, University of Sussex, Brighton, August 1992.

Subrahmanyam, K, (ed), *Nuclear Myths and Realities: India's Dilemma*, ABC Publishing House, New Delhi, 1981.

————, *India's Security Perspectives*, ABC Publishing House, New Delhi, 1982.

————, *India and the Nuclear Challenge*, Lancer International, New Delhi, 1986.

————, *Nuclear Proliferation and International Security*, Lancer International, New Delhi, 1986.

Subrahmanyam K, and Air Commodore Jasjit Singh (eds), *Global Security: Some Issues and Trends—An Indo-German Dialogue*, Lancer International, New Delhi, 1987.

Subramaniam, RR, *India, Pakistan, China: Defence and Nuclear Tangle in South Asia*, ABC Publishing House, New Delhi, 1989.

Sundarji, General K, *Blind Men of Hindoostan: Indo Pak Nuclear War*, UBSPD, New Delhi, 1993.

Talbot, Phillips, and SC Poplai, *India and America: A Study of their Relations*, Harper and Row, New York, 1958.

Talbot, Phillips (ed), *South Asia in the World Today*, University of Chicago Press, Chicago, 1950.

Taylor, Jay, *The Dragon and the Wild Goose: China and India*, Praeger Publishers, New York, 1987.

*The Challenges of Nucler Weapons to India's Foreign Policy*, Select Readings, School of International Studies, New Delhi, 1966.

*The Story of Defence, 1947-1972*, Ministry of Defence, Government of India, 1972.

Tharoor, Shashi, *Reasons of State: Political Development and India's Foreign Policy Under Indira Gandhi, 1966-77*, Vikas Publishing House, New Delhi, 1982.

Thomas, Rāju GC, *The Defence of India: A Budgetary Perspective of Strategy and Politics*, Macmillan, New Delhi, 1978.

Thomas, Raju GC (ed), *The Great Power Triangle And Asian Security*, Lexington Books, Lexington, 1983.

————, *Indian Security Policy*, Princeton University Press, Princeton, 1986.

————, (ed), *Perspectives on Kashmir: The Roots of Conflict in South Asia*, Westview Press, Boulder, Colorado, 1992.

Tinker, Hugh, *India and Pakistan: A Political Analysis*, 2nd edn, Pall Mall Press, London, 1967.

Tully, Mark and Satish Jacob, *Amritsar: Mrs Gandhi's Last Battle*, Rupa, Calcutta, 1985.

Varma, B, *Insurgency and Counter-Insurgency*, Uppal Publishing House, New Delhi, 1988.

Varma, Shanti Prasad, *Struggle for the Himalayas: A Study in Sino-Indian Relations*, University Publishers, Jullundar, 1956.

Varma, SP and KP Misra (eds), *Foreign Policies in South Asia*, Orient Longman, Bombay, 1969.

Venkateshwaran, AL, *Defence Organisation in India*, Publication Division, Government of India, New Delhi, 1969.

Verma, HN and Amit Verma, *Decisive Battles of India Through The Ages*, 2 vols, GIP Books, Campbell, California, 1994.

Wallace, Paul (ed), *Region and Nation in India*, Oxford and IBH, New Delhi, 1985.

Wilcox, Wayne, *India, Pakistan and the Rise of China*, Walker and Co, New York, 1964.

Wilcox, Wayne, Leo E Rose, and Gavin Boyd (eds.), *Asia and the International System*, Winthrop Publishers, Cambridge, Mass., 1972.

Wilson, Jeyaratnam and Dennis Dalton, *The States of South Asia: Problems of National Integration*, The University Press of Hawaii, Honolulu, 1982.

Wirsing, G, *The Indian Experiment: Key To Asia's Future*, Orient Longman, New Delhi, 1972.

Wolpert, Stanley, *A New History of India*, Oxford University Press, New York, 1977.

————,' *Roots of Confrontation in South Asia: Afghanistan, Pakistan, India and the Superpowers*, Oxford University Press, New York, 1982.

Wood, John R (ed), *State Politics in Contemporary India: Crisis or Continuity?*, Westview Press, Boulder, Colorado, 1984.

Woodman, Dorothy, *Himalayan Frontiers: A Political Review of British, Chinese, Indian and Russian Rivalries*, Bassie and Jenkins, New York, 1970.

Younghusband, GJ, *Indian Frontier Warfare*, Anmol Publications, Delhi, 1985.

Ziring, Lawrence (ed), *The Subcontinent in World Politics: India, Its Neighbours, and the Great Powers*, Praeger Publishers, New York, 1978.

*Journals*

*Agni* (Forum for Strategic Studies, New Delhi).

*Strategic Analysis* (Institute for Defence Studies and Analyses, New Delhi).

*USI Journal* (United Services Institution, New Delhi).

*International Studies* (School of International Studies, Jawaharlal Nehru University, New Delhi).

# CONTRIBUTORS

## Author

GEORGE K TANHAM was a Vice President and Trustee of the RAND Corporation. He has recently authored *The Indian Air Force: Trends and Prospects*, Vision, 1996.

## Commentators

KANTI P BAJPAI is Associate Professor at the School of International Studies, Jawaharlal Nehru University. His latest publications are *Brasstacks and Beyond: Perception and Management of Crisis in South Asia*, Manohar, 1995 and *Interpreting World Politics*, Sage, 1995.

AMITABH MATTOO is Associate Professor at the School of International Studies, Jawaharlal Nehru University. His latest publications include *India and the Bomb*, University of Notre Dame Press, 1996 and a study on South Asia for the Carnegie Commission on Deadly Conflict.

RAHUL ROY-CHAUDHURY is Research Officer at the Institute for Defence Studies and Analyses (IDSA), New Delhi. His publications include *Sea Power and Indian Security*, Brasseys, 1995.

VARUN SAHNI is Associate Professor at the School of International Studies, Jawaharlal Nehru University. He has written a paper on an affordable defence for India, and has contributed to the *Cambridge History of Latin America*, Cambridge University Press, 1995. He is completing a book on the Argentine Navy.

WAHEGURU PAL SINGH SIDHU is presently doing research in International Relations and Security Studies at the University of Cambridge. He was, for several years, a defence correspondent for *India Today*.